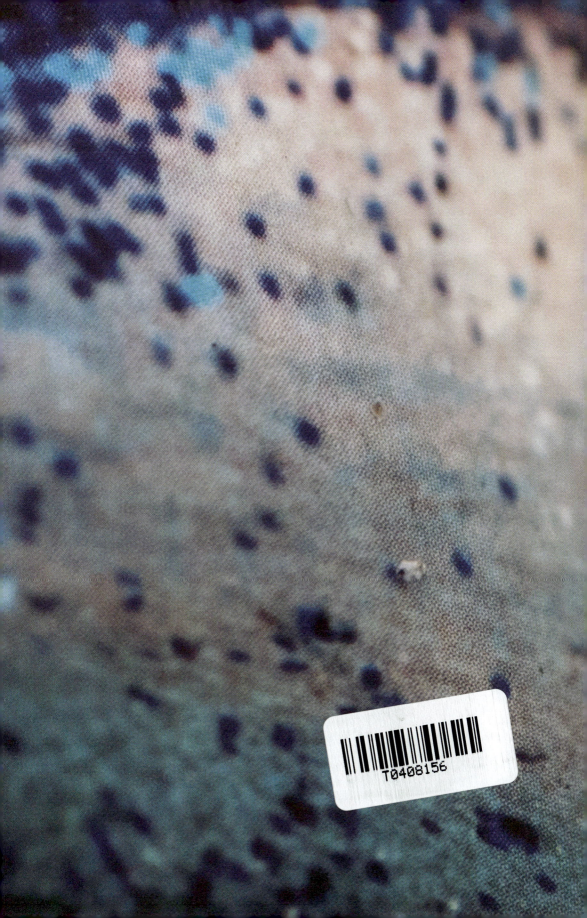

In Smithereens

In Smithereens
The Costume Remains of Lea Anderson's Stage

Mary Kate Connolly

intellect
Bristol, UK / Chicago, USA

First published in the UK in 2024 by
Intellect, The Mill, Parnall Road, Fishponds, Bristol, BS16 3JG, UK

First published in the USA in 2024 by
Intellect, The University of Chicago Press, 1427 E. 60th Street, Chicago, IL 60637, USA

Copyright © 2024 Intellect Ltd

All rights reserved. No part of this publication may be reproduced, stored in a retrieval system, or transmitted, in any form or by any means, electronic, mechanical, photocopying, recording, or otherwise, without written permission.

A catalogue record for this book is available from the British Library.

Copy editor: MPS
Cover designer: David Caines
Cover image: Rik Pennington
Production manager: Julie Willis (Westchester Publishing Service UK)
Book designer and typesetter: David Caines

Hardback: 9781835950524
Epdf: 9781835950548
Epub: 9781835950531

To find out about all our publications, please visit our website. There you can subscribe to our e-newsletter, browse or download our current catalogue and buy any titles that are in print.

www.intellectbooks.com

This is a peer-reviewed publication.

HAMM: You're a bit of all right, aren't you?

CLOV: A smithereen.

Endgame by Samuel Beckett ([1957] 2009: 10–11)

Acknowledgements	viii
Beginning	1
Smithereens: Ghosts, detritus and performance's return	23
Disintegration	43
Preservation	101
Transaction	173
Display	233
Ending	275
Bibliography	286
Biographies	297

Thank you

There is the actual book that you have in your hands or on your screen, if you're reading this bit. That takes some putting together, by some people. There are the hijinks this book describes (films made, exhibitions mounted, interviews given). They take some doing too: generosity and patience on the part of whoever gave me their time, didn't suck their teeth as I faffed with technical equipment, tripped on my questions or sent one last – totally final, honest (never final) – draft for feedback. There is also the time this book project traversed and the life that gets in the way, gets lived, gets shared along the way. The people who sustain this part – they do a lot. Holding the thread, holding the baby, holding the phone, holding your tongue. Whilst writing a book can feel like a solo endeavour, it is far from that and there are therefore many people to thank. Too many. If your name is not listed below, I hope you've already recognized it above, by implication.

This book arose from my doctoral research and so first thanks go to my doctoral supervisors, Ann R. David and Tamara Tomić-Vajagić. I am privileged to have benefited from their wisdom, wit and unerring enthusiasm for this project from its earliest incarnation.

Without Lea Anderson and her treasure trove of works (and their costumes) this book wouldn't exist. The significance of The Cholmondeleys' and The Featherstonehaughs' contribution to the dance world goes without saying. What does need to be mentioned is my deep gratitude to Lea for her generosity and openness to my continual poking and prodding in the archive, and all that has unfolded as a result. We continue to work together and I continue to come away from our encounters feeling that anything is possible. Happy birthday to The Cholmondeleys in this, their 40th year.

Many creative professionals associated with the companies were similarly generous to me in sharing their insights. To Jay Cloth, I remain indebted for your Wardrobe Mistress and Door Whore expertise. And for working diligently with me as we all set out enthusiastically to destroy a precious costume from the archive. To the designers, composer and dancers who took time out to speak with me – Sandy Powell, Simon Vincenzi (who laughed indulgently in the face of our attempts to destroy his costume), Steve Blake, Luca Silvestrini, Makiko Aoyama (who put her own body on the line in the cause of the aforementioned destruction) and Anna Pons Carrera – I am ever so grateful. Your voices have profoundly shaped this book. There are many other interviewees too, who allowed me access to their worlds of expertise – museum conservation rooms, props workshops, auctioneer houses – indispensable glimpses snatched from the front lines.

For all those involved in the mounting of the exhibition *Smithereens: A Collection of Fragments Considered as a Whole* (2021), thank you. Karsten Tinapp, who humoured both me and my design whims as we plotted technical requirements with egg boxes and string in his kitchen – and who went on to mount it in style, with the skilled assistance of Paul Panayi. Angela Kerkhof for the sewing of infernal materials and invaluable advice. David White, who didn't flinch in the face of petrol shortages, successfully transporting a baboon suit, those silver dancing shoes and everything else from one end of the UK to the other. Keran James and Michael Keenan at studio 1.1, London, who insisted that the show must and would go on despite all the pandemic delays. As indeed it did, in the end.

Thank you to Rik Pennington for his wonderful photos and willingness to jump right in, faced with anything from a moving dancing target to a three-piece suit. The images form a backbone of the practical research in this book, alongside the wonderful *Cholmondeleys* and *Featherstonehaughs* legacy held in the catalogue of photographs by Chris Nash, Pau Ros, Matilda Temperley and Pete Moss who have generously allowed their inclusion. Without these images the text would founder altogether. The publication costs of these images has been vitally supported by a Society of Theatre Research grant.

You'll find Joe Kelleher's name in the acknowledgements pages of many good books. I feel lucky to include it here. As examiners of my Ph.D., both he and Helen Thomas opened up the potentials of the project for me and the possibilities of where it could journey to next. That voyage has taken some time and Joe has been there in the boat, however inadvisably, all the way. Bailing the misplaced commas and much more besides.

David Caines is the only person I could have dreamt of designing this book. This marks another one of many collaborations together – each of them enriched by his artistic talent and good-humoured forbearance in the face of that last (never last) amendment.

Huge thanks to Jessica Lovett, Laura Christopher, Rosie Stewart, Julie Willis, and all at Intellect who have made this book happen. It is wonderful to have it in our hands. Sincere thanks also to the anonymous peer reviewers whose incisive feedback spurred the book on to that final, necessary stage of adjustment and redrafting.

That holding of phones, tongues and babies that I mentioned… In no particular order: Julianne Roche, Tarryn Oberholzer, Terry Clark, Emma Redding, Laura Blazy, Charley Webb, Hans Georgeson, Clare Taylor, Gerrie ter Haar, Medea Vaczy, Ariana Kireilyte and lastly 'The Dudes' (if you know, you know).

To David Taylor for the Proustian attention to the little things that makes for a life well lived, and the late Barbara Taylor whose support and female solidarity never wavered, coming as it did, wrapped in the gently anarchic gesture, the practical gift, the joyously subversive observation.

To Ann and Jerome Connolly – there from the beginning. I mean the very beginning. Unfailingly encouraging and supportive of these archival adventures, as they have been with all the ones that came before. To William Taylor, fellow wayfarer nonpareil. To Finn, Greta and Aveline – bright flames, Professors all.

ix

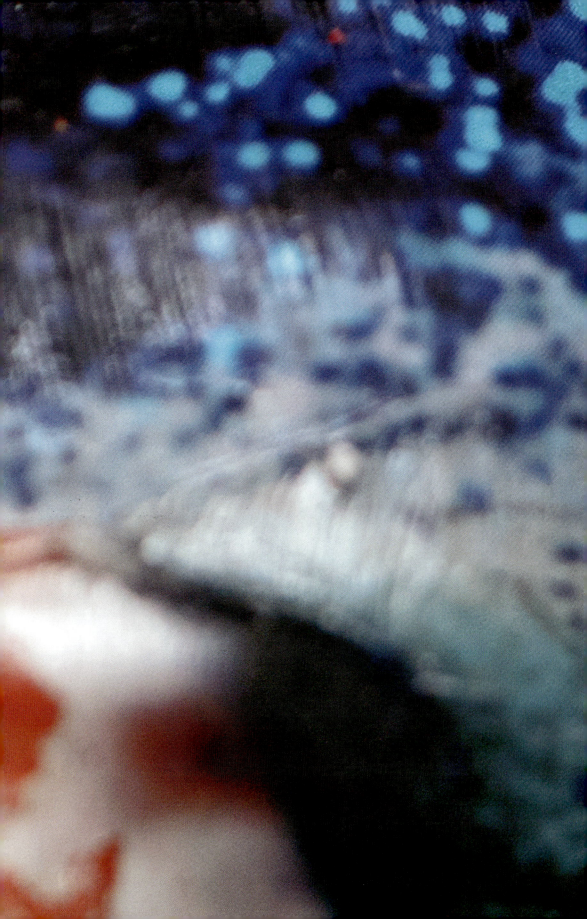

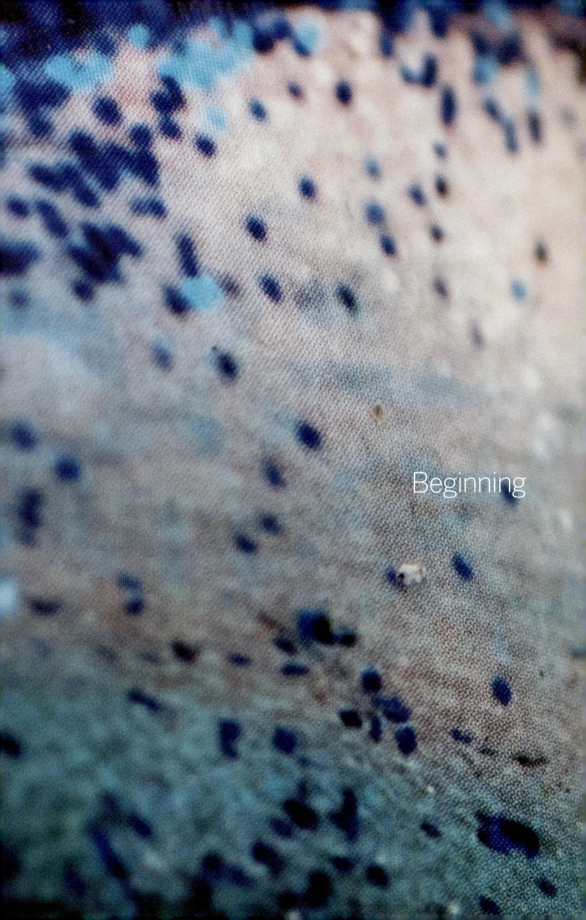

Deep in London's southern periphery down a warren of suburban streets, there is a lockup. Utilitarian, industrial, not much to look at, with a heavy duty padlocked door which slides upwards, disappearing into the recesses of the concrete ceiling. Heaving the door up reveals a portal to another world. Despite a slight damp smell and the pall cast by a bare lightbulb, from the moment of entering this cold cavern, you are confronted with the world of theatre. Here stored away, are the fabric remains of the stage. To be exact, the remains of the work of British choreographer Lea Anderson (1959–present). Distributed between this lockup and another elsewhere, are the trappings of well over 30 years of contemporary dance performance by her companies *The Cholmondeleys* and *The Featherstonehaughs*, who performed regularly from the mid-1980s until Arts Council funding cuts stalled their performances in 2011.

All along one wall, stacks of clear packing boxes reveal fake breasts and silver shoes piled neatly inside. Moveable costume rails are crammed with black clothing bags. Here, a see-through cover contains a polystyrene wig-head adorned with an elaborate pearl and satin headdress. There, a box of fabric samples bears several labels in assorted handwriting, some peeling or with words crossed out. It is a heady mix of highly theatrical garments and the trappings of industry – the everyday labour of lugging things around, of storing and cataloguing. An old Persil box houses a spare battery pack for a light-up costume, coils of industrial cabling hang on rails adjacent to those laden with tailored suits and satin dresses.

This netherworld, whilst captivating, is not unusual. From lockups and attics, to the prestige of environmentally controlled archives in major museums, a similar picture emerges of the fabric remains of theatre and performance. Secreted beneath tissue paper and protective covering, they are rendered silent – severed from the performances in which they came to life. Preservation within heritage collections focuses on protecting and sustaining the garments (Coffey-Webb and Campbell 2016). In doing so, a kind of disappearance can be enacted. For costumes which are excluded from archive collections deemed important or historically valuable, there is sometimes a total lack of visibility.

In the face of this vanishing, questions arise concerning the ephemerality of performance, the nature of costume as a generative and partially [re]constitutive document of performance, and the ethics of preservation and/or disintegration. If preservation of costumes in the traditional archival sense results in a 'disappearance' into storage or protected conditions, it becomes pertinent to consider whether (and how) costumes might continue to 'perform' beyond performance.

This book centres on the private costume archive of pioneering choreographer Lea Anderson, an artist whose work has slipped somewhat from visibility since the cessation of *The Cholmondeleys*' and *The Featherstonehaughs*' performances in 2011. Like the slow degradation of the costume artefacts lying mute in their cold storage, so too a similar degradation is being wrought on the legacy of these performances. Small erasures and gaps in knowledge are growing – multiplying almost imperceptibly, like treacherous moth holes in wool. Material degradations of garments vary greatly according to their composition. Plastics can eventually leach toxins, rubber will shrivel and crack, silk may shatter in place, into smithereens. In addition to the material deterioration at work in Anderson's costume archive, I would argue that there is a corresponding conceptual slippage of understanding and context of her work. It is perhaps most akin to that of a shattered silk blouse – the fragments are there, but now separated from one another – lacking a vital connective thread.

Placing Anderson's costume archive at its heart, this book maps alternative after-lives for a selection of costumes, proposing that the costume archive can function as a site for invention as well as an alternative materiality of performance. Such an approach does not aim to mend these ruptures (both physical and conceptual) but rather to gesture to the fissures and holes. To use the costumes themselves as interlocutors of past performances now gone, witnesses to current erasure, and sites for creative ingenuity. As such, the book represents an attempt to see justice done for a select few totems of performance whilst also unpicking the complex predicaments surrounding artefacts which survive long after works which are no longer performed.

The significance of costume in Anderson's work and its role in the devising process of her choreography is something which she herself discusses in detail (Connolly 2017). My longstanding interest in her use of costume has led to a further curiosity on my part, about the fate of dance costumes more generally, particularly outside the realms of repertory theatres or prestigious cultural institutions. What does happen to them once the performances have ended? My own embodied encounters with costume (particularly in my work with Donatella Barbieri as part of the research collective *Wearing Space*) signalled to me early on the potential of disused garments such as the ones populating Anderson's archive.[1] I had no prior grounding in costume making or costume-specific scholarship when I first started working with Anderson's costume archive, so was largely ignorant of the mechanics required to create, house, store, preserve, exhibit or indeed dispose of, used costumes post-performance. My limited interactions with costumes post-performance had largely been in the context of viewing traditional costume exhibitions which displayed costumes on mannequins, and backstage theatre tours I had attended. I was also struck by Barbieri's work within the archives of the Victoria & Albert Museum, London, entitled *Encounters in the Archive*, in which she emphasized 'the absent body and the traces it leaves behind in the lived in and performed in costume', arguing that costumes 'are not only memories but acquire agency in the "dialogue" with an engaged viewer in the here and now' (Barbieri 2012: n.pag.). Barbieri's investigations contributed to growing areas of dress and costume scholarship which point towards the ties between garments and memories, and the entangled nature of garments and embodied experience (Grew 2019; Hodgdon 2016; Barbieri and Crawley 2013; Monks 2010; Taylor 2002; De La Haye and Wilson 1999).

Discussing costumes post-performance, Barbieri argues that 'Separated from its context costume becomes redundant, yet as an object it is marked with a creative process which mediates between performance, its crafting, the body and the gaze of the audience' (Barbieri 2012: n.pag.). The esteem in which I hold Anderson's work underscores a sense of dismay at the gradual disappearance of both her work and its surrounding context. I have wondered about this redundancy which Barbieri refers to, and the seemingly narrow ways in which costumes can live on post-performance as objects for interpretation within museums, or forgotten totems locked away in storage.

In 2016, Anderson was invited by the Victoria & Albert Museum, London, to create a performed costume exhibition *Hand in Glove*, featuring over 300 of her costumes and accessories with dancers performing vignettes from a number of her key works. This exhibition, which I will discuss in further detail later in this book, occupied the V&A's Raphael Court for several days. Dance scholar Ramsay Burt heralded *Hand in Glove* as having 'the ambiance of a club night with live and pre-recorded music ... with decor by Raphael' (Burt 2016: n.pag.). The event occupied a nether-world between the former performance lives of the costumes and the space of exhibition. Through being performed (with their original music and with original choreography), these costumes seemed to resist the mummification which can come with being presented as artefacts for exhibition. Whilst occupying a wholly different space to that of the theatre, *Hand in Glove* nonetheless retained an undeniably theatrical aspect and thereby arguably eschewed interpretation in a traditional museological sense, reasserting the costumes' potency as agents of performance. After this brief exposure in the spotlight the costumes were once again returned to the lockup. Whilst Anderson is loath to part with any of them, the logistical and financial burden of sustaining them in storage is not insignificant. It was at this time that she remarked, only somewhat flippantly, to me that:

> Sometimes I think I will burn them all and that will be a work, or perhaps auction off a few at Sotheby's to fund a new work, or maybe I should give some of them to somewhere like the V&A after all.
> (Anderson 2016: n.pag.)

Whilst these were slightly playful remarks, they nonetheless sharply summarize the dilemmas which emerge in the face of costume's long survival post-performance. Questions arise concerning the nature of costume as an archival remnant, economies of value and the concept of costumes operating as trace repositories of knowledge. This conversation was to become a guiding light within the methodological and conceptual core of this book. It is one I returned to instinctively when devising the practical interventions to be carried out within the archive. Anderson's quandary chimes with my own observations of the costumes as having great creative potential and yet suffering from lack of visibility. A key aim of this book is to effect renewed visibility of an artist whose work has been somewhat erased and to highlight the potential for costume to serve as an eloquent, if fragmented, remnant of performance within an experimental archival framework. The costumes in Anderson's lockup are significant not only in terms of their materiality and design, but as the vestiges of a particular creative era within British contemporary dance. Anderson and her collaborators such as designers Sandy Powell and Simon Vincenzi, performer David Hoyle and composers Drostan Madden and Steve Blake created highly stylized performances which mobilized design and costume in a manner rarely seen in contemporary dance of that time. The costumes (if we view them as interlocutors of this period in contemporary dance) hold information regarding the works themselves and also the particular constellation of creative individuals who created them.

In the presence of ghosts?

Taking up a conceptual position which regards costumes as interlocutors invites an immediate problem: how to find the means of listening to what they might have to tell us about the vanished performances in which they once lived. Following my own observations of the costumes within *Hand in Glove*, and subsequently confronting them in the cold damp of Anderson's lockup, inevitably perhaps I was struck by what I might refer to as their ghostliness. The uncanny nature of a lifeless mask moulded from the contours of a dancer's face or the strange [dis]embodiment of a nylon stocking still stretched into the outlines of a foot. My immediate impression of these costumes as being somehow haunted is not an uncommon observation. As Barbara C. Hodgdon (reflecting on 'Spectral Traces in the Archive') puts it: 'If live performances are already embodied ghosts to prior material exigencies, to prior performances, and also to performance memories, then the material remains surviving performance are ghosts ghosting ghosts – and they come not in single spies but in battalions' (Hodgdon cited in Abel and Holland 2021: 279).[2]

'The empty costume', as Aoife Monks has proposed is 'an incomplete body, brimming with potential and memory, imprinted by a body but no longer of it and offering a ghostly and inanimate outline of a body of its own' (Monks 2010: 141). The ghostly and sometimes uncanny nature of costumes post-performance had been touched upon by various scholars – both in terms of how repertory costumes may be handed down and reused (Taylor 2003; Arnold 2017), and in the ways in which uninhabited costumes become complicated totems – illuminating disappearance rather than successfully recapturing performance. As Monks has described, 'when we actually confront this object in the archive [...] it has transformed itself behind our backs, turning itself into a memento of loss rather than being a reliable piece of evidence' (2010: 140).

When asked in interview what a particular costume (*Dead Skin* costumes from her 2006 work *Yippeee!!!*) now represents for her, Anderson replied that she viewed the costumes as:

> inanimate objects like a discarded skin [of] an insect or a snake: dead and uninhabited. And it doesn't really mean anything to me. In my head, I know the missing parts of it – there's missing parts (it's not a thing in itself). It's not real until the dancer is in there. And it's not real until the dancer is in there doing it correctly in the right place. [...] So it's a kind of pointer. An arrow to something else [...] I'm usually looking at it for a different kind of reason like 'How we are storing this?' 'Is it worth storing it?' 'Where shall I put it?' 'Where does it need to be?' 'Will we ever use it again [...] what is using?' 'Will we need it to show someone?'. 'Is it worth keeping in case we do it again?', So that's the kinds of

things I think of when I see the stuff now from the show but I didn't think that before. Before it was full of potential and imagining.
(Anderson 2017: n.pag.)

Thus costumes post-performance possess an innately tricky duality – that of the logistics of preserving their bulky material form which persists in the face of performance's disappearance, and the total inability of that form to reconstitute the performance.

Or ineloquent, shattered remains?

Contemporary dance performance, often categorized as ephemeral, arguably leaves even fewer decipherable material remains than for example classical ballet repertory (where works are remounted and notated) or written plays where early written drafts and annotated scripts might still be accessible. However, costume and scenography often play a key role within the creation of dance performance. There have been iconic collaborations between choreographers and artists/designers, including Merce Cunningham working with Robert Rauschenberg (Potter 1993), Regine Chopinot with Jean-Paul Gaultier (Saillard 2010), William Forsythe with Issey Miyake (Tomić-Vajagić 2021) and Michael Clark with fashion duo *BodyMap* (Nothing Concrete 2020). Given the scope and importance of these collaborations, it is not unreasonable that costumes may come to be regarded as potentially potent *remains* of dance. The material realities of archival storage however – whether in museum holdings or the damp cold of a concrete lockup – run as a counter-current to any potential we might wish to project onto the garments themselves. For Anderson, the 'potential and imagining' of the garments is something that came before and is now submerged by the logistical quandaries of what to do with the material remnants of her performances (Anderson 2017). In the face of these constraints, an inevitable consideration emerges: whether to sustain or destroy these fabric remains that, in the 'here and now', have in fact come to represent for Anderson a vanishing or total loss of potential.

It is worthwhile noting that many of Anderson's works (from the 1980s for example) existed originally in a largely pre-digital age, where digital technologies were only emergent and therefore only photographs, playbills and other ephemera now remain of the works. Acknowledging the ever-expanding ways in which dance can be captured, represented and documented, evidenced in digital projects with choreographers such as William Forsythe (Zuniga-Shaw 2011) and Siobhan Davies (Whatley 2017), the 'remains' of many [pre-digital] dance works sit outside of any such structures. In the case of a work which was neither notated (through a recognized dance notation system) nor filmed/archived digitally, items such as costumes may well seem to present as valuable and intriguing ciphers, yet in all sorts of ways they remain as stubborn detritus. Whatever their shape-shifting appearance when initially liberated from the confines of a dark packing box, they can remain exasperatingly partial and ineloquent in terms of evoking the performances now lost.

The costumes within Anderson's archive were designed and tailor-made for each individual production. Their specificity of design renders them mostly unfit for subsequent reuse and there exists no text or score to anchor them thematically within a wider performance heritage. They were unique to each work performed by *The Cholmondeleys* and *The Featherstonehaughs* – they lived and died with them. Costume and design have long been central elements in Anderson's works, not only influencing the choreography, but at times fundamentally altering the dancing body. Jessica Bugg (2020) cites Anderson's work with costume as representing a markedly different approach to that of many contemporary dance choreographers. She argues that, in the main, costume for contemporary dance 'has remained largely body conscious, prioritising ease of movement and functioning as visual enhancement' (Bugg 2020: 353). As part of a study on the 'lived experience of dress and its agency in the collaborative process', Bugg interviewed a number of choreographers and dancers including Anderson and her collaborators to illuminate how 'a deeper engagement with the corporeal experience of dress can activate costume as more than an applied visual overlay' (2020: 354). She cites Anderson as saying that 'I will not present anything in dance pajamas, and I will not present anything in bare feet. I just don't understand what that means apart from you just got out of bed or I'm not dressed?' (Anderson cited in Bugg 2020: 356).

Collaborations with designers such as Sandy Powell and Simon Vincenzi (among others) play a vital role in Anderson's work, and her devising process of allowing the physicality of the costumes to disrupt or alter the choreography sets her work apart from many of her contemporaries in the dance world of that time. The visible investment in costume in works such as *Smithereens* (1999), which featured costumes made by highly skilled professionals including a tutu maker from Royal Opera House, London, demonstrates the value Anderson places on costume. Encountering these costumes in the lockup however, their previous vitality and potential appears emptied out, or, displaced elsewhere. Conceivably, this displacement opens a further insight into Anderson's own indecision about whether to embrace the destruction of these costumes and be free of their inconvenient material bulk, or whether to continue preserving them for an imagined future to come, of remounted work or museological display. These questions arguably travel alongside a more complex one, of where, exactly, the legacy and history of past performance works such as these ones might reside. Is there a need to gather together and reanimate the material shards of vanished performances in the hope of a resurrection of sorts? Or, working from an acknowledgement of their innate partiality, might further fragmentation of these smithereens in fact prove a more provocative way to reveal both the losses and the material persistence of performance legacies?

Framework for an after-life

There's a familiar posture that gets adopted in the lockup. Like two character actors in an abstract material landscape of sequins, plastic oddments and grime. The artist and the scholar. She, poring over a costume or a sketchbook or a mix-tape with illegible biro listings scrawled on the back, and I, standing aside, pen or camera-phone in hand, not wishing to break the reverie. Waiting for the object to be contextualized for me; for it to come alive and drop down into legibility via her reminiscences of the history it is connected to. Some of these objects and costumes are already familiar to me – recognizable from the works I am acquainted with. Others are completely without context; a recording of found audio samples, say, by composer Drostan Madden, still in its large reel to reel format, the tape coiled round the plastic spool and encased in a battered cardboard cover. These objects speak to the sheer non-biodegradable hulk involved in recording things at that time – what it took to harvest sounds or images for an imagined future work, or capture aspects of an already-made work for posterity. Exclamations of 'Oh My God!' or 'I don't believe it!', or 'Oh yes, I remember this …' are all commonplace punctuations of our meditative scenes together in the archive. Our relationships to the materials to hand and the legacy which arguably lies therein, or elsewhere, are wholly different, but our impetus in what we attempt to mine these materials for is not so dissimilar. There is something at stake in these moments. We try to make the most of what we find. Make the most of what it can tell us, of how we might use it and where (if anywhere) it could travel to, for the future.

My initial curiosities with regard to costumes post-performance, the logistical plight of these seldom-seen garments, and questions of legacy and displacement bound up with fabric remains gradually distilled into an archival project design. Myself and Anderson decided we would try to 'do something' both physical and conceptual with the costumes in order to unfurl these dilemmas and identify new ways forward for her archive. We began with the basic idea of choosing three costumes which could be used as case studies to investigate the creative potential of costumes post performance. These were chosen by myself in collaboration with Anderson both as an extension of her original somewhat playful ideas as to what to do with her archive, and also as a result of encountering them physically in the costume lock-up. As we opened box after box in that freezing space and I held up each garment in turn under the bare lightbulb, I felt their storage was enacting a kind of banishment. I wondered whether they could be given an after-life other than these boxes, and if so, what it might entail. I speculated whether they could be used as test-cases for Anderson's throwaway remarks about the 'problem' of costume remains, and if so, which items would be best to choose and what we might physically do with them. Anderson was very open to the idea of working directly with the costumes to test whether their ineloquence as fabric remains in a packing box could be transformed into something else. An alternative after-life drawn from the past performances in which these costumes lived, which could frame these costumes in relation to the fundamental considerations which crop up for fabric remains: their materiality, value, legacy and potential for further dissemination.

The three costumes we selected were chosen with Anderson's words still echoing in my mind – that they might one day be destroyed in any case, or perhaps end up in a prestigious museum, or, if possible, could be monetised through sale 'at Sotheby's to fund a new work' (Anderson 2016 : n.pag.). Dwelling first on the idea of material destruction, we discussed the possibility of allowing (or in fact, causing) one costume to disintegrate as a means of hastening the inevitable material decline of the fabric remains in the archive. Fragmenting them further, in other words, to highlight their inherently partial nature – the ways in which they already operate as smithereens and will continue to fragment further over time. To this end, the most suitable costume was deemed to be a Dead Skin costume from Anderson's 2006 work *Yippeee!!!*. The Dead Skins are bodysuits which relate to concerns of decay and vanishing both narratively (in relation to the themes of *Yippeee!!!*) and physically (in their extensive staining, wear and tear and the visible bodily imprints which remain in them). Hence, the Dead Skin was the first costume we chose to work with.

In contrast to exploring material destruction, it seemed fitting to also investigate ways in which it might be possible to adopt museological and archival preservation and conservation methods within the physical and economic restraints of Anderson's personal archive. Essentially we wished to utilize the material preservation of costume remains for posterity as a means of recognizing their totemic importance, or indeed imbuing them with such via their careful archival care. These considerations led quite naturally to the selection of the full set of 36 moulded and hand painted masks from *Smithereens* (1999). These masks are richly crafted and long held in high esteem by Anderson as valuable objects, so it felt appropriate that they would be materially-cared for in order to secure their longevity towards a potential future of museological display or reconstruction of work.

Next, the notion of monetizing elements of the archive via sale was discussed. Would it be possible, for example, to sell some costumes at Sotheby's, London, or an equivalent auction house? If we were to test this possibility the chosen costume would need to be one which Anderson was willing to auction off and therefore part with forever. It would also need to be a costume of aesthetic or historical value in order to attract potential buyers. Anderson selected a three-piece painted suit from *The Featherstonehaughs Draw on the Sketchbooks of Egon Schiele* (1998 and 2010) for this third costume intervention. We aimed to sell the costume as a means of determining the economic value of the suit itself, but moreover the potential (if any) for economic transaction of costumes such as these more generally.

A final strategy for intervention emerged quite organically from those already described – that of further dissemination via display or exhibition. Unlike the after lives afforded through conservation and heritage collections (such as at the V&A museum or National Theatre, London), I was conscious of the small-scale 'make-do' aspect of the archive collection with which I was dealing. From early on in the project I became concerned with how it might be possible to make visible the after-lives which we were seeking to create for the costumes. In answer to this question I decided to mount an exhibition of the fabric remains of Anderson's archive. This provided a means of investigating the transitions from live performance, to archival storage, to dissemination in alternate form (via exhibition or film, for example) which costumes such as these often undergo. The process of mounting this exhibition will be explored in more detail alongside Anderson's own exhibition, *Hand in Glove*, in relation to a wider frame of dissemination, in the chapter entitled Display.

The overarching strategies in this book of disintegration, preservation, transaction and display are each radically different from one another and could potentially be regarded as inherently contradictory. Deliberately setting out to disintegrate a costume is arguably as far as one can get from archival cosseting and museological storage for the imagined ages to come. What unites these strategies, however, is the implicit acknowledgement of their current predicament in the lock up: their invisibility, the erasure of legacy and their gradual but inevitable material decline. If this book is to scratch at underlying questions concerning the location of legacy for performances now lost, or indeed attempt any recuperation of that legacy outside of the largescale mechanisms which sustain cultural heritage, it needs to begin by mobilizing the ineloquence of these remains as a petition for something new. It must bind any imaginative potential which they might possess together with their impotence, and the numerous losses which their material persistence alerts us to. It requires adopting a view of the costume archive not as an ordered repository of past performances preserved in material form, but as the awkward, scattered remains of legacy blown apart into disembodied unequal shards. Smithereens of things – shows, ideas, choreographies – harvested at the end of the run, sprayed with Febreze to keep odours at bay, stuffed into bin bags, peppered with handwritten labels, catalogued in the best way possible at-the-time, with whatever time and money and storage was to hand. Smithereens, then, which have travelled, by staying immobile in their lockup, to the *here* and *now*, and which can, if we allow them, demand an alternative after-life that disrupts the vanishing inflicted on these costumes and the companies who danced in them.

Archival paradox

There is no hierarchy to the interventions outlined in this book – they are each separate avenues of exploration and, like the archive they work with, were carried out within the confines of whatever logistical and economic realities prevailed at the time. These included the habitual restraints of limited funding and the non-habitual interruption of a global pandemic which occurred midway through the project. I make no attempt either, to suggest that these strategies should be considered as representative of 'best-practice' for every costume archive. Rather, this book prioritizes a close engagement with the particular archive at stake, and in doing so seeks to stage a specificity of engagement which could be regarded as a fruitful means of unlocking the potential for costumes to live on in individualized after-lives. The interventions within this book could thus be considered as being akin to labelled archive boxes stacked next to one another. Each one contains the remnants of a material journey, and the attendant knowledge and memories unfolded in the process. Engaging with these chapters as a reader is designed to mimic the sense of opening a selection of archive boxes (conceptually at least, if not physically), and peering at the materials entrapped within. The actual boxes in Anderson's archive are not uniform – some are large plastic tubs with lids, others repurposed cardboard boxes which once contained Freed dance shoes or Sony cassette tapes. Garment bags hang alongside the towers of stacked boxes, which in turn sit next to other uncatalogued heaps of audio equipment, folders of letters, and lastly, those omnipresent cellophane bags of spare zippers, fabric oddments and dye swatches. Useless detritus? Or, just possibly, the essential clue to what the original fabric or fastenings of a costume looked like, before repeated wear and dry-cleaning rendered it an altogether different hue. What to do? What to do with all of this *stuff*? Here in this book there is a deliberate attempt to present the remains of these costumes (both the actual costumes and the relevant information concerning them) as a site for encounter rather than a closed historical narrative. The holes and fissures which I have referred to earlier are at work and intentionally kept within the frame. The aim is not to close over these voids or fill in the gaps, but rather to gesture to the partial legacy left behind in these garments, and suggest ways in which they can be activated beyond their cold storage in the anonymous lockup.

Discussing her cross-disciplinary project *Mishandled Archive*, Tara Fatehi Irani outlines that the 'concept of the archive makes use of the passions and tensions of keeping, losing, conserving, destroying, listing, erasing, repeating and re-imagining moments for futures which may never come' (Fatehi Irani 2020: 13). Centred on a rare collection of Iranian archival photographs and documents, *Mishandled Archive* challenges conceptions of history and belonging via a 'mishandling' and displacement of archival artefacts. Fatehi Irani argues that within the conceptual space of the archive, '[r]igorous knowledge, imagination, fantasy and affect all cohabit and intermingle' (2020: 13). Her embracing of the paradoxes of the archive chimes strongly with the ethos of the interventions carried out within this project. Each one engages with specific remnants of the costume archive as an attempt to highlight their potential as generators of knowledge and imagining for alternative after-lives, but also, the inherent partiality and sometimes doomed futility of the archival gesture. In summary – this book does not wish to 'replace' the shattered smithereens of this archive with a polished scholarly account of Anderson and her work. Instead, the physical interventions prioritize the close encounter – they aim to pick up the remaining shards and turn them over, gleaning what fragmentary knowledge they impart and allowing their material nature to dictate the direction of their afterlife. Anderson's works (outside of the three selected costumes) are not discussed at length nor is there an attempt to categorize the legacy of *The Cholmondeleys* and *The Featherstonehaughs* within broad subject-matter categories (thematic concerns or late twentieth-century contemporary dance, for example). There are gaps and blind spots in this approach – in taking a position so 'up-close' both to the garments and the creative individuals associated with them. These are acknowledged as an inexorable element of this alternative approach to the costume archive. At times the methodology dips toes into film making, dress-conservation, auctioneer appraisals and more, yet it succeeds in mastering none of these. The interventions merely walk those paths as far as possible to test the potentials for these particular costume smithereens.

Partners in thought

The theoretical framework for this book has unfolded through working directly with the costumes as interlocutors at the heart of the project. Interactions with the costumes prompted further encounters with performers, designers, tailors and conservation experts. These meetings were carried out in a variety of settings – from noisy cafes to the hushed concentration of work rooms, and the bustle of a theatre costume department with rehearsal calls echoing out over the tannoy, obliterating the audio recording I was attempting to make. Due to the adaptive and process-based drivers of the project, the theoretical framework emerged in tandem with my work with the costumes and as a general rule I sought to avoid reaching immediately towards pre-ordained concepts from theory or particular fields of study (dance and costume studies, for example).

Photographic documentation of the selected costumes and my subsequent interviews with makers of the works in question give further shape to the after-lives of the costumes, suggesting both additional physical actions to undertake with the garments and avenues of theoretical exploration to pursue. I allow the physical actions carried out to point towards frames of reference which might prove apt partners in dialogue with the costumes. For example, with transaction the chapter looks to the visual art world to provide a suitable framework of valuation in relation to the three-piece Schiele suit. The *Smithereens* masks require a different approach and are greatly influenced by the conversations I have had with conservation experts, alongside broader perspectives towards artefacts within heritage and preservation contexts.

The conceptualization of 'the ghost' as it has emerged both within costume scholarship and wider sociological and cultural discourse also provides a useful backdrop against which to place the costume smithereens of this research (Monks 2010; Gordon 2008). The ghost can be utilized as a figure of unruliness: uncanny in nature, with the capacity to travel across time and across context. These conceptions, conversant as they are with my earliest impressions of the costumes and their stymied potential, operate as helpful counterparts to think through both the potentials and inertia of fabric remains.

Following on from this opening chapter I unpack in greater detail the conceptual underpinning of ghosts, and in contrast, the idea of fabric remains operating as forms of archival detritus, both of which assisted me in laying the ground for the practical material interventions I would go on to undertake – the 'doing something' with the costumes which Anderson and I had agreed to. This section explores tensions between ghost discourse as a useful provocation and conduit towards representational repair and the ways in which this constructed position must yield to the practical, economic and cultural conditions of Anderson's archive. It emphasizes the notion that any haunting or alternative after-lives this book might set out to create begins with physical actions grounded in the *here and now* of the actual fabric remains. The conceptual tug of war between viewing the potential of these garments as being able to enact a haunting, and on the other hand the undeniable physical realities of their material inertia, accompanies the journey of these smithereens from beginning to end of this book. As the physical actions unfold through disintegration, preservation, transaction and display in the intervention chapters, these ideas continue to crop up and become configured in relation to the needs of the individual costume remains in Anderson's archive.

From time to time, practical upskilling has been required in order for me to realize the project – garnering the fundamentals of film making, sound recording and editing, for example. Carrying out these actions, largely as a novice with no prior experience, is in fact a crucial element of the work that this book describes. The role of the novice tentatively finding the way forward fast became a generative position to occupy; allowing for curiosity and openness to prevail. Each physical gesture undertaken nudges on the research journey, conceptually shapeshifting the fabric remains and increasing the sense of my own entanglement with them. Alongside Anderson, I became implicated by the costumes early on – subservient to them – and no option remained but to carry on the journey of these smithereens as far as possible.

Roads not travelled

What paths does this book not take, and why? These are numerous. Despite the multi-tentacled nature of the research framework, there are many directions left untouched – set aside for future journeys. It would be impossible to track all of these here – the hunches, the sparks of interest found in surrounding conceptual worlds and fields of practice. It feels important to acknowledge their existence however, as important partners within the thinking of this book.

A chief area to be mentioned is that of the worlds of material culture and history of fashion and dress. Whilst the project does at many times crossover with these areas of scholarship and co-opt certain strategies and skills from within them (such as my training in dress handling and basic conservation), I must concede that the interaction with these areas of knowledge and practice has largely been at a limited, discreet level. This is partly born out of pragmatism – each of these areas (material culture, fashion and dress history) are vast in and of themselves. Moreover, there is a conscious decision to foreground a dance-specific perspective and to embrace the role of the uninitiated novice, allowing the research to delve *from there* into unfamiliar worlds. To give an example: deduction work utilized by dress researchers and conservators is often used to discover or validate the provenance of a historical garment for which there is little documentary evidence beyond the garment itself. Thus, museum specialists might look to discern details of who designed or made a garment, or for what purpose and by whom it might have been worn. With Anderson's costumes, the garments do not suffer from a comparable lack of verifiable historical information. Multiple memories and facts are still held, both within the material artefacts themselves, and the memories of the professionals who worked with them. This will not always be the case – the garments will eventually perish, and so too the individuals linked with their performance lives. The work of this book is therefore not about guesswork, but in fact about the gathering and collation of memories, traces and residues. This has been largely carried out via a dance-specific lens. The book prioritizes the encounter with the costumes as the key to unravel these associated histories and draw them together, but it does so with the sensibility of a dance historian or performer, rather than that of a dress history specialist. In the case of Anderson's costumes, we already know where the bodies are buried so to speak – I began the work with useful knowledge of the catalogue of works I would be investigating. In this sense, the guess work and intuition generally employed by a costume specialist (when confronting an unknown garment) is utilized, but in a different way. There is an aim not only to gather relevant historical information surrounding the garment, but also to call up the partial embodied recollections and insights of the individuals involved with the garments which, if not documented now, will certainly slip out of reach of historians eventually, as time passes.

There were further pathways that could have been traversed, such as an investigation of the histories of the fabric used to make some of the costumes. The Dead Skins fabric, for instance, was purchased from a now closed-down establishment on Goldhawk Road in London, an area with a rich history of fabric shops, frequented by theatre designers and costume makers; another interrelated world similar to that bound up with the tailor's shop in Soho where the Schiele suit was made. Potentially deeper work could be done here in tracing the histories of the individuals and processes involved in the original base materials of the costumes, and the economic and cultural worlds of their production. There would be much to discover in these worlds which speak to the concerns of this book – different kinds of precarity, economic variability and dedicated, expert, craft and labour. Additionally, whilst the interviews with dancers threw up rich observations on the specific embodiments and reciprocal relationships engendered between costumes and bodies (and how these differed between dancers), further investigation could be made into how these differences may or may not have shaped the spectators' perception of the works and how the choreography was embodied differently by individual dancers. This is just a further sample of a pathway not followed in depth. There are many more potential avenues like this one to be explored.

The journey taken

In acceptance of the roads not taken, the false trails and the 'if onlys', what might be the benefits of the up-close, adaptive, encounter-led approach adopted in this book? Such an approach is inarguably one which inculcates blind spots. Yet it also allows the necessary up-close engagement which can facilitate an interlocution of the semi-vanished performance histories bound up in the garments under investigation. It foregrounds a specificity of attending to the archive in question, moving away from the categorical cataloguing and summative historical approaches sometimes favoured in more traditional archival contexts. It gestures towards the ruptures – the metaphorical shattering (akin to silk) of the legacy of Anderson's work. It seeks neither to repair these ruptures nor to turn away from them. It advocates a sense of care – a prioritizing of the smithereens – the 'little bits'. A *being-with* the materials as a means of conjuring half-remembered entanglements and the reciprocal relationships between costumes and bodies once in full flight. It acknowledges the inevitability of material transitions, the steady march of degradation, the uncountable losses and yet still presses on. Up close. Picking over the shards which remain. It utilizes one small archive and just three individual costumes to excavate and illuminate the wider structures at work in their after-lives – physically, socioculturally, economically. It carries out this labour, not only as a work of illumination, but more optimistically as a means of divining a further sympathetic or fit-for-purpose framework for the interlocution and care of fabric remains. It could arguably be regarded as a ridiculous gesture – one that, in its futility and excess, deems these costumes to be materially frail, conceptually rich, ever changing and meriting our care.

Beginning again

But first, to begin once more. Here offered is an encounter with smithereens – the material remains of performances now largely ruptured but not entirely vanished from view. The writing attempts as far as possible to set these fragments on a new course towards their alternative after-lives. It is hoped that within this text, the methodological approaches, dead ends and attempts at interlocution all radiate outwards from the up-close material details of the garments themselves – just as they did during the work itself.

Afterword: The lockup continued

I am certain I can smell a trace of damp and tentatively ask Lea 'Is it damp in here?' 'No I don't think so', she replies. 'Though maybe it is a little. I prefer it to be slightly damp than dry but with moths!' She recounts a story of the 'Yellow Box' storage facility she once used to store costumes which was very dry because it had fans, but then moths got in through the vents and ate holes in all the garments.

The lockup curves round to the left where there are piles of metal stage supports, chairs, stage lights (from *Yippeee!!!*), and more rails and rails, boxes and boxes. We spend the next hour and a half opening boxes, peering through suit bags, stacking and restacking. Lea greets each garment with the hesitance of one reacquainting herself with dear but distant friends. 'Which one is this? *Baby Baby*? No – these are the *Las*

Lea Anderson at the costume lockup. Photos: Mary Kate Connolly

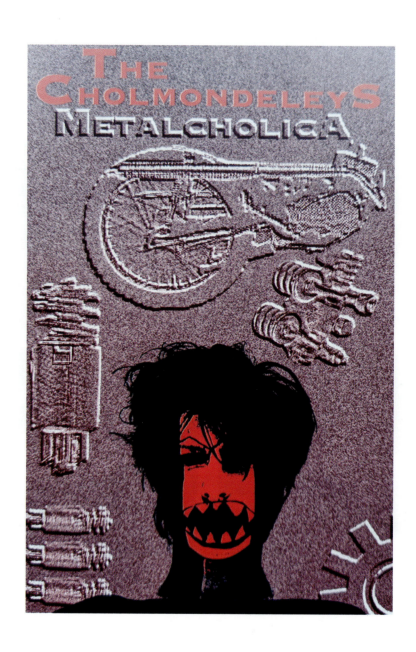

Publicity poster for *Metalcholica* (1994). Featuring Gaynor Coward with makeup by Cash Aspeek. Photo: Chris Nash

Vegas jackets! They were amazing.' Anecdotes inevitably tumble out with each new item that she looks at. I am interested in the traces of the dancers' bodies which are left behind in the costumes, which become uncannily inescapable when Lea picks up the *Smithereens* masks cast from the faces of each individual dancer. Some mime-artist white, some decorated with Hannah Hoch-style collages overlaid on the features from the dancers' faces. Even without the scribbled name tags inside I can identify some of the dancers I am familiar with.

Later we turn up more masks – this time from the 1994 work *Metalcholica*, in which Lea herself performed. The black and white leather masks were based on a photograph of a face-painted Bronislava Nijinska. Lea looks at them. 'Teresa? Is that her? Where am I? Oh there I am!' She holds her own mask to her face. I ask if it still fits. 'Yes, pretty much, although actually I seem to remember that this bit never actually fit quite right over the eyes'. As she wrestles to close the heavy duty padlock on the door, Lea tells me that just after the last *Featherstonehaughs* performance the lockup was burgled – everything thrown around, cameras and equipment stolen which contained the films of the final performances. There is something at odds, or jarring, about locking up this storeroom of theatrical wonders which has the aura of a shrine, and emerging once again into faceless suburbia. Walking away and waiting impatiently in the cold for the next train to spirit you away from this soulless place. Alice-in-Wonderland style. Almost as if it never happened …

Notes

1. Projects devised for Prague Quadrennials 2011, 2015 and 2019 which comprised several approaches to using costume and objects as embodied partners in the choreographic and design process. These were in step with other research interrogating the interplays between costume and movement, including Jessica Bugg (2014, 2020), Sally E. Dean (2011, 2020) and Michèle Danjoux (2014, 2020).

2. Hodgdon has explored not only ghostliness and the presence of the actor's body within costume, but also within other material remnants such as prompt scripts and rehearsal photographs. See Hodgdon (2016) and Abel and Holland (2021).

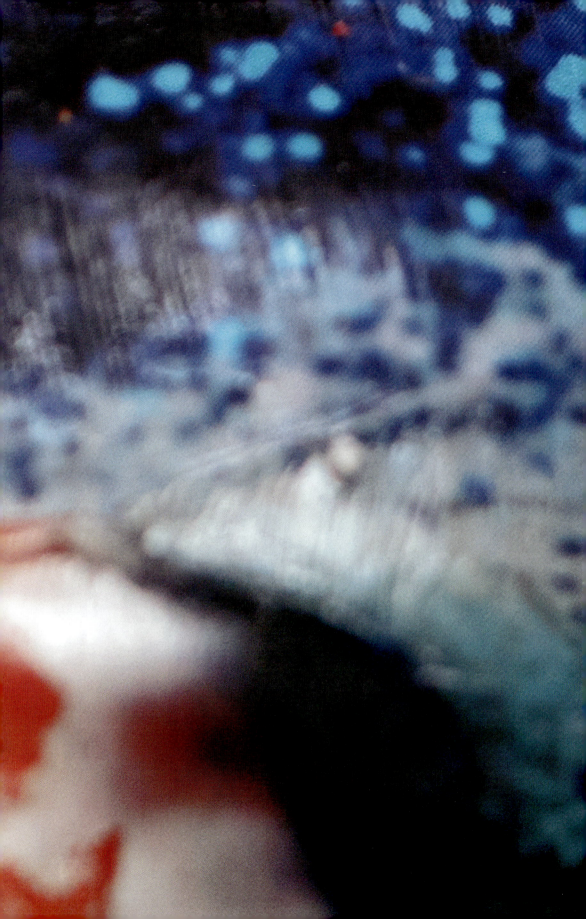

SMITHEREENS:
Ghosts, detritus and
performance's return

When I began my work with Anderson's archive it was essentially motivated by a need for something-to-be-done. An attempt at physical actions which could reframe the fabric remains therein, or creatively mobilize them to enjoy an after-life beyond that of their archival boxes. These boxes alone, if we dwell with them for a moment, implicitly frame these costumes contradictorily as both historically rich, loaded with potential and worth preserving, and as bulky inconvenient 'stuff' in storage – detritus, arguably. They are also wholly invisible to anyone outside the padlocked door of the lockup. Enhancing the visibility of some of these remains runs in conversation with the deeper undercurrents of this project; of indirect, partial recuperation of the legacy of a catalogue of performance work which is slipping beyond our view. As outlined in Beginning, the theoretical partners in thought which unfold in this book are arrived at via direct interaction with the costumes. From the outset however, I was tempted by an instinctual positioning of the costumes as ghosts. And it seems helpful to dwell a while on the concept of ghosts, given its seeming ready applicability to fabric remains such as Anderson's, before it can become transfigured through the physical interventions in the chapters which follow. This chapter, which centres on the joys and contradictions of costumes as ghosts and as detritus, unpacks the construction of ghosts and haunting across a range of fields (sociological, literary, museological and performance). This is undertaken in order to foreshadow the work of hands-on figuration that this book is concerned with: the *doing-something* with fabric remains which Anderson and I embarked upon in her archive. Against a backdrop of erasures, quests for disruption, representational repair and performative return – and no less than the practical interventions on stubbornly material smithereens that will be set out in the chapters that follow – ghost-summoning is revealed as an active, constructed and unavoidably partial enterprise.

Troubled by ghosts

Conceptualizing the costumes in Anderson's archive as ghosts was initially motivated by my overriding sense of these garments enacting a haunting in some way. This impression formed in the immediacy of encounter as Anderson and I hunted through the lockup, disinterring garment after garment from their temporary archival burial sites. On further reading it is of course apparent that this hunch around costumes as appearing haunted is far from uncommon (Hodgdon 2006, 2016; Barbieri and Crawley 2013; Monks 2010). However, given the inherently 'haunted' nature of costumes post-performance, it still seems worthwhile to unravel this idea further: to intentionally position Anderson's costumes as ghosts in order to ask specifically what kind of haunting might be provoked within *this* particular archive. 'If haunting describes how that which appears to be not there is often a seething presence, acting on and meddling with taken-for-granted realities, the ghost is just the sign [...] that tells you that a haunting is taking place' (Gordon 2008: 9).

It seemed to be the *ghost* in particular that I was searching for in the early stages of this work; a figure capable of inciting physical actions with the costumes and unlocking hidden performance histories. Essentially, a ghost was conjured in my mind's eye in order to make manifest the haunting or provocation which I felt this material legacy of performance work could potentially gesture towards (as Gordon alludes to above). Positioning Anderson's costumes as ghosts was a helpful step in establishing their role as interlocutors of performance histories, and celebrating the inherent complications of their status as material remains of an ephemeral art form. The instability of the ghost was wholly embraced; conceived as a conceptual figure commandeered in a quest for visibility, whilst remaining open to the unexpected and only partially visible within its archival field. There was a conscious attempt to allow the costumes alone to provoke a cascade of relevant concerns, to potentially disrupt assumed practices of archiving and documenting, and to enhance the visibility of garments which are currently hidden from view and discourse. The material realities of the selected costumes (as I encountered them), their performance histories and insights from across a range of disciplines have fed in to the creation of the figurality of the performance costume foregrounded in this book. I owe a debt of gratitude in this endeavour to these diverse perspectives, in particular the work of Avery F. Gordon (2008) and Aoife Monks (2010). Tracing a path from literary and sociological theory (Del Pilar Blanco and Peeren 2013), to curatorial practices and performance discourse (Clark 2017; Lepecki 2010), the ghost figure has appeared as a persistent, problematic repository of body memories and performance folklore replete with absence. The ghost has allowed for the inherent contradictions or complications of garments such as these to be acknowledged, whilst also selecting a delineated focus of enquiry.

But why might it be useful to summon ghosts in Anderson's archive in the first place? Establishing Anderson's costumes as ghosts can certainly be seen as a useful first step in seeking to explicate artefacts which by their nature are mercurial and shape-shifting. The Dead Skins from Anderson's *Yippeee!!!* (2006) for example, when held aloft, still bear the makeup streaks and physical stained contours of the dancers' bodies. In one sense they look indeed like a discarded skin, utterly lifeless and inanimate. They also seem unmistakably haunted by the body which hollowed out those contours and is no longer present. Witnessing this absence is almost to imagine the body still present, suspended somehow by the hollow shell of the fabric. Rebecca Schneider, responding to the work of Peggy Phelan (1993), influentially questioned whether 'in privileging an understanding of performance as a refusal to remain [...] we ignore other ways of knowing, other modes of remembering, that might be situated precisely in the ways in which performance remains, but remains differently?' (Schneider 2011: 98). In conjuring the ghost here, there is no suggestion that costume offers a body to *stand-in* for the performance which disappears, but rather that it offers up the possibility of costume as a locus and generator of particular (and potentially untold) knowledge of the performance which brought it into being. Anderson's fabric ghosts, if such they be, operate *across* time as being artefacts of performance which came alive in the late twentieth or early twenty-first century, but which are now acted upon and interpreted within the context of the present-day. This ability of the costumes to operate within two spheres underpins the value in beholding them as entities that can, as it were, haunt the present moment and, in doing so, unearth concerns relating to value, visibility and preservation.

Ghost problems

It is high time to note also that to venture into the realm of ghosts and haunting comes with inherent risks. Strewn with the bear traps of academic gimmick and cultural commentary bandwagon, it is challenging to find a path of argument that has not already been well trodden. Yet it is also no small thing to walk in company with a rich variety of voices and ideas, congruent and divergent, spanning a cross-section of fields from literary to sociological. *The Spectralities Reader*, edited by María Del Pilar Blanco and Esther Peeren (2013), emphasizes the variety of questions and approaches that can be enriched by ideas of spectrality. In their introduction, the editors outline the ways in which ghosts were transformed (in the 1990s in particular), from the world of fiction and lore into 'influential conceptual metaphors permeating global (popular) culture and academia alike' (Del Pilar Blanco and Peeren 2013: 1). They chart the emergence of the ghost as a conceptual tool for interrogation, analysis and knowledge production. Pivoting from the cultural moment precipitated by the publication of Jacques Derrida's *Spectres de Marx* (1993) (and the subsequent English translation in 1994), which has become known as 'The Spectral Turn', Del Pilar Blanco and Peeren sketch out the cultural and theoretical landscape before and after Derrida's text and the elevation of the spectre from metaphor or allegorical figure, to conceptual tool which disrupts, illuminates and categorizes within the respective fields of its employ.

Despite labels such as the Spectral Turn, the editors of *Spectralities* are keen to stress that Spectrality or the use of spectres for enquiry is far from being a delineated or controlled field or science.

'The ghost, even when turned into a conceptual metaphor, remains a figure of unruliness' (Del Pilar Blanco and Peeren 2013: 9). It is just this unruliness and shape-shifting which, again, might point to the potential of the ghost figure in relation to the costumes of Lea Anderson. However, to utilize the term ghost is to evoke an unstable metaphor, subject to interpretation. Due to the variability of ideas which the ghost or spectre could be seen to represent, the need for specificity of context and framework becomes imperative. Del Pilar Blanco and Peeren suggest that

> the ghost also questions the formation of knowledge itself and specifically invokes what is placed outside it, excluded from the perception and, consequently, from both the archive as the depository of the sanctioned, acknowledged past and politics as the (re)imagined future.
> (Del Pilar Blanco and Peeren 2013: 9)

On the face of it, the capacity for the ghost to meddle with established histories, and to haunt both the stage and the stability of the archive itself, might seem appropriate for the fabric remains of the work of a female choreographer which are currently both physically and metaphorically *disappeared* from the lexicon of dance and performance culture. Again, though, in attempting to locate and give shape to these costume ghosts it is necessary to acknowledge the caveats in such an endeavour. Firstly, to clarify that the ghost and concept of haunting as it is referred to here is fundamentally a western-centric cultural construct. In the face of the cross-pollination which has occurred as ideas of spectrality have traversed continents (despite the Judeo-Christian and western bias of Derrida's conception of the spectre in *Specters of Marx*, 1993), Del Pilar Blanco and Peeren highlight the need to 'insist on taking seriously the disarticulations that remain even as a spectral Esperanto seems to be emerging' (Del Pilar Blanco and Peeren 2013: 92).

In the introduction to his edited volume, *Spectral America: Phantoms and the National Imagination* (2004), Jeffrey Andrew Weinstock attempts to unpick the profusion of haunting which, as he observes, has sprung up in American popular culture and academia around the turn of the millennium. For Weinstock, 'phantoms haunt; their appearances signal epistemological uncertainty and the potential emergence of a different story' (Weinstock 2004: 7). Weinstock places the fascination with phantoms inside the context of (American) millennial angst and uncertainty for the future, and also emphasizes the contingent nature of the ghost in how it relates to contemporary culture and politics. 'Ghosts', according to Weinstock, 'do "cultural work" but [...] the work they perform changes according to the developing needs of the living. Phantoms participate in, reinforce, and exemplify various belief structures' (Weinstock 2004: 8). There is accordingly, an underlying instability and shape-shifting nature of the ghost operating across a web of associations within social, cultural and geographical contexts. Weinstock also reveals some unease with the proliferation of ghosts at the moment of his writing, asserting that the ghost has become 'a privileged poststructuralist academic trope' (Weinstock 2004: 4), even as he underlines the continued value of the ghost for compelling us towards the continuation of cultural memory. He suggests that 'the alternative to their presence is even more frightening [...] without ghosts to point to things that have been lost and overlooked things may disappear forever' (Weinstock 2004: 6). Ghosts can, therefore, be potentially helpful figures in alerting us to the work required in remembering, and where necessary, attempting to enact representational repair or interrupt the predominant cultural and historical discourse. How, though, do these aspirations for the ghost figure meet with the material realities of the stained bodysuits, stuffed packing boxes and near total invisibility of Anderson's archive? How might ghosts be used in the face of the contradictions of these objects which oscillate between being cast as invaluable cultural treasure and the inconvenient 'junk' of performance remains?

Detritus, visibility and representational repair

> instead of the archive's instability and compromised authority being an inevitable accident, can it be transformed into the central motif of a live performance archive celebrating transformation and fluidity?
> (Reason 2003: 87)

Matthew Reason (2003) is arguing here a case for an archive of performance detritus (objects left behind in performance's wake). An assemblage which could, in its incompleteness, provide traces which chime with the audience's memories of a performance as it took place, rather than attempting a faithful documentation of a performance now gone. He concludes by suggesting that

The idea of detritus as archive is also not so far from the state of all archives: but the archive as detritus turns around the presumptions of neutral detachment, objectivity, fidelity, consistency, and authenticity – instead claiming partiality, fluidity, randomness, and memory. And having abandoned claims to accuracy and completeness, such an archive is able to present archival interpretations, proclamations, and demonstrations, consciously and overtly performing what all archives are already enacting: dumb objects not allowed to speak for themselves, but spoken for.
(Reason 2003: 89)

It serves me well to remember the 'dumb' element of archival objects which Reason describes, before I begin merrily ascribing all sorts of eloquent capabilities to the objects – masks, suits and artificial dead skins – at the heart of my research.[1] Undoubtedly this book 'speaks for' these costumes, but such ventriloquism arises from the aim of altering the narrative of erasure and fixed historicity which already attended these garments – the ways in which they were spoken for (through silence, invisibility or fragmentary theatre reviews still traceable online). The costume-as-interlocutor becomes a means through which the conversation can be extended, and the after-lives for these costumes reimagined. To this end, a particular utilization of the ghost figure is called for. Various conceptions of ghosts have been justifiably generative in the theorizing of theatre costumes and their post-performance afterlives (a topic which sits at the heart of this book), but if I am to borrow from ghost discourse for Anderson's costumes in particular, I'm drawn most to the work of Avery F. Gordon (2008), which is grounded in the field of sociology and deals in particular with instances of historical erasure, subjugated knowledge and representational repair. These elements, whilst transplanted from a field of study far removed from dance and costume scholarship, nonetheless seem (to me) to speak to the concerns of disappearance, the fractures of archival remains and recuperation of performance legacy at the centre of my work with Anderson's costumes.

Gordon outlines a concept of 'writing ghost stories, stories that not only repair representational mistakes, but also strive to understand the conditions under which a memory was produced in the first place, towards a countermemory for the future' (Gordon 2008: 22). Her book *Ghostly Matters: Haunting and the Sociological Imagination* offers a complex and highly creative framework of haunting mobilized as a means of disturbing closed historical narratives and worrying at, if not overturning, disappearances enacted via traumatic sociological ruptures and oppressive political regimes. However, for Gordon: 'Haunting is not the same as being exploited, traumatized or oppressed although it usually involves these experiences or is produced by them' (2008: xvi), and these provide the topics of her investigation. Clearly the subjects of her enquiry differ greatly from contemporary dance costumes within a private archive, but the multilayered complexity of her approach nonetheless has much to offer in the realm of imaginative archival work and attempts at enacting visibility. Whilst Gordon is writing from the field of sociology, she emphasizes (in her introduction to the book's second edition) that her work doesn't set out to critique this field but rather 'to learn from subjugated knowledge' (2008: xviii), turning to the novels of Toni Morrison and Luisa Valenzuela, among other sources, in this venture. The spaciousness of Gordon's approach suggested to me that there could be room to accommodate my utilization of the ghost in step with hers. I was aiming after all, to unfurl stories which are irreparably fragmented through archival dispersal, yet which can still operate as a kind of echo or eloquent trace of performances now vanished. Crucially, Gordon's ghost figure is, in ways, also a troublemaker who demands our attention. Gordon:

> Haunting was precisely the domain of turmoil and trouble, that moment [...] when things are not in their assigned places, when the cracks and rigging are exposed when the people who are meant to be invisible show up without any sign of leaving, when disturbed feelings cannot be put away, when something else, something different from before, seems like it must be done.
> (2008: xvi)

Gordon cites a key goal of her book as being 'to get us to consider a different way of seeing, one that is [...] more willing to be surprised, to link imagination and critique' (2008: 24). An intriguing example of this linkage of imagination with critique can be found in her second chapter which centres on a 'detour', as Gordon categorizes it – essentially a ghost hunt, which begins with her happening upon a photograph in which a certain woman should be, but who is not there. The photograph is from the 1911 Psychoanalytic Congress in Weimar and the missing woman is Sabina Spielrein, famously associated (or indeed entangled) with both Carl Jung and Sigmund Freud in ways both personal and professional. Thus begins a journey in the book towards representational repair, in which the preoccupation with Spielrein's absence in the photograph (with what is not visible) becomes mobilized as a conduit to understand all the other elements which might also be missing, and how they might have been disappeared. Spielrein's significant contributions to the field of psychoanalysis, for example, which become elided in the representational absences and the more salacious stories which now *stand-in* in their stead.

Returning to the context of Anderson's archive, this approach prompts renewed concern for me, in unpacking what is there and what is not there. What can be seen and how we (interpreting the archive) might be seeing it. Anderson's archive contains embodied materials which remain alongside (or as prompts for) the memories of those who wore, maintained and stored them. Though the costumes held in the lockup remain largely invisible to wider public view, a close attending to their current material state, and a gathering of the stories of their creation and the embodied memories of those who wore them, can begin to enact a renewed visibility. To put stories back in where they are missing – to allow a haunting, or perhaps more accurately, a disruption of closed narratives, to take place.

For Gordon, 'haunting, unlike trauma, is distinctive for producing a something-to-be-done' (2008: xvi). A ghost can thus be employed as a provocateur to spur us towards new action, or the creation of an alternative account; a new way of seeing things. In the case of Anderson's archive, co-opting the fabric remains into conjuring a haunting of sorts provides the impetus for radical action with the costumes. Physical actions such as for example, intentional disintegration of a costume, which might seem to run counter to the widespread assumptions of how an archive might sustain or repair legacy. Borrowing from Gordon's utilization of the ghost in a battle against erasure can also be helpful for a project such as this, which champions visibility as a central motivator. The visibility of the costumes as archival document and interlocutor in and of themselves is foregrounded but, equally, there is also an aim to make visible the structures (archival and performative) which have entrapped these costumes and rendered them into a state of disappearance. In this endeavour it becomes necessary to first quantify *what* visibility is aimed for. What indeed has been subject to erasure? Primarily, the costumes in their physical state, hidden away in a distant anonymous lockup to which only Anderson herself has the key. But there are wider considerations here too – there is also a sense in which Anderson herself, as a choreographer who at one time enjoyed acclaim and visibility within the contemporary dance community in the United Kingdom and internationally (Hutera 2011), has in effect disappeared from this terrain.

With the funding cuts her companies suffered in 2011 came a significant change. *The Cholmondeleys* and *The Featherstonehaughs* largely ceased performing and making new work. Her dance works, once featured on the GCSE and A-Level syllabi in the UK secondary schools, are no longer part of the dance studies curriculum. Scholarship concerning her work tends to dwindle in the years prior to her companies' disappearance (Hargreaves 2007; Burt and Briginshaw 2009; Briginshaw 2009). There is an ongoing lack of in-depth interrogation of her more recent works (such as *Ladies and Gentlemen* 2015; *Laberinto* 2019; *Elvis Legs Quarantine Mix* 2020), and in terms of the legacy of the catalogue of performances produced from the 1980s until 2011. Her work did feature for example in the BBC 4 documentary *Dance Rebels: A Story of Modern Dance* (BBC 4 2015), but she does not enjoy the visibility and acclaim of some of her male contemporaries such as choreographers Matthew Bourne and Michael Clark (whose works have continued to be programmed at Sadler's Wells [Bourne] and The Barbican [Clark][2] and across the United Kingdom).[3] A complex set of economic, cultural and aesthetic factors have undoubtedly conspired in this partial erasure of Anderson and her work, and an unravelling of these sits outside the feasible scope of this book. It is however an aspiration that by allowing the costumes to articulate their specific narrative, a wider picture may emerge, creating a dynamic and contemporary discourse around certain elements of her work and legacy.[4]

The volume of information on an artist which is available and the ease or difficulty for researchers, writers and others to access it (particularly within an online realm), exerts considerable influence on the ways in which artists are kept within, or excluded from, the cultural sphere. The resources required for maintaining a prominent continual online presence,[5] however, can be burdensome. Whilst choreographers such as Bourne, Clark and other counterparts such as Wayne McGregor have companies equipped with administration to sustain a well-designed informative web presence, Anderson does not currently possess the infrastructure to maintain her website as a dynamic archival resource. Likewise, whilst the aforementioned companies engage with the wider community through outreach projects,[6] Anderson no longer has such an engagement. With the removal of funding for her companies, came the end of their outreach work, and education partnerships.[7] Thus, whilst the scholarship and press reviews which exist in the public domain might create the illusion of full visibility of this artist, in fact there is a great disparity between the accessible information on Anderson and her work, and that of many of her UK contemporaries. Whilst surveying this aspect in detail is beyond the remit of this enquiry, there are nonetheless aforementioned gaps and fissures which this book aims to point towards. Gordon (2008) draws attention to the concept of 'hypervisibility' in contemporary culture – the ways in which the selectivity of representation is no longer highlighted, or rather that the selectivity and distinctions between the visible and invisible have been abolished. She suggests that '[i]n a culture seemingly ruled by technologies of hypervisibility, we are led to believe not only that everything can be seen, but also that everything is available and accessible for our consumption' (Gordon 2008: 16). Such an assumption risks missing the overlooked, the not-seen, the forgotten, or taking for granted the absence of forgotten histories.

In an archival context such as Anderson's – a padlocked anonymous lockup where, without intervention, no haunting or visibility whatsoever could be realized – how might it be possible to counteract the disappearance which has befallen these costumes and their wider performance legacy? Gordon suggests that we must seek to redress the overlooked, 'to start with the marginal, with what we normally exclude or banish or, more commonly, with what we never even notice' (Gordon 2008: 24–25). The performative nature of the dance costume demands a creative strategy for the (re)writing of its history. Beginning with the bare traces and memories that Gordon alludes to, the stories told in this book arise directly from the materiality of the costumes, and seek in the telling to give shape to the absences which these fabric remains point towards. Rather than producing a set of rules or strict methodology Gordon suggests that her method 'involves producing case studies of haunting and adjudicating their consequences' (Gordon 2008: 24). This is used as a ploy to investigate, or as a way of seeing 'what happens when we admit the ghost – that special instance of the merging of the visible and the invisible' (Gordon 2008: 24). The deliberateness of Gordon's approach does two things: it ushers in the ghost as a useful figure for disruption, but also clearly outlines the intentional labour involved in writing ghost stories and attempting a redress of sociological and cultural disappearance. Similarly, this book does not assume the presence of costume ghosts or any inherent eloquence of fabric remains; rather it regards the ghost figure as providing the impetus or indeed the alibi for specific material actions to be carried out on the costumes. Interventions which arise from their various core concerns of material decay, iconic status, logistical inconvenience, invisibility and rich creative potential. In initially positioning the costumes as ghosts in order to devise alternative after-lives for them, the central motivation has been to place the costumes in a new context and then attend to the ways in which they appear to articulate their condition. This essentially provides a means of opening up new ways to think about disintegration and vanishing, totemic significance, economic exchange, dissemination and legacy.

Performance's vanishing and return

Directing focus more specifically towards dance and performance archives, there is a rich body of scholarship concerned with the disappearance of performance, and with the traces it leaves behind (Taylor 2003; Reason 2006; Lepecki 2010; Schneider 2011). These include pertinent considerations of the roles, functions and limitations of the performance archive, and the oscillations between live performance and live mediatized performance (Auslander 2008). Peggy Phelan famously stated in *Unmarked: The Politics of Performance* that 'performance's only life is in the present' (Phelan 1993: 146). Making a clear distinction between the present moment of performance and any other attempt to reconstitute it (such as a repeat of the performance, a video of the performance), she argued that '[p]erformance's being [...] becomes itself through disappearance' (Phelan 1993: 146). This assertion and its subsequent rebuttals by scholars such as Rebecca Schneider (2001, 2011) and André Lepecki (2006) are by now well-rehearsed. The potency of the idea of the loss and death of performance nonetheless prevails as an intriguing concept, albeit as one against which to pose the physical reality of Anderson's fabric remains. Their stubborn yet fractured materiality which persists in the face of performance's vanishing.

In addition to scholarly discourse on performance and ephemerality, there are rich explorations of alternative archives, such as the body itself as archive (Lepecki 2010), and investigations of specific fragments and remains of performance such as image, video and text (Pavis 2003; Reason 2006). Hodgdon (2006, 2016) and Monks (2010, 2013) have looked towards items of the kind of 'detritus' which Reason (2003) refers to: stock costumes which bear uncanny traces of previous actors, stage props such as skulls (Monks 2013) and swords (Hodgdon 2006), rehearsal images and prompt scripts (Hodgdon 2016). Lepecki (2010) also touches on performance remains such as the lipstick of Martha Graham and her costumes (though not as the main object of focus, and in the specific context of re-enactment). The rich insights provided by these studies put forward a solid grounding for an approach towards a dance costume archive which employs a similarly forensic level of attention towards costumes as a means of retrieval of vanished histories across a specific canon of work. Costumes which are not handed down as they are in repertory theatre or stock costume holdings (which Hodgdon and Monks explore), but rather as custom-made garments which lived and died with their individual performances.

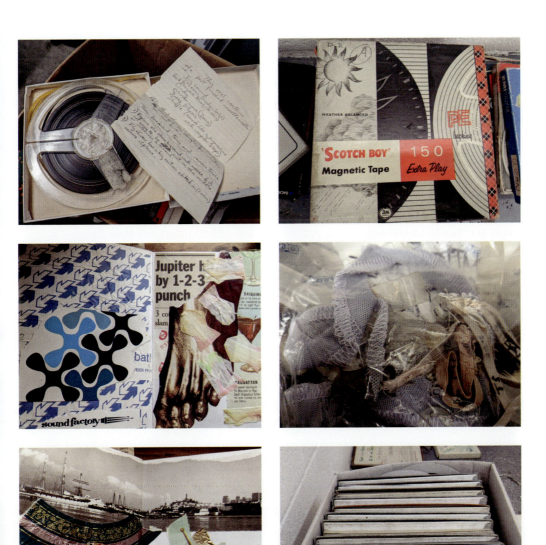

Reel to reel audio tapes, fabric remnants and pages of Lea Anderson's notebooks from *The Cholmondeleys* and *The Featherstonehaughs* Archive. Photos: Mary Kate Connolly

35

The Dead Skins, for example, viewed by Anderson as 'an arrow to something else' (Anderson 2017: n.pag.), differ greatly in any haunting which they might enact to the masks from Anderson's 1999 work *Smithereens*. Moulded individually to the dancer's faces, these masks operate far more in the realm of a totemic object. They perceptibly bear the exact features of each face, and without difficulty Anderson can recognize each dancer from the past as she holds their masks in her hands. They were hand painted (some by the performance artist David Hoyle), and as such can be regarded as craft or art objects in and of themselves. Rather than being a partial, hollow shell which is unreadable out of context, the mask could be appreciated in an alternative material way when viewed outside of performance. Nonetheless their inherent contradictions prevail, as, whilst they are 'whole' in the way in which the face is fully rendered as an object, they simultaneously conjure the absence of the face which made the mould in the first place. Anderson outlined in interview that

> the masks [...] are something that I look at. And because they look like the dancers that were in them, I have a fondness for them as an artefact and an object. A sort of totemic thing. And it's very different from the Dead Skin. (Anderson 2017: n.pag.)

Thus the conjuring of memories and illumination of absences which each individual costume can perform varies according to their materiality and the conceptual ways they are viewed by those directly linked to them. Any retrievals of lost performances in this context are unavoidably partial and differ greatly between each of the fabric remains. They present on the whole, therefore, as a collection of smithereens which can nonetheless be mobilized to make visible the unique characteristics of each costume and how they relate to their wider performance history and place in the archive.

Take, for a moment, the example of the Dead Skin as a case study to adjudicate. The costume, when examined closely, reveals details which speak back to the body which inhabited it and the choreography it performed. The dancer's bodily imprint is immediately visible through the slightly stretched contours and sweat stain discoloration. Footprints are etched onto the fabric where, once, a dancer's feet would have been. The absence of shoes and accessories is foregrounded by the tell-tale snags and rips left behind – threads of fabric which once became ensnared in a pearl necklace or the button of a shoe. And so, appraised in this close-up way, the costume begins to reveal its legacy. Not only the body or bodies which inhabited it and the items which were worn to adorn it, but indeed, specific elements of the choreography have equally left their marks. The smears of dark face makeup on the shoulders, for example, echoing a movement when dancers (during a sequence from *Yippeee!!!* called *Wavy Arms*) swayed together, with their chins tucked closely to their shoulders, flicking their heads from side to side. It is also possible to find many wiry curls from the pubic wigs (which the dancers wore inside the Dead Skins) still trapped in the tiny holes of fabric. The wide area in which they can be found across the torso and down the legs retraces the way in which these wigs would begin to roam about the body during performance, leaving dark trails under the Dead Skin. These clues offer much information as to the past histories still literally held within the garment itself. Thus it can be enabled to operate as a transmitter of information concerning these legacies. The hands-on interventions devised in response to these close appraisals of the costumes aim to bring forth these past histories to offer a fractured but vivid encounter with fabric remains, and to attempt a partial return of lost performance and legacy. In the case of the Dead Skin, this involved a speeding up of material decline and the creation of new archival artefacts including photographs and film. The interventions do not assume that haunting can be enacted in an overarching or uniform way, but instead attend to the minutiae of the costumes to find the way forward for their alternative after-lives.

Archival acts and blindspots

Rather than uniformly positioning the costumes as ghosts, I felt compelled instead to use the 'ghost' as a motivator to *act* upon the costumes. This is an active, rather than passive 'attending to' the archive, and it therefore risks imposing certain conditions and 'truths' onto the materials therein. 'To be haunted', writes Gordon, 'is not a methodology or a consciousness you can simply [...] adapt as a set of rules [...] it produces its own insights and blindness' (Gordon 2008: 22). This is certainly true of any conjuring of costume ghosts. I am not suggesting that the garments themselves speak to us of their own accord – rather it becomes about adopting an attitude towards artefacts which then endows them with a voice. In entering into this attendance, I, as the researcher, am in a sense surrendering the objectivity of distance in favour of the details and narratives which being up-close can reveal. And in doing so it is necessary to embrace the potential 'blindness' which Gordon refers to, along with the 'insights'. It seems important to reiterate that this book seeks to open up a specific framework for thinking about the fabric remnants in Anderson's archive – to allow the archive to speak back and articulate the concerns (historical, artistic, archival) of these individual garments. In light of the popularity of spectrality within scholarship, and the resultant suspicion of the term as either an academic ploy, or a suitably opaque catchall cultural term, it becomes a somewhat perilous project to adopt the use of ghosts wholesale within this archival endeavour. Instead, ghosts (as provocateurs towards action) travel along companionably with the practical work described in the chapters which follow. They provided a useful partner in thought from time to time, reminding me to prioritize visibility and the aim for representational repair in any after-life which I sought to achieve for the costumes.

Literature scholar Julian Wolfreys' ideas of how the immaterial qualities of written texts (or equally I would argue, material objects) traverse time and live on are of relevance here. In the preface of his 2001 book *Victorian Hauntings*, Wolfreys explores the ways in which texts and the textual can be considered haunted. He suggests that texts, whilst appearing material, are also intricately engaged with the spectral and subject to careful construction in the ways in which texts live on through time, imbued by us the readers with a sense of the immortal. Wolfreys lays bare the mechanics by which texts are afforded a life and voice beyond the material reality of the page. He suggests that we anchor the materiality of books through the structures of 'heritage and tradition' and the archive, in a perhaps naïve disavowal of their spectral nature and active maintenance:

> We announce in various ways the power of texts to survive, as though they could, in fact, live on, without our help, without our involvement as readers, researchers, archivists, librarians, or bibliographer [...] we keep up the plot, the archival burial ground, saying all the while that the life or afterlife of texts is all their own, and not an effect of the embalming processes in which we engage. (Wolfreys 2013: 71)

The dynamic processes of reading and archiving which Wolfreys illuminates, and the structures of archive and tradition in any enactment of haunting, are wholly relevant to this study. They also echo with a dilemma of impossible survival as described by Giulia Palladini and Marco Pustianaz in *Lexicon for an Affective Archive* (2017: 13–14), a publication containing a diverse range of archival encounters which unfold the affective and critical ways in which memories and archival histories are constructed in the space of archival encounter. The responsibility of what to preserve and how to preserve it, which any archival researcher faces. The visible and invisible biases which influence the choices made. Whilst undeniably, the *active* nature of my archival interventions with Anderson's costumes produces intrinsic blindnesses and imposes structures on the costumes, it also seems fair to suggest that the costumes in their archival state were already being acted upon. They are wholly at the mercy of the structures of archive (exclusion), preservation, heritage and the ravages of time. In being subject to cultural erasure due to their disappearance into storage, they are already being animated by a host of cultural and economic narratives. They are already spoken for. This project essentially seeks to make visible these structures and suggest alternative ways in which these fabric smithereens could be 'performed' or acted upon. In addition, I aim to unearth more specific information concerning the choreography, the bodies of the dancers who inhabited them and the creative processes involved in the making of the works. Viewing the costume as a locus or provocative remnant of a performance affords an exploration of costume on its own terms, rather than being overly directed by scholarship on the past performance works, or traditional conceptions of archival preservation. It allows an expanded view of costume to emerge: as a site of memory or archive in and of itself. This in turn speaks back to the original performances in which they came to life, offering partial but dynamic ways of understanding Anderson's work anew.

This approach is influenced by ideas put forward by performance scholar and curator André Lepecki, regarding performance work which re-enacts performance and utilizes the body itself as archive (Lepecki 2010). Discussing performance artist Julie Tolentino's work in which she archives a series of performance works (from artists such as Ron Athey) within her own body through performance,[8] Lepecki suggests that this shift towards the body itself as archive releases fresh possibilities by moving away from previous conceptions of the archive as a system of management of the past. In particular, Lepecki argues that using such an unstable and transitory medium as the body also frees it from 'the author's intention as commanding authority over a work's after-lives' (Lepecki 2010: 35). Whilst arguably, not all reinterpretations or re-staging of works place author's intention as their governing principle as a rule, Lepecki's discussion on the instability of the body is nonetheless of relevance here. Loosening the costumes from their authorial moorings in a sense provides an opportunity to unpick the potency of costumes post-performance, and discover alternative ways in which they can live on. This, in turn, opens up a debate about their material and philosophical constitution, and their relationship to 'a supposedly past work, which is never ever dead. Instead it is always haunting' (Lepecki 2010: 40).

In activating Anderson's costumes, I hope that not only the garments themselves will be made visible, but also the wider context in which they operate. The unique characteristics of the fabric remains as delineated for this study (from the sterility and death of the Dead Skins to the totemic nature of the *Smithereens*' masks), directly influences what kind of after-life might best befit each costume. Disintegration, preservation, transaction and display become consequently selected as the 'something to be done' (Gordon 2008: xvi). There is an acknowledged leap of faith in this process: an active attending (or submitting to archival seduction) giving way to a creative attempt at animating these garments beyond their current material state, to something other. Gordon's concept of the ghost and writing 'ghost stories' as being about 'putting life back in where only a vague memory or a bare trace was visible to those who bothered to look' (Gordon 2008: 22), provides further impetus for these active, deliberate strategies.

In the epilogue of her book *The Actor in Costume*, Monks suggests that in the face of costume's unstable nature as a document post-performance, 'we could imagine a different form of archival work that might make a new performance out of a reconstruction of the scars and stresses, the dirt and odours, of the costume itself' (Monks 2010: 142). She questions what this performance might look like, deciding that whilst it would not 'resemble or rediscover the performance it reconstructs through the fabric of the costumes', perhaps performance onstage is always 'a failed attempt at archaeology, a gesture to what is gone, a performance of memory, presence and loss' (Monks 2010: 142). In a sense, Anderson's fabric remains could be regarded as holding within their aged and worn fibres all those layers of loss which Monks outlines. The series of practical interventions which are to follow, however, intend to move beyond solely gesturing towards the losses of performance itself. The archival action which this book describes adopts a practical, hands-on approach towards garments which are often categorized solely from the perspective of their related performance histories or preservation status. Here, instead, the material reality of these costumes in their current state is utilized as a conduit towards new knowledge and the devising of a conceptual way forward for this costume archive. Drafting an experimental framework to illuminate the performative traces of these fabric remains, the aim is then to go further and reinsert them as (partially) visible and powerful interlocutors within and outside of the archive.

Notes

1. For further discussions on the illusions and seductive properties of the archive (and the contingent and conditioned nature of interpreting archival materials), see Freshwater, H. (2003), 'The allure of the archive', *Poetics Today*, 24:4, pp. 729–58 and Bradley, H. (1999), 'The seductions of the archive: Voices lost and found', *History of the Human Sciences*, XII:2, pp. 107–22.

2. In 2020, The Barbican mounted an exhibition dedicated to Michael Clark's work entitled *Cosmic Dancer*.

3. Whilst these three choreographers differ greatly in style, Bourne and Clark are selected as illustrative examples due to the fact that they are her contemporaries in age (within a three-year age difference) and location. They were born in the United Kingdom/Scotland and like Anderson, trained in London. Clark trained at the Royal Ballet School, and Bourne was a student alongside Anderson at the Laban Centre for Movement and Dance.

4. Whilst this research is focusing on Anderson and the partial erasure of her work, it is important to acknowledge that many other choreographers suffer from greater lack of visibility within the dance landscape and struggle to access opportunities and funding to make work. A 2016 annual diversity report by Arts Council England for example, stated the need to increase Black and Minority Ethnic visibility and recruitment of people with disabilities within the UK arts and museums sector. Statistics for employment within arts council portfolio organizations during 2020–21 ran as follows: 49 per cent were women, 14 per cent were Black, Asian and Ethnically Diverse, 10 per cent were LGBTQ+ and 7 per cent were disabled.

5. See waynemcgregor.com, new-adventures.net, and www.michaelclarkcompany.com. Accessed 12 January 2024.

6. A requirement for companies in receipt of public funding such as Arts Council Funding.

7. For example, a 2011 partnership agreement with Trinity Laban, to co-deliver a master's programme where students could work directly with *The Cholmondeleys* and *The Featherstonehaughs*.

8. This formed part of Tolentino's ongoing performance project *The Sky Remains the Same* which began in 2008 (Tolentino 2017).

Overleaf: Costumes from *Yippeee!!!*. Photos: Pete Moss

Disintegration

We hunch, bent forward from the waist, over the plastic packing box. The space is dimly lit and damp with cold. I am once again with Lea Anderson in her costume lockup. After several unsuccessful hunts which have thrown up velvet dresses, offcuts of material and bags of swimming goggles, this box appears to be the one we are looking for. Nestled inside in an unprepossessing heap lie the Dead Skins: translucent mesh bodysuits with buttoned spines. Sliver-thin and slinky, they formed the 'skins' of the dancers in Anderson's 2006 work *Yippeee!!!* Stuffed with copious pubic and underarm wigs, they were further transformed by a host of appendages and adornments which evolved during the performance (with the help of Jay Cloth, wardrobe mistress) in full view of the audience.

In a previous conversation Anderson has described the Dead Skins now as looking like 'dead insect wings' (Anderson 2016). This image has already imbued the skins in my mind as possessing something of a corpse-like or deathly quality. Gingerly lifting them one by one out of the box, I see what Anderson means. I'm immediately confronted by their strangeness. Rolled all together they look indeed like discarded dirtied skins or the ossified wings of dead insects on sunny windowsills.

Yet they aren't wholly inanimate either – the outline of the stitched seams, seemingly still accommodating the contours of the bodies which once inhabited them, have left clear traces behind. They appear seductive in their translucent ephemeral quality – the mesh is almost slippery to the touch. The relative attractiveness of this is underscored, however, by the functional operations of the garment, and its aged, tired nature. The skins are laundered (a scent of fabric conditioner hovers) yet indelibly marked by wear, sweat and the stains of makeup. Hasty repairs are in evidence.

Despite the see-through softness of the garments, there is an undeniable harshness to them too; the tight elastic loops worn over the middle finger to keep sleeves in place, the raised ridged seams traversing the feet with holes in the bottom to anchor the Dead Skin inside the silver dancing shoes. Tiny black curls of pubic wig hair still remain ensnared within the holes of the fabric here and there. These elements speak to the labour of the dancers who performed in them. The restrictions of elastic looped tight over extremities swollen from exertion, the rub and itch of a synthetic hide worn on sweating skin. The inertia of these sad garments seems only to emphasize further their exile from the performances in which they first lived. Rather than seeming distant from them, they appear to vibrate with the elements that are no longer present.

The bodies, the stage lights which would have rendered their colour altogether different, the accessories which transformed them by turns throughout *Yippeee!!!*

From my earliest encounters with the Dead Skins from *Yippeee!!!* (2006), I have perceived them as reverberating with the histories of their past performance life. The material realities of the garment in the archive alongside its functions and narrative motivations within *Yippeee!!!* itself unfurl a set of possibilities for its after-life. An after-life perhaps more fitting than the Dead Skins' archival existence as a shapeless heap within a plastic packing box. Selecting one Dead Skin (as a representative example of the twelve Dead Skins in the archive) makes it it possible to regard the material garment as evidence of the sense that what appears to be absent or distant is indeed (in the words of Gordon), 'a seething presence' (Gordon 2008: 9). The resilience of these tough garments is immediately identifiable, but so too, an impotence and fragility in terms of their lack of possibilities (aesthetically and logistically), to be reborn in another performance life. Their particular aesthetic and custom-made measurements, along with their signs of wear (etched into the mesh fabric that, by its very material nature, cannot safely endure significant alterations), renders them somewhat uninspiring to look at alone in their box. However, their associative history and distinctive markings do suggest potential for them to operate as interlocutors, rendering visible the unique characteristics of the Dead Skins, and also revealing the specific context of their performance histories.

The Dead Skin selected for investigation is that worn by dancer Makiko Aoyama. She performed in it in original *Yippeee!!!* performances, and more recently as a performer in the exhibition *Hand in Glove* (2016), when excerpts of the choreography were remounted. I appraise the garment in detail noting each of its distinctive markings – every snag and smear of makeup. The overall shape and impression of the garment as being representative of the chorus of Dead Skins (as they were viewed in the original performance work) is also to be taken into consideration.

As outlined in Beginning, the Dead Skin has been chosen as a garment which could realize an after-life centred on creative destruction or disappearance. Echoing Anderson's sentiment that sometimes she felt she might wish to 'burn' the costumes in her archive, the Dead Skin's materiality becomes a vehicle through which to explore an after-life which attempts to escape archival entombment through hastening its own, inevitable disintegration. Each of the costumes in the archive will be subject to material transition, even if just left in their packing boxes. Quite immediately, this intervention chimes with what Giulia Palladini describes as 'the act of ripping the whole', in relation to dealing with artefacts which form part of an archive (Palladini 2020: 235). Discussing issues of incompleteness and forms of mishandling in relation to Tara Fatehi Irani's performance project *Mishandled Archive* (as referenced in Beginning), Palladini suggests that:

> A form of estrangement is always at stake in gestures that deliberately interrupt the context in which archives exist as a whole: the act of ripping the whole, which supposedly presides over the fragments manipulated in production, is necessary in order for items to be used, dealt with, manipulated and reorganised. (Palladini 2020: 235)

It has been apparent from the outset that a proposed intervention centred on effectively destroying an object from an archive is a potentially contentious one. Such an action creates a rupture: the complete set of twelve Dead Skins reduced to an incomplete eleven. This sense of peril is at times reinforced by the feedback I receive when presenting my proposed research at conferences. A particularly memorable response comes when I present at a symposium at the Gulbenkian Foundation, Lisbon, entitled 'From the pleasure of preserving to the pleasure of displaying: The Politics of Fashion in the Museum' (2017). A museum director from Lisbon finds my proposal quite distressing, beginning his comments in response by saying 'wonderful presentations but I am so upset by this Mary Kate Connolly'. How *could* you? is the essence of his question to me. How could I indeed? The idea of an after-life motivated by disintegration becomes unavoidably entangled in debates around the (ultimately impossible) permanence of material objects, and the means by which certain objects are 'saved' through the mechanisms of conservation, or conversely, discarded as detritus. A 2019 publication *The Explicit Material: Inquiries on the Intersection of Curatorial and Conservation Cultures* (Hölling et al.), sets out to interrogate the tensions and increasingly blurred boundaries across curatorial and conservation agendas within museum and gallery cultures. In their introduction, the editors outline two distinct types of materiality – that of temporal materiality and relational materiality:

> Temporal materiality [...] has to do with time, time passing, the chronicity of objects, the events of interventions, and the temporality of museum vaults and

displays in relation to the time lived outside the institutional walls. Relational materiality indicates, first, that the material state of an artefact can only be grasped comparatively, in relation to something else. An artefact can be in a better 'state' or 'condition' only comparatively to another condition (perceived, deduced from a documentary material, or imagined).
(Hölling et al. 2019: 4–5)

These two conceptions of materiality go some way to illuminating the motivations behind selecting an after-life for a Dead Skin which involves disintegration, and perhaps ultimately, the disappearance or transformation of its original material form. Both temporal and relational elements vibrate within the fibres of the garments – physical encounter with them renders these relations almost physically manifest. For the editors of the publication, artefacts are regarded as 'complex entities with a power to convey meaning and to signify themselves' (Hölling et al. 2019: 8). They go on to note that objects 'often preserve physical traces of the process of creation, re-creation, maintenance, distribution, and usage, revealing multifarious potentialities involved in materiality' (Hölling et al. 2019: 8). This is certainly true of the Dead Skin – the stains and rips illustrate a specific and layered material history. A history of interaction and reciprocal transformation – a garment touched by many hands, inhabited by a certain dancing body, worn in particular performance contexts. These marks point towards a partially vanished history. Like the stubborn traces of Willem De Kooning's pencil marks which remained in Robert Rauschenberg's iconic 1953 work *Erased De Kooning Drawing* (despite Rauschenberg's efforts to erase every trace of De Kooning's previous work on the canvas), these smears and tears stubbornly signal the presence of a previous life of the costume which has been rendered largely invisible by the mechanics of storage and the ending of their performances.

Holding the Dead Skin in my hand, its slippery tainted mesh tumbling through my fingers, feels like witnessing both the past and the future. The markings direct my attention to the now irreproducible past, and the inexorable march towards its future vanishing act. As historian of conservation and heritage, the late David Lowenthal, put it, 'nothing can be preserved forever. Every inanimate object, like every living being, undergoes continual alteration, ultimately perishing. Cumulative corrosion extinguishes every form and feature. Things either morph into other entities, dismember into fragments or dissolve into unrecognizable components' (Lowenthal 2019: 16). This eventual morphing into something else, or the final disintegration of the Dead Skin might not be possible to observe in my lifetime, or that of Anderson's.

But that final vanishing act is ultimately coming. It is these visible signs embedded in the ragged materiality of the Dead Skin (seemingly pointing towards a predetermined final act of disintegration), which mark it out for an alternative after-life. Intervening through an act of creative destruction, then, becomes a hastening of a profoundly inescapable reality rather than a false creation of it. The after-life seeks merely to render more visible the ravages of time, the histories and the material future of the garment.

In a world now dominated by mass-produced objects with obsolescence accelerated by the discontinuation of product lines, Lowenthal argues that objects which display decay and the markers of time are often not greeted with pleasure by the viewer, suggesting that 'wear and tear usually portend grievous or repugnant loss of function, senescence, imminent demise, posthumous decay' (Lowenthal 2019: 24). He does however acknowledge the exceptions to this observation, found for example in the 'wabi-sabi' aesthetic of Japan which he describes as resting on 'three simple principles: nothing lasts, nothing is finished and nothing is perfect' (Lowenthal 2019: 25). What might such principles have to suggest in the context of the Dead Skin? Perhaps that by embracing and honouring these qualities of the artefact, an alternative after-life might arise, freed from the stasis of the protective but suffocating realities of the plastic packing box in the lockup.

But back to 'how could I?' for a moment. The visual art world provides some windows onto, if not the motivations behind the actions, then at least other instances of creative destruction, of 'how could you?' moments. From Robert Rauschenberg's aforementioned erasure of Willem De Kooning's artwork, to artist Cornelia Parker's exploded and reconstituted garden shed in *Cold Dark Matter: An Exploded View* (1991), many works have been created through the destruction of other matter or other artworks. Some works are intentionally self-destructing – Banksy's *Girl with Balloon* (2006), which was shredded seconds after its auction at Sotheby's in 2018 is an infamous more recent example. The print had an inbuilt hidden shredder in the picture frame which was activated seconds after the auctioneer's hammer came down, having secured a sale price of £1.04 million. The work has since been renamed *Love is in the Bin* (Busby 2018). Artist Michael Landy famously destroyed everything he owned (including his passport and birth certificate) in his 2001 work *Break Down*. In 2010 he staged *Art Bin* – an exhibition in which works of art were destroyed. Artists were invited to contribute their artistic 'failures' for destruction. Gillian Wearing, Damien Hirst and Tracey Emin were among those to contribute works to the bin. Each of these examples operate in a wholly different realm to that of the Dead Skin. Yet in a fundamental way they are also self-referential to their own contexts, specifically the caprices and value systems of the visual art world. They provoke questions about what should be kept and what should be destroyed in the context of artistic archives and modes of display. They also operate as signposts to the impermanence of things, to the ruptures and transformations brought about by embracing destruction, and the morphing of one object or art work into quite another entity.

This chapter outlines some of the Dead Skin's histories drawn from interviews, existing scholarship and reviews, before engaging with the garment itself as an interlocutor of performance histories, and the rationale and process behind the disintegration intervention of this research. This is laid out in reverse order to that of the actual research process as it has been carried out, in which a close engagement with the garment preceded engagement with production reviews and scholarship. Here however, the production history is outlined first in order to contextualize the Dead Skin and go some way towards understanding the critical reception of the work at the time of its inception, and the ways these histories continue to live on in the material details of the garment. Exploring the Dead Skin costume (which the dancers wore throughout the performance of *Yippeee!!!*) provides a window onto the numerous ways in which the dancing body was originally constructed and performed in the work. Consequently, this chapter also explores contagion within performance design and choreography, and the ways in which costume disrupted or re-choreographed both bodies and movement alike.

Yippeee!!! production history and critical appraisal

Yippeee!!! was a visually arresting full-length work, inspired in part by the dance films of Hollywood choreographer Busby Berkeley, with a cast of twelve dancers and an original score performed live. Inspiration, according to Anderson, was also drawn from 'evolution and multiples in many different ways in terms of spatial multiples and time multiples, doppelgängers, and bad copies of bad copies that degenerate and deteriorate' (Anderson 2017: n.pag.). There were many other influences at work in the production, emanating from a broadly similar timeframe of early twentieth-century performance – ranging from 1930s nostalgia to avant-garde writing and visual art. These included Herman Hesse's 1927 novel *Steppenwolf*, collages from artist Hannah Höch, and a sequence from comedic duo Laurel and Hardy. Of particular significance within the context of the costumes however, is the confluence of old Hollywood

Yippeee!!! Maho Ihara and company. Photo: Pau Ros
Yippeee!!! Company in performance. Photo: Pau Ros

Yippeee!!! Company in performance. Photo: Pau Ros

images of glamorous showgirl chorus lines, with the degeneration of copies and the relentlessness of cyclical patterns. Anderson said at the time of production that there was an idea that 'these dancers have been doing show after show after show, and as one drops, they are replaced. Through these generations of dancers, the silver shoes [which form part of the costume] become more important than the flesh inside them' (Hargreaves 2007: 26). Anderson also outlined the direct relationship between bacteria, evolution, genetic engineering and the work of Berkeley:

> Berkeley's kaleidoscopes resemble microscopes, with the dancers like bacteria, which change as they reproduce. I'm half looking back, with all the 30s nostalgic references, but also half looking forward, with images of genetic cloning – it's another idea about multiples but in an apocalyptic, futuristic way, with mutations [...] The movement development has been modelled on viral infection, and so have the costume changes. Something appears, then spreads, changing as it is copied.
> (Hargreaves 2007: 25)

This element of looking back and also forwards, described by Anderson, is equally evident in the material realities of the costumes as they are now in the lockup. As touched on earlier, they gesture towards their performance pasts and their inescapable material future of degradation. This dual perspective was explicitly inbuilt into the creative elements of the work – the historical referents combined with a contemporary (to 2006), sensibility of anxiety around mutations and scientific enhancement. The production was contemporaneous to a significant outbreak of BSE (more commonly known as 'Mad Cow Disease')[1] in the United Kingdom, and some costume elements reference the trappings of outbreak and contagion (such as velvet face masks shaped like vulvas, rubber gloves, rubber boots and cows tails). These images become newly relevant and striking viewed as they are now, through the lens of the recent coronavirus pandemic (2020). In addition to this looking forward and back, there is also a sense of nostalgia and the uncanny about the costumes. At the very least, the Dead Skin renders the bodies of the dancers corpse-like.

Originally named *Yippeee!!! (2006)*, in reference to *Whoopee! (1930)*, (a musical and film directed by Thornton Freeland, with choreography and staging by Busby Berkeley), *Yippeee!!!* premiered on 5 October 2006 at South Hill Park, Bracknell (Berkshire, United Kingdom). *Yippeee!!!* was a high-profile work, which enjoyed two UK tours –

Yippeee!!! Csongor Szabo. Photo: Pau Ros

Yippeee!!! Ryen Perkins-Gangnes and Macarena Campbell. Photo: Pau Ros
Yippeee!!! Company in Performance. Photo: Pau Ros

the first included performances at Sadler's Wells (3–4 November 2006), as part of the Dance Umbrella festival, before travelling across the United Kingdom to locations including Sheffield and Brighton. The second tour took place in 2007 and it was at this point that the show became known simply as *Yippeee!!!* (removing the date 2006 from the title). For this tour there were some casting changes and the running time was shortened (from 100 minutes to 90 minutes) due to choreographic edits. The final performance of the work was at the Hackney Empire, London in June 2007. This performance was filmed live, and made commercially available on DVD (*The Cholmondeleys* and *The Featherstonehaughs* 2007).[2]

The cast of *Yippeee!!!* was made up of both *The Cholmondeleys* and *The Featherstonehaughs*. There were twelve dancers in addition to Jay Cloth (performing onstage in costume) as wardrobe mistress, and an assistant.[3] Costumes were designed by Simon Vincenzi (marking the first of a number of collaborations between him and Anderson). Production design and lighting was created by Simon Corder, featuring a shiny mirrored floor and banks of stage lights which were wheeled around on stage by the dancers as part of the performance. The music was composed by Steve Blake and performed by Blake and his collaborators (Simon King and Pat Thomas), as the *Yum Yum Band*, a group specially formed for *Yippeee!!!* During the course of the making of the work, the work's 'costume bible' (a notebook containing all details of costumes, makers, fabrics, dyes, etc.) was lost (Anderson 2017; Vincenzi 2017). As a result of this, some details regarding individual costume makers for *Yippeee!!!* and the process behind the costumes have been forgotten by the creative team and certain production details are difficult to verify.

Despite positive preview interviews (such as Mangalanayagam [2006]), and a London-dance review declaring it as 'just what dance in the twenty-first century should be, exciting, enthralling and controversial' (Haight 2006: n.pag.), overall critical reception among the British press was decidedly negative. Summing up dance critics' responses at the time including the texts by Debra Craine (for *The Times*) and Judith Mackrell (for *The Guardian*), journalist Louise Radnofsky opened an article for *The Guardian* blog entitled 'Yippeee!!! It's a Flop!' with 'It may have lived up to its promised weirdness but Lea Anderson's latest has been panned as "mind-numbing", a "cacophonous scrawl" and "at least an hour too long"' (Radnofsky 2006; Crane 2006; Mackrell 2006). Fundamentally, it appears the work did not match critics' expectations of what a dance work inspired by the films of Berkeley (known for aesthetically pleasing costumes and catchy musical scores), might entail. Dance critic for *The Observer*, Luke

Jennings, was equally negative. His descriptions of the costumes nonetheless offer helpful windows onto the visual landscape and embodiment of *Yippeee!!!*:

> Visually it's weird – at times nightmarishly so. The dancers' faces are horribly stained around the mouths, their smiles are glassy, and their prosthetically modified teeth glint in the klieg lights [...] The costumes are equally disturbing, as baby-doll nighties alternate with gas mask-and-pearls ensembles. One tableau sees the entire cast enter with bandaged arms and blood-covered hands [...] and another offers a wrenching hate-filled duet for a couple who, in the place of noses and mouths, have red velvet vaginas.
> (Jennings 2006: n.pag.)

The costumes appear as key drivers of the thematic and aesthetic language of the work in this description. Costumes and choreography clearly subverted critics' assumptions of what an Anderson work inspired by Hollywood glamour, would look like. These sentiments were expressed by Mackrell, who admitted that 'when [...] *Yippeee!!!* came advertised as a homage to Berkeley it seemed we were in for a visual treat', before lamenting the costumes as having been designed 'through the mind-set of an alien – with diaphanous trousers from which dangle an extra leg, ropes of pearls that come accessorised with gas masks and padded taffeta skirts that sport kangaroo tails' (Mackrell 2006: n.pag.). These press reviews have since been criticized by some dance scholars who seek to situate *Yippeee!!!* within the performance histories which it referenced, underscoring its value as an innovative work (Briginshaw 2009; Burt 2016). Writing in response to the 2016 performance of extracts from *Yippeee!!!* (as part of the performed exhibition *Hand in Glove*, V&A Museum) Ramsay Burt argued that:

> *Yippeee!!!* was a brilliantly surreal mash-up of Weimar girl-kultur and in particular the collages of Hannah Höch, with a queer adaptation of Busby Berkeley [...] It was a really sophisticated piece, which showed up the ballet critics' severe lack of understanding: there were headlines [in 2006] like 'Yippeee!!! It's a flop' in the Guardian of all places.
> (Burt 2016: n.pag.)

Whilst the critical reception to *Yippeee!!!* is not of foremost concern within the context of this book, the overt negativity in press reviews nevertheless provides some clues as to the ways in which the costumes functioned within the work.

Yippeee!!! Macarena Campbell and Gary Clarke. Photo: Pau Ros

Yippeee!!! Design drawings by Simon Vincenzi

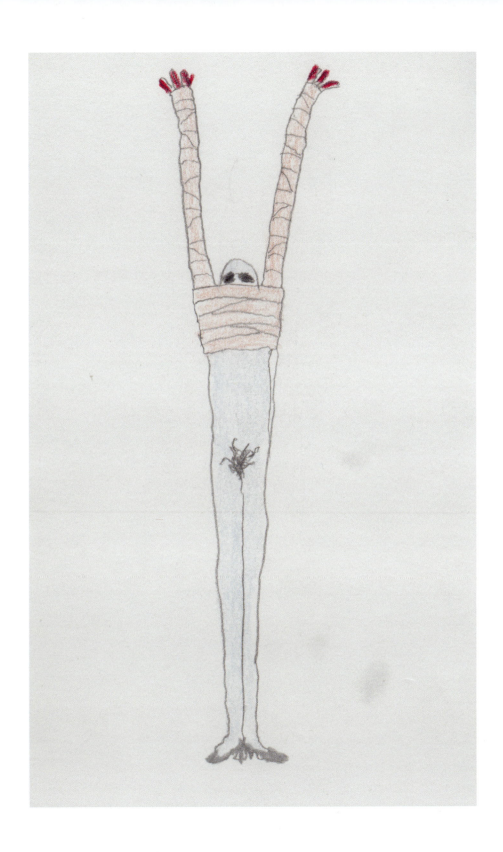

Yippeee!!! Design drawings by Simon Vincenzi

The constructed world of *Yippeee!!!*

There were well over a hundred costumes and accessories in *Yippeee!!!* – they were wheeled around on rails throughout the performance, and dancers changed in full view of the audience. The Dead Skins formed the central base costume for the work; worn throughout by all twelve cast members, dressed identically. The Dead Skin itself was made from performance mesh fabric (also known as 'power net' – traditionally worn by showgirls and used to look invisible on the skin). It appears thin and flimsy, but is extremely tough when put under stress in that it doesn't tend to rip, and has only minimal stretch (as opposed to a fully stretchy mesh like that of nylon tights). It is more prone to ladders and small runs in the fabric than large structural damage. Tailored to be skin tight on the body, the Dead Skins were worn stuffed with copious black pubic and underarm wigs (which trailed all across the torso and down the legs beneath the mesh). Dancers also wore metal, and sometimes diamond studded, prosthetic teeth, silver bowed dancing shoes (similar to tap shoes) and heavy face makeup. The makeup was that of the kind sold in fancy dress shops – a white chalky base, overlaid with smudges of dark purples, blacks and yellows from oil-based makeup pencils (such as might be worn as part of a Halloween costume).

Beginning from this base layer of Dead Skin, shoes and makeup, performers were further transformed by the addition of an array of aforementioned accessories – from pearl necklaces and silver discs, to gigantic tongues and gas masks – depending on the dance number they were performing. There were sparkly green dresses for example, for a '42nd Street' chorus dance number (in homage to the 1933 Berkeley musical film of the same title), which hooked over the shoulders of the dancers, still encased in what appeared to be dry cleaning bags. There were also tight black sparkly bodysuits which were sometimes worn over the Dead Skins. The effect of these numerous additions and costume changes created the sense of a series of show-stopping dance routines, like those you would encounter in a Berkeley-style film. Yet the images were simultaneously complicated by the eeriness of the costumes, and uncanny presentation of the dancers with their metal-toothed smiles.

Intrinsic to the choreography and the costumes in *Yippeee!!!* is the sense of the production of anonymous theatricalized bodies within dance. The chorus is visually striking yet oddly faceless as they don endless numbers of costumes, performing dance number after dance number. The snaking chorus lines in *Yippeee!!!* are recognizably creations of the dance stage, yet in their strangeness, they fail to comply

Yippeee!!! Inn Pang Ooi. Photo by Pau Ros
Yippeee!!! Tim Morris, Valentina Formenti and Frauke Requardt. Photo: Pau Ros

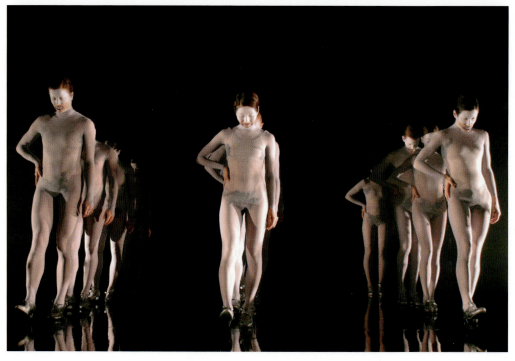

Yippeee!!! Maho Ihara, Kath Duggan and Inn Pang Ooi. Photo: Pau Ros
Yippeee!!! Company in Performance. Photo: Pau Ros

with the assumed framework in which they operate. The chorus execute endless patterns, faces constricted into twisted showgirl grins, heeled silver buckled shoes clacking on the stage. Here, the viewer is not only encountering glitzy remnants of the world of Berkeley, but also a sense of disenchantment, akin to that described by Weimar-era writer Siegfried Kracauer in his renowned essay, 'The mass ornament'. In response to the proliferation of chorus line and mass patterns (exemplified by performers such as The Tiller Girls, and gymnasium demonstrations) which he identified in Germany in the 1920s and 1930s, Kracauer interrogated what he termed 'surface level expressions', of the culture. He posited that 'surface-level expressions [...] by virtue of their unconscious nature, provide unmediated access to the fundamental substance of the state of things' (Kracauer 1995: 75). For Kracauer, the ornaments of these large group performances were emblematic of a deeper disassociation at work in society, as the march of capitalism and fascism encroached ever further into the social choreography of the Weimar Republic.[4]

Crucially, he argued that the 'the ornament is an *end in itself* [sic]' (Kracauer 1995: 76). He suggested that the 'mass movements of the girls [...] take place in a vacuum; they are a linear system that no longer has any erotic meaning but at best points to the locus of the erotic' (Kracauer 1995: 77). Here is perhaps a clue to the kind of doubleness found in *Yippeee!!!*. The chorus lines continue to point towards the locus (as Kracauer would have it), of their origins as being rooted in the early twentieth-century dance and film canon. These references are instantly complicated however, by the ways in which the costumes exemplify (in an outward, visually unmistakable fashion), the contradictions and hollowness of these original chorus lines, as contemporaries such as Kracauer originally observed. Kracauer noted a hollowing out in the presentation of chorus lines – still standing as an emblem of eroticism, yet now devoid of eroticism itself. A cipher now, or an empty gesture. The costumes of *Yippeee!!!*, in particular the Dead Skins, seem to bind these two elements together – flashy escapism with a visibly sinister underpinning. The performers are thus rendered somewhat monstrous as they perform routine after routine, dancing far beyond exhaustion towards an immortal, never-ending performance. Anderson had noted (as cited earlier under 'Production History and Critical Appraisal'), the idea of the dancing shoes becoming more important than the bodies inside them. Like the obliteration of the individual which Kracauer identified in factory production lines, and the performed equivalent in Tiller Girl chorus lines, the costumes themselves supplant the actual dancers – in a sense they stand in as the epicentre of the work.

The bodies inside are merely conduits towards an inexhaustible, ever replicating performance.

The dancing body was forged in *Yippeee!!!* through a reciprocal relationship between costume and choreography. The intersection of design, costume and movement created a hyper-theatrical, potentially beyond-human, dancing body. A dancing body as an end in and of itself, rather than a human body which performs dance. In this interplay, there is already a sense of the ghostly inscribed in these figures, which gesture towards the production of chorus lines and the endless replication of choreographic multiples. They come to represent the idea of chorus lines per se, rather than embodying them in an uncomplicated manner for the viewer. Here, the bodies are merely channels, existing only within the context of the performance itself. Kracauer observed a similar subjugation of individuality with the chorus lines of the 1930s. 'The Tiller Girls', he argued, 'can no longer be reassembled into human beings after the fact. Their mass gymnastics are never performed by the fully preserved bodies, whose contortions defy rational understanding' (Kracauer 1995: 78).

The role of the Dead Skins is significant here, in the ways in which they present a somewhat 'recognizable' human body, complete with flesh tones and pubic hair. Yet these bodies are also unknowable – seemingly corpse-like and ghostly, grotesquely exaggerated (with their metal-toothed grins and swathes of body hair), and also rendered as units within the larger machine of choreography. The costumes therefore disallow a comfortable enjoyment of spectacle. The viewers are invited to contemplate the uncanny nature of these chorus lines, moving as one. Barbieri writes that

> the emergence of identically costumed dancers in the chorus line of showgirls from the late 19th century onward, is significant [...] in its controlling and directing of groups of female bodies on stage, which project a version of femininity, produced socially, mechanised, and even militarised.
> (Barbieri 2017: 50)

Barbieri here is illuminating ways in which bodies have historically been co-opted to project a symbolic iteration of an idea. The notion of the militarization of female bodies is of particular relevance within the context of Berkeley's work. It is an oft cited fact that his early career as a Lieutenant in the US army (directing military troop parades and conducting aerial reconnaissance) may have influenced his choreographic sensibilities. Mackrell (2017) argued that

Berkeley offered his female actors and dancers up to the camera with a mathematical exactness that could border on ruthlessness. One of his signature tricks was to zoom, in rapid succession, over the faces of the chorus line, but far from individualising the women it simply confirmed their conformity to type (usually blond and china-doll cute). As a device it was no more humanising than Berkeley's favoured shots of disembodied legs, busts, feet or arms.
(2017: n.pag.)

The 'chorus girls' (made up of *The Cholmondeleys* and *The Featherstonehaughs*) in *Yippeee!!!* do not possess Berkeley's requirements of doll-like cuteness, but they nonetheless clearly conform to a standard within *their own* performative construct. That of replication, continuous production of performance, and a strangely familiar yet repulsive construction of the dancing body, mechanized as a conduit of choreographic logic. Kracauer suggested that mass chorus lines produce an alienation on the part of the viewer. That '[t]he more the coherence of the figure is relinquished in favor of mere linearity, the more distant it becomes from the immanent consciousness of those constituting it' (Kracauer 1995: 77). This perhaps hints at what I mean when I suggest the chorus figures become somewhat unknowable to the viewer, or somehow 'beyond-human'. They are trapped within their own performance framework and cannot exist outside it. Thus, it becomes nigh impossible to view the performers as individual dancers with discreet identities. They are entrapped by *Yippeee!!!* and can only exist through performing it. This suffocating reality for the performers, created largely through the interaction with costume, is central to *Yippeee!!!*. It is also uncomfortable to bear witness to, as evidenced in the negative press reviews of the time. For Anderson, Berkeley was '[a] much misunderstood choreographer' (Anderson 2006: n.pag.). She noted in interview with *The Independent* dance critic Zoe Anderson, that his 'black-and-white work is the most beautiful – all the very, very surreal dance sequences that come from nowhere. Halfway through them, you think, "Where did this start out? How on earth could this possibly be fastened to any Hollywood narrative?"' (2006: n.pag.).

Both these perspectives on Berkeley's work (that of the surreal beauty created by his lavish productions, and also the dehumanizing elements and bodily control exacted from his female dancers), offer some insight into the construction of the chorus figures in *Yippeee!!!*. It is perhaps within these contradictions between sublime beauty and exaltation of the dancing body, and the denigration of the doomed chorus girl, that the power of the Dead Skin operates. Exploring these elements through an

Hand in Glove, V&A. Makiko Aoyama with Third Year Student Performers from London Contemporary Dance School. Photo: Pau Ros
Dead Skin. Photo: Rik Pennington

appraisal of the costume in various settings, from performance onstage to the exile of the archive box, reveals a mercurial garment.

Encountering the Dead Skin

In approaching the Dead Skin it is crucial to consider how its appearance differs depending on context. From performance onstage to performance in a gallery space (at the V&A during *Hand in Glove*), and from being photographed in the archive, to being held in the hand. In each of these contexts, the costume performs differently, remains differently, offering up a fresh perspective on the performances in which it lived.

Viewing the costume photographed in performance onstage reveals a familiar theatrical image – that of the emblematic chorus girl, but one which is unsettling, somehow unseemly. The light from the spotlights (wheeled around onstage by the dancers) bleach the body to a ghoulish flesh-coloured glow, across which the dark trails of pubic hair and purple face makeup appear as disquieting smears. Watching the costumes performed in the V&A's Raphael Court (as part of the exhibition *Hand in Glove*, 2016), however, the effect was somewhat different. The overall colour darkened due to the different lighting, and viewed in such close proximity (which the costumes were not originally designed to be), the actual flesh and details of the body were highlighted. The texture of the pubic hair became far more visible, and watching up-close was almost to experience discomfort in empathy with the dancing bodies encased in such skin-tight sheaths of fabric. It was also possible at this close range to see the details and trimmings of the costume, the stitching along the seams and the minute loop of elastic worn over the middle finger to keep the sleeves tight.

Disconnected from these performances in which it 'lived', the costume truly does take on the mantle of a 'Dead Skin'. The outline body shape (fitted precisely to the dancer's measurements), along with the translucent nature of the fabric, creates the impression of a hollow body – a skin peeled straight from the dancer, now lifeless and devoid of movement. Held in the hand without the addition of stage lighting, the fabric surprisingly appears lilac or blue in colour. It is thicker in texture than appears when stretched across a moving body, and, whilst light, is not weightless as it seemed on the dancers. The tiny holes which make up this net fabric are also somehow unexpected, as they do not show up when worn on the body. Allowing the fabric to move reveals its fluidity, and also the ways in which the tiny holes can cross over one another, creating swirling patterns which appear to have a choreography all of their own.

Under close examination, the costume in its current state reveals details which speak back to the body which inhabited it, and the choreography they performed. At first glance, the dancer's bodily imprint is visible. Sweat discoloration marks streak the underarms, crotch and feet. The footprints of the dancer's feet are etched onto the fabric, not only revealing an outline of the ball and heel of the feet, but, if compared across costumes, potentially highlighting individual differences in anatomy and technique. For example, a pronounced staining on one part of the foot suggesting where an individual dancer placed the majority of their weight. Shoes and accessories have also made their marks. From the outlines of the stains on the foot, it is possible to map the shape of the shoe. Tiny snags and rips can indicate damage from particular accessories which caught on a thread of fabric.

Examined thus, the costume can also begin to conjure specific elements of the choreography which have left a trace. The shoulders of the Dead Skins tend to feature pronounced stains for example. These blemishes point to certain moments in the performance of *Yippeee!!!* such as a sequence midway through the work entitled *Wavy Arms* when dancers with arms held aloft sway left to right in a cluster. Slow sustained movements give way at other points in the work to frenzied quick turns of the head, with chin tucked closely to shoulder. These movements not only streaked the costumes with dark purple marks from the dancers' makeup, but in turn the dancers' makeup became further smeared and distorted by this interaction, conspiring to render the chorus girl figure ever more disconcerting. In a similar reciprocal metamorphosis, the choreography (as it increased in range and speed of movement), prompted the untethered pubic and underarm wig hair to roam about the body inside the Dead Skin, leaving trails across the torso. Thus the dancing body transformed the costume, and was simultaneously altered as the costume distorted the vision of the dancing body. Through tracing the specificities of the materiality to hand in the archive in this way, the Dead Skin can be mobilized to serve as interlocutor between the performance's life in the present (now disappeared), and the historicized accounts and pictorial evidence which persist in the face of performance's vanishing. The *taken-for-granted* lifelessness of the costume and assumption of total obliteration of the performances now gone can be brought into question, allowing for a partial recuperation to take place.

In addition to the evidence held in the Dead Skin (of the body which occupied it, and the choreography which was performed), the repairs and alterations built into the costume further reveal its particular heritage. Whether it is one of the original

Dead Skin. Photo: Rik Pennington

Wavy Arms. Company in Performance. Photo: Pau Ros

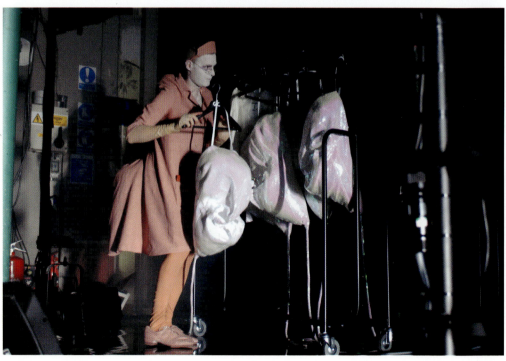

Dead Skin. Photo: Rik Pennington
Jay Cloth as The Wardrobe Mistress. Photo: Pau Ros

Yippeee!!! costumes for example, or whether it is a replacement, whether it has played host to only one dancing body, or been altered slightly to accommodate a new physical form. Original *Yippeee!!!* costumes have a detailed stitched 'spine' where the costume unbuttons, whereas replacements were more hastily made, with large plastic popper buttons sewn on without stitched borders. Name tags adorn the garments, sometimes bearing more than one name. These tags betray the individuality and intimacy of the skins – they are rendered literally legible as historical documents. In addition to major repairs or alterations carried out in between shows, the costumes in *Yippeee!!!* were also mended during live performances when necessary. Wardrobe mistress Jay Cloth (in costume and character), moved the costumes around on rails during the performance, helping dancers change costumes in view of the audience. At times he also carried out speedy repairs if a costume had become damaged and required immediate attention. More significant repairs and alterations were undertaken by costume makers in between shows. Evidence of some of these repairs still remain, tracing the life of the individual costume and bearing material witness to the scars of the performances in which it danced. As such we can begin to see the costume as an archival document of sorts, retracing the embodied histories which inhabited the fabric, illuminating moments of calamity and emergency in performance, alongside the wear and tear wrought by touring and rehearsal.

Interview encounters and emergent characteristics of the Dead Skin

The key characteristics which these appraisals reveal (alongside my earliest conversations with Anderson concerning the fate of the archive), go on to form the basis of the interviews which I subsequently carry out with Anderson, Vincenzi, Jay Cloth and Aoyama. Each interview centres on the interviewees' first impressions, embodied experiences and current relationships with the Dead Skins. When I undertake the interviews there is a deliberate effort to remain open to the ways in which the conversation might unfold. They aim to eschew the creation of a smooth historicized narrative of the costumes, and instead ascertain how their presence might have affected the work in which they lived.

Each interviewee has differing perspectives on the costumes, yet certain characteristics emerge as shared across all interviewees. Several elements appear the most crucial in terms of illuminating the characteristics of the costume as it lived in performance and how its embodied histories can still be traced. In response to this emergence of shared characteristics, I devise a series of headings to illustrate these key themes within my interpretations of the interviews. The first of these is the costume as an adversary – a mercurial shape shifter. The Dead Skin seems to exude simultaneously both precariousness, and strength. The second is the question of hiding in nakedness – being rendered invisible by a nonetheless very physically-revealing design. The sense of the costume being both present and absent at the same time appears to be part of this dynamic. Finally, the reciprocal and negotiated relationships between costume and movement, and also costume and body, seem significant. Each of these elements appear to play a role in constructing the chorus girl figure of *Yippeee!!!* as both an actual physical entity, but more especially, as a cipher for the chorus girl in and of itself. A figure both undeniably of the dance stage and simultaneously strange and somewhat unknowable, trapped within the constructed visual world of *Yippeee!!!*. It seems helpful to explore these elements individually in order to unpack the ways in which contagion and mutual influence evolved the chorus figure further.

Costume as adversary

A recurring theme of conversation across interviews centres on the difficulties and tricky nature of the costumes as a whole in *Yippeee!!!*. To begin with, there were well over a hundred costumes which were wheeled around on rails throughout the performance, with dancers changing onstage. For Jay Cloth, the challenge arose from the sheer number of costumes and their management on and offstage. For the dancers, there were various situations in which it was necessary to 'work against' the costume, whether due to discomfort (of, for example, the prosthetic teeth or tongues they had to wear), or the way in which the costume exposed their bodies. Aoyama describes the physical realities of dancing at full exertion whilst needing to hold her prosthetic teeth in place by sucking in her lips, and the difficulty of having a mouth full of saliva, or perhaps dribbling all down one side of her face, but all the while having to maintain a rictussed full smile. The smile, she adds, wasn't a '*smile* smile', but became more like a 'silent scream' (Aoyama 2017: n.pag.). She also touches on the feeling of exposure that came with wearing such a translucent garment, and the itchiness and extra heat created by the pubic wigs (2017: n.pag.).

The Dead Skins appear to possess an inherent duality – that of precariousness and resilience. On the one hand, garments that were sometimes held together with sellotape (in emergencies during performances) and popped open unexpectedly, but that on the other hand were tailor-made, long lasting and easy to mend. They weren't

Yippeee!!! Kath Duggan, Tim Morris, Valentina Formenti and Inn Pang Ooi. Photo: Pau Ros
Yippeee!!! Valentina Formenti and Frauke Requardt. Photo: Pau Ros

subject to large structural damage and, due to the composition of the mesh, ladders or small holes in the fabric could be picked up and stitched easily with a needle and thread. Whilst large alterations might not have been feasible, small repairs were relatively simple to do in between performances. Jay Cloth jokes that Vincenzi 'has this great knack of making it look like they have been destroyed. Or that they are on the verge of falling apart but they never do [...] They look worn, look tattered but they are still going' (Jay Cloth 2017: n.pag.). This precariousness and resilience appears to speak to the narrative world of *Yippeee!!!* – that of a dancing troupe caught in an endless loop of glitzy routines with no escape. Vincenzi describes how he considered the dancers as being dead, and that over the years trapped in a theatre, the figure of the chorus girl had endlessly replicated and mutated, evolving to have extra dancing legs and odd appendages (Vincenzi 2017: n.pag.). These sentiments speak again to the beyond-human or not-quite human aspect of the chorus figures. Whilst Anderson described the costumes (which prevail in the face of bodily decay) as more significant than the bodies which inhabit them, narratively speaking, Vincenzi also built in literal bodily morphing to the design of the costumes. Here the dancing bodies mutate through means of evolutionary adaptation, in response to the demands of the chorus line. They become equipped with extra legs or appendages, which are all in service to the performance (as seen in the accompanying images).

Costume-as-adversary is perhaps unsurprisingly, not necessarily viewed as a negative element. Each interviewee describes the adversarial nature of the costume as spurring on the evolution of character embodiment. The costume prompted the dancers to work against it, and in doing so, reach new depths of embodiment and transformation, working as a formative and positive tool. Jay Cloth mentions the costume 'keeping you on your toes' by adding an extra productive layer of risk to the performance (Jay Cloth 2017: n.pag.). The dancers worked extensively with the costumes in rehearsal, and yet by their very nature, the costumes' inherent precariousness remained within the moment of performance. This seemed to maintain an 'edge' within the performance space, prompting a pushing of boundaries to occur anew during each performance. It could not be rehearsed out.

In addition to the adversarial nature of the costumes operating in an 'unseen way' (e.g. when Aoyama had to persevere with her smile despite the discomfort of saliva on her face), there were times when the mercurial nature of the *Yippeee!!!* costumes was made visible to the audience, and deployed as a performative/narrative tool. The previously mentioned '42nd Street' dresses for example were dazzling garments, very much associated with Hollywood chorus girls. They were worn however over the Dead Skins (around the dancer's necks), still seemingly in dry cleaning bags, and only covering the front of the dancers. When viewed from the front, they look like glitzy showbiz dresses, but when the dancers turn upstage, the audience can see that the dresses are mere illusions which leave the back of the dancers exposed – naked in their Dead Skins. It is an intentional performative slip – a moment of failure, and is yet another way in which the adversarial costumes complicate the figure of *Yippeee!!!*'s chorus girl. The costumes reference the aspirational illusions propagated by early twentieth-century dance films, but mires them amid images of decay, nakedness and bodily function.

This oscillation between sublime illusion and the grimier trappings of degradation and repair which the *Yippeee!!!* costumes reveal is a dynamic at work in many theatre costumes. As garments designed to be viewed within a proscenium theatre, at a distance and under stage lights, it is not unusual for them to disappoint the viewer if encountered at close range, in a museum display cabinet or backstage. Monks cites an early evocative example of this disappointment from Samuel Pepys' diaries which describes his surprise at encountering theatre costumes backstage. He laments the difference between 'how fine they show on the stage by candlelight and how poor things they are to look at now too near to hand' (Pepys cited in Monks 2010: 139). What Pepys is describing can be attributed to the change in context, lighting and proximity between backstage and onstage, and how this reveals the costume in literally a whole new light. As already described, this is also true for the Dead Skins (which look very different onstage, in a gallery, and in the archive). What is remarkable about the costumes in *Yippeee!!!* however, is that they succeeded in communicating this discrepancy within the actual moment of performance. The use of the '42nd Street' dresses worn over the Dead Skins for example, lays bare the inherent gaudiness and theatrical falsity at work in the moment of performance. They shift from being transformative, (in actually accomplishing a transformation of the dancers) to appearing theatrically grotesque. Thus the costume-as-adversary operates within the *Yippeee!!!* costumes on a subtle functional level for the dancers, but also as a performative trickster in and of themselves, for the audience.

Clothed in nakedness

Aoyama describes the Dead Skin as an 'extra skin that feels quite exposed but protected at the same time. You feel it's there but totally fits your body so it gives the sense of freedom, as if you are naked' (Aoyama 2017: n.pag.). Contradictions between exposure onstage and freedom seem key elements in the nature of the Dead Skin. These contradictions were at the heart of the second element of the costume – the question of hiding in nakedness and being invisible within a very revealing design – of costume being both present and absent at the same time. Monks' chapter 'Undressing: The disappointments of nudity' considers various interplays bound up with the naked body onstage, and the ways in which stage nudity, constructed as it is, can be considered as a costume in and of itself (2010: 99–118). Putting forward the idea that in the main, nudity on the dance stage is 'indigestible' for audiences, Francis Sparshott (writing in 1995), suggests that 'the medium [of dance] calls rather for suggestion or symbolism. To represent nakedness by nakedness would be amateurish' (Sparshott 1995: 306). With the Dead Skin, the importance of costume as 'standing-in' for the naked body, or rather creating a hybrid naked dancing body (with corpse-like pallor and unruly body hair), appears significant. These were recognizable, yet clearly theatrically augmented bodies on display. Inside this illusion there was a possibility of disappearance for the dancers into costume (despite their bodily exposure).

Discussing his design of the work, Vincenzi speaks of what he saw as 'a sort of fetishisation over the body in dance and a sexualisation that a lot of the time is quite unpleasant' (Vincenzi 2017: n.pag.). Wanting to avoid 'taking a dancer's power away' he continues,

> I knew that I wanted this fictional troop to be naked [...] But there was no way I wanted them to be [actually] naked [...] I didn't want [them] to feel vulnerable [...] The Dead Skins give them a strength in their body rather than not wearing anything in that context [...] They are naked but they are still clothed in a sort of fiction.
> (Vincenzi 2017: n.pag.)

By all accounts it seems that the first time the dancers saw themselves in the Dead Skins, it was a shocking experience due to the level of bodily exposure. But this initial

Yippeee!!! Anna Pons Carrera and Inn Pang Ooi. Photo Pau Ros surprise gave way to the realization that it was nonetheless possible to hide within the design – to have anonymity and power within the costume. Anderson describes how she found it

> quite shocking [...] because it was much more translucent than I expected the textile. But it was much more effective [...] everyone looked naked and everyone looked like they were dead. The bluish mauve tinge [...] looked like [...] cold slabs of white flesh.
> (Anderson 2017: n.pag.)

The exposure and constructed nakedness of the Dead Skins thus imbued the performers with both strength and vulnerability. Whilst undoubtedly the power which Vincenzi felt the costumes attributed was in evidence, Anderson also makes reference to the fact that many of the dancers began losing weight after the introduction of the Dead Skins. Whilst she acknowledges stress and the physical toll of the choreography as factors, clearly she also considers increased bodily awareness to be an influential factor in the weight loss (Anderson 2017: n.pag.). In her study into the 'aesthetic and politics of practice clothes and leotard costumes in ballet performance', Tamara Tomić-Vajagić illuminates similarly opposing elements at work for performers dancing in skintight costumes. As an illustrative example, she cites ballerina Deborah Bull's observations that the increased bodily awareness which certain costumes bring can influence the way in which a performer approaches a performance. Given the variability in how a dancer might feel about their body, and the fluctuations this could be subject to over time, Bull commented that '[d]epending on how you might feel about your body', this type of costume may 'set one up to start the performance with a sense of vulnerability, or from a stance of power' (Bull cited in Tomić-Vajagić 2014: 93). In the case of the Dead Skins, it seems that both these elements were at work at different times in the creative process of making *Yippeee!!!*.

Anderson stresses that the most powerful aspect of the costume was the way in which it rendered the dancers very similar. She describes having

> to really stare at hips and the pelvises of people to see really whether they were male or female [...] it wasn't just the shocking-ness of it, it was also that maybe an audience member couldn't pick out who was who.
> (Anderson 2017: n.pag.)

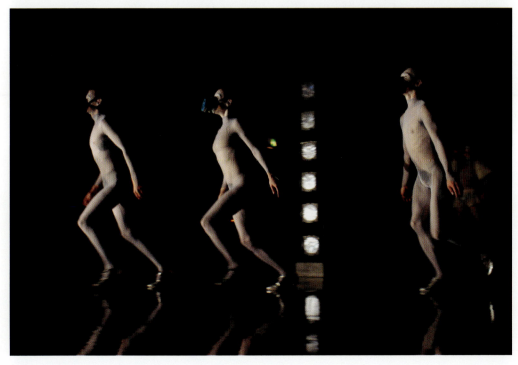

Yippeee!!! Anna Pons Carrera & Inn Pang Ooi. Photo Pau Ros
Yippeee!!! Company in Performance. Photo: Pau Ros

The hybrid nature of the chorus figure in *Yippeee!!!*, operating as a specific performative construct of the dance stage is evident in this description. It also highlights a significant choreographic interest of Anderson's, which is concerned not with any physiological markers of gender per se, but much more specifically, inherent differences between bodies. Whilst the figures in *Yippeee!!!* execute movements akin to those that might be performed by early twentieth-century chorus girls (at times possessing a coquettish air and emphasizing stereotypically 'feminine' movements such as swaying hips and delicate curving arm movements), they are performed by a cast of both men and women, each dressed in the naked semi-uniformity of the Dead Skins. The shocking nature of the costumes and the nakedness (recognizable as human form, but nonetheless otherworldly and uncanny), serves to emphasize the differences in bodily movement and proportions between dancers. This seems significant to Anderson:

> the style of their movement and the differences between them became [...] how they could differentiate from each other, which is what I wanted. I wanted the idea of a repeated pattern with slight variations but the variations don't come from mistakes [...] just little differences in style. Very slight differences – the kind that you can't choreograph but comes from the angle of your limbs and how it moves with your particular body, the kind of differences you can't iron out become greater, which was part of the thematic material of the work.
> (Anderson 2017: n.pag.)

Here again is an example of how the visual language of the Dead Skins fed very directly into the choreographic and thematic landscape of the work – extending the ideas of the choreography and presenting the dancing body in a dance-specific constructed framework. It is a moment where the language of the Dead Skins departs somewhat from Kracauer's conception of 'The mass ornament'. For Kracauer, the system behind the orchestration of mass ornaments was one 'oblivious to differences in form', which, he argued, 'leads on its own to the blurring of national characteristics and to the production of worker masses that can be employed equally well at any point on the globe' (Kracauer 1995: 78). For Anderson as the creator of *Yippeee!!!* it is not an obliviousness to differences but rather an acute awareness of minute physical characteristics (which render each dancer's performance unique), which occupies the heart of the choreography. Anderson here is not attempting to smooth over these differences, but instead to use the constrictions of a uniform framework in order to call the viewer's attentions to the tiny failures to comply with the construction. The

Dead Skin thus operates as a double once again – both suggesting uniformity and highlighting difference. The Dead Skins appear present and absent at the same time. Absent in the sense that the viewer is presented with the illusion of seeing a naked human body, but utterly present, in their strangeness, their anonymizing effect and the ways in which they refuse to comply with the aesthetics of the Hollywood canon they are referencing. In Hollywood musical films, power net costumes would have been employed in a genuine attempt for them to appear invisible to the viewer.

Reciprocal influence

Finally, it is important to consider the relationship between costume and movement, and costume and body – the ways in which contagion and mutual influence evolved the chorus figure ever further. The costumes in *Yippeee!!!* had a profoundly reciprocal relationship with the dancing bodies inside them, and the ways in which those bodies moved. In the examples already outlined there are crossovers between the three elements I have described – the '42nd Street' dresses for example, demonstrate how the dancing body was altered by costume. The previously mentioned *Wavy Arms* section of choreography further illustrates some of the ways in which the relationship between costume, movement and dancing body is endlessly intertwined.

There are also instances in which the costume 'solved' Anderson's choreographic problems, for example in *Wavy Arms* when the chorus sway together in a group, arms held aloft. Anderson wanted the focus of the audience to be directed towards the hands of the group during this sequence. The dancers found it difficult to translate this into embodiment until they were given red gloves to wear, which immediately highlighted the hands for the viewer, and also therefore for the dancers. Anderson also spoke of the effect of the Dead Skins in *Wavy Arms*, when dancers' faces were obscured by bandages but otherwise unadorned.

> [Y]ou could tell the dancers were *very* very aware of their entire bodies and the musculature and what they were presenting. It gave a heightened feel to that exposed portion of their bodies [...] which worked totally with the dance. And it gave detail to it that was very difficult to talk about when they're wearing their sloppy rehearsal clothes. But it happened in an instant when they [could] [...] feel the cool air around their midriffs [...] and feel that they were very close to each other. (Anderson 2017: n.pag.)

Hand in Glove, V&A. Third Year Student Performers from London Contemporary Dance School. Photo: Pau Ros

In other moments, choreography and movement were indelibly altered through their interaction with costume (as previously described), when movements not only streaked the costumes with purple marks from the dancers' makeup, but in turn the dancers' makeup became further smeared and distorted by the physical interaction, and the pubic wig hair began to leave their trails inscribed across the torso.

Ideas of becoming or transforming through costume are not unique to *Yippeee!!!*. What is unique about these costumes however, is the peculiar way in which they achieved this transformation. They oscillated between disguising the mechanics of transformation, and also laying them bare when the costume (deliberately) revealed its material precariousness to the audience. They evolved, degraded and mutated as part of the performance. Thus their material appearance referenced (and continues to reference), both life and death – individuality and anonymity. The chorus girl confronts us and eludes us all the time – refusing the annihilation of the traditional chorus line, whilst simultaneously being a victim of it. The Dead Skins oscillate between sublime beauty and the uglier trappings of decay and contagion: makeup streaked grubbily across the Skins, pubic hair snaking around limbs. Within these oscillations, both the illusionary aspirations of theatre and its tawdry mechanics hover. The transcendent idea of the performer and the leaking realities of unruly bodies exist side by side within a continuous slippage of imagery, shuttering rapidly past as in an old Hollywood movie.

Partial listening and ghost figures

Anderson referred to the Dead Skin as being akin to dead insect wings. Vincenzi's design conceived of deceased dancers. The interviews and conversations, however, reinforce the impressions of a mercurial shape-shifting garment, which combined transcendence with decay, and strength with vulnerable exposure. Jay Cloth, for instance, describes in detail the way in which he can 'see' the garments in his imagination, still retaining the contours of the individual dancers who wore them.

JC: Yeah they kind of do take on the shape of the person. Frauke [Frauke Requardt, a cast member of *Yippee!!!*], I can really see Frauke's in my brain as we are talking. [...] Because I'm so familiar with the shape of the cast it's quite easy to fit that costume to that person.

MKC: When you say you have Frauke's in your mind, do you see it just as the costume?

JC: Yes, I can see – I can see the shape of Frauke's costume. [...] It's just exactly how it was when she had it on. It's funny because her legs were a bit baggy because I always remember her pulling them up so I can always see it in the legs, in her one. Gary's [Gary Clarke] was always dirty around the neck. And he doesn't have to be wearing it, I see it just as the photos for the book [when the costumes were pinned to be photographed]. I see them all like that.

MKC: And so in a way they've got the embodiment of the dancer – the outline or the contours, but the dancer isn't there when you see them?

JC: No no. I could put a head on them but I am just seeing the costume.
(Jay Cloth 2017: n.pag.)

Here Jay Cloth seems to visualize or conjure the costume as a ghost body in and of itself. The Dead Skin stands in for the body which usually inhabited it, and indeed, the Dead Skin seems to hold priority in this visual hierarchy, rather than the body which it signifies. He also describes how he can see the pubic wig hair of the dancers in his mind's eye, and the particular shapes and ways it would be arranged on individual dancer's bodies. He even goes so far as to link the arrangement of how the pubic hair looked with individual traits of the dancers and the characters they played, demonstrating again how these 'identical' costumes gave rise to small variations and differences across multiples, accentuating the physical nuances across dancers.

The ghost figure seems thus to crop up in these considerations, and even to point towards the potential for an alternative after-life. However, in critiquing her own approach of utilizing haunting within a socio-historical context, Avery Gordon acknowledges that

> [t]he intermingling of fact, fiction, and desires as it shapes personal and social memory situates us on the border of the social sciences and makes me wonder What does the ghost say as it speaks, barely, in the interstices of the visible and the invisible? (2008: 24)

She also recognizes the inescapable reality that the writer of these ghost stories – the listener to any ghost's voice – is inextricably entangled in the interlocution. As Gordon puts it 'for better or worse: the ghost must speak *to me* in some ways sometimes similar to, sometimes distinct from how it may be speaking to the others'

(2008: 24). Given the fact that an after-life of disintegration is being prioritized in the interlocution of the Dead Skin, the partiality of my 'listening' as researcher needs to be acknowledged. This costume ghost figure would for example undoubtedly speak differently to the museum director for whom I caused distress in my seemingly reckless bent towards material destruction. Despite this caveat, the thematic elements and embodied nature of the Dead Skins as I have outlined in this chapter nonetheless reinforce the deficiencies of their current archival situation, and can be marshalled to suggest ideas for an alternative after-life.

The question of value unavoidably emerges in this consideration. What of the after-life of this garment – how might it be appraised financially? Whilst dance costumes worn by icons such as Nijinsky have attained almost totemic status (albeit many years after their original performances), these Dead Skins do not share such prestige or economic 'value'. They remain hidden in Anderson's personal archive over a decade and a half since the premiere of *Yippeee!!!*. In economic terms, they do not appear to be of much worth (in that they are not particularly aesthetic garments, and were not worn by iconic figures such as Nijinsky, which would add monetary value). Their distinctiveness and specificity of purpose render it impossible to reincarnate them into a new role. Their potential to serve as archival documents or sources is hugely hampered by their stasis in the lockup – they are protected from extreme decay but obliterated through lack of visibility. In the face of these concerns, what after life might befit the Dead Skins best?

Disintegration as an assertion of visibility

Despite being protected from severe degradation the ravages of time are nonetheless at work on the Dead Skins. The costumes bear visible marks and wear from performance and loss of condition from time spent in the lockup. They serve to illustrate both the scars of performance, and the effects of time, albeit in a very gradual minor way. Taking into account their plight of immobility and their physical nature, it becomes possible to envisage an alternative after-life for these skins, or at least, for one of them. An after-life which might allow a transcendence post-performance for the costume – one which is more appropriate to its genesis and life. Perhaps in the case of the Dead Skin, not preservation but in fact *disintegration* could prove a more fitting after-life. This strategy becomes largely concerned with time – attempting a gesture towards disintegration contains the implicit aim of speeding up, or making visible in real time, the gradual degradation that the costume will eventually suffer if left abandoned in its packing box. Taking a radical gesture towards disintegration also feels in step with my earliest conversations with Anderson regarding the archive. When she had casually remarked that '[s]ometimes I think I will burn them all and that will be a work' (Anderson 2016: n.pag.), Anderson was hinting at the underlying potential for a radical gesture to prove more fitting in honouring the potency of these garments, than sealing their anonymity and slow decline within the lockup. Disintegration was thus one of several equally valid hypotheses which Anderson put forward for the after-lives of the costume archive (transaction and preservation being the other two). In the case of the Dead Skin, disintegration seems most befitting.

Allowing the costume to disintegrate or be altered materially also allows for the creation of alternative archival remnants (through the use of photography and film). These would not be employed to purely document the garment as museum specialists would do in the creation of catalogue entries for their collections, but as a way of allowing the costume to speak differently through a medium other than archival storage or traditional display on mannequins. How, then, might one implement a strategy of material disintegration? Rendering the costume into sculptural form and leaving it outdoors to disintegrate (exposed to the elements over time) would be aligned to that of visual artists employing creative destruction, but in a different vein to those already mentioned such as Landy (2010) or Banksy (2018). Gradual and inherent disintegration would broadly walk more in step with works such as Leopoldo Maler's H2OMBRE (1982) – an ice sculpture (of himself) left to melt in a gallery space, or Zoe Leonard's *Strange Fruit (for David)* (1992–97) consisting of sutured and repaired fruit skins which slowly degrade on the gallery floor. Philadelphia Museum of Arts (who now hold the work) present it with an accompanying interpretative note which reads: 'The fruit skins – emptied, dried, faded, repaired, and ornamented – have the feel of relics, almost like photographs. Transformed by the artist's delicate mending, they are subject to effects of time that are as unpredictable as they are inevitable' (Philadelphia Museum of Art n.pag.). Quite aside from the lengthy timeframe required for a work such as Leonard's, these works also differ greatly from the Dead Skin in that they were created solely for the intended art work, rather than having a previous incarnation like the Dead Skin's past performances. Yoko Ono's 1961 *Painting for the wind* attempted to speed up destruction by encouraging the viewer to expose the work (which had seeds embedded inside) to the wind, thereby scattering the seeds inside the artwork. Such an action would solve the timeframe quandary but nonetheless remains in a canon outside that of the Dead Skin.

An intervention employing strategies such as these examples appears on reflection to be too drastically disconnected from the world of the Dead Skin (in particular the specificity of its life within performance and with a particular group of individuals). Whilst the creation of an alternative after-life is ultimately a construction of the research and therefore unavoidably involves imposing a set of conditions onto the garment, the aim is nonetheless that the after-life should be sympathetically linked to the conditions of the costume and its embodied histories. In keeping with these sentiments, it seems a logical step to devise a performed intervention whereby Makiko Aoyama could perform segments of the *Yippeee!!!* choreography repeatedly in a Dead Skin costume until it changes from its visibly recognizable form, to something *other*. Whilst it is impossible to predict exactly what might manifest through this process, the aim is to create an archival document 'written' by choreography and the dancing body. This strategy acknowledges the disappearance and exile which the storage archive can impose, and attempts to reinsert the costume within a visible archival arena. The Dead Skin's disintegration began in the moment of performance when choreography, dancing body and costume conspired together to mutually evolve and distort one another. It seems fitting therefore for the Dead Skin's potentially final obliteration to be at the mercy of dancing body and choreography, rather than rendered mute and disappeared into the cavern of the lockup.

Disintegration intervention

The creative team (consisting of myself, Anderson, Aoyama, Jay Cloth, Anne Verheij [filmmaker] and Rik Pennington [photographer]) assembles early on the appointed day, in the studio I have chosen at the Laurie Grove buildings in New Cross, London.[5] It has grey dance flooring and exposed brick walls painted white with no mirrors. Skylights give sufficient natural light to film without the addition of overhead lights which seems useful in distancing this new after-life which we are seeking to create, from the previous incarnation of the Dead Skin which would have always been viewed under stage lighting. Daylight produces a distinctly different effect to that of electric lighting and emphasizes the material details and quirks of the costume (which would usually be obliterated by the strong spotlights). I am mindful that the studio setting should provide as neutral a backdrop as possible for the film and photographs. I want at all times to highlight the distinction between the after-life intervention and the costume's previous life in order to avoid any resultant footage looking like an attempt to 're-stage' the costume.

I have devised the intervention with the Dead Skin as a one-day session whereby Aoyama will revisit sections of the choreography of *Yippeee!!!* (in particular ones that might put the Dead Skin under stress structurally), and perform these repeatedly in the studio setting. This is in order to explore both what might happen to the Dead Skin when stressed repeatedly, but more significantly, to reveal the embodied negotiations that occur between costume and body within *Yippeee!!!*. This will not be performed within a 'true' performance setting – there will be no stage lights, other cast, live music or the adrenaline which comes with live stage performance. Nonetheless the key elements of body, choreography and costume will be at work in reciprocal exchange. We have decided to focus on a section called *Grid* from the early part of the work which was performed by all cast members. *Grid* features a number of torso twists, leg kicks and rolling on the floor and as such is representative of the more strenuous choreography from *Yippeee!!!* as a whole. A recording of the music from composer Steve Blake plays on repeat.

Jay Cloth has been involved from the early stage of the process, sourcing extra accessories such as pubic wigs and face makeup which matched the originals (now no longer usable due to age or having been disposed). He is on hand today helping Aoyama to dress, checking her costume, hair and makeup, just as he would have done within *Yippeee!!!* itself. Whilst the order of the day and plans are ostensibly led by myself, the way in which the intervention progresses evolves collaboratively with all the individuals involved. Just as I have consciously avoided being led by previous scholarship and reviews of photographs of *Yippeee!!!*, so too I am unwilling to presuppose the outcome of what might happen to the costume during this intervention, or how I might wish it to appear in film or photographs. With this in mind, we employ a gathering approach to the documentation with the aim of creating a collage of film and images which will be further shaped and edited to become new archival documents. A variety of images with different styles are compiled including close-up footage of the garment in ways which one might not be accustomed to viewing it, sometimes rendering it abstract. I ask for moving shots, out of focus sections, and still images, along with more conventional wide shot framing, and close ups of particular details such as nametags on the garment. Aoyama is photographed as she dresses, does her hair and makeup and applies her prosthetic diamond studded teeth. After running the *Grid* section a number of times, we alternate between full run-throughs of the segment to small repeated actions, paying particular attention to the costume as it moves, wrinkles, snags and is strained during these movements. The fast pace of the movements makes it challenging for the photographer and film maker to capture the costume – even the effort involved in this endeavour bears witness to its mercurial nature and the reciprocal relationship between costume and body.

It is a punishing challenge for Aoyama too – the demands of the choreography, including for example maintaining the rictussed smile, seem exaggerated by the low key nature of the setting. Rather than being buoyed up by the adrenaline of live stage performance and theatrical additions such as lighting, the white daylight and somewhat clinical studio setting makes for draining and pared-back surroundings, which expose the harsher elements of the Dead Skin in performance.

Reciprocal degradation begins

The role of makeup in the alteration of the dancing body fast becomes apparent as large purple streaks begin to emerge on the arms and shoulders. The pubic and underarm wigs begin to shift slightly and on close examination, more and more tendrils of hair can be found protruding through the tiny mesh holes on the torso and legs of the costume. During the course of my interview with Vincenzi, he has emphasized that the Dead Skins are made from a particularly durable performance mesh (the type worn by performers in Las Vegas or the Folies Bergère in Paris). As such, he feels that they should be almost indestructible as the fabric was designed to be incredibly strong despite its translucent, delicate appearance. He has expressed amusement at our attempts to speed up a disintegration of the costume, and feels we might have our work cut out to achieve this goal. His confidence in the resilience of the garment as a whole is proven to be well founded. Whilst Aoyama's Dead Skin does indeed look (in the hand) like it might begin to disintegrate at the least stressing of the fabric (due to its aged, delicate appearance), in fact it proves incredibly resilient. What becomes apparent instead are the structural vulnerabilities of the garment – the poppered spine and the stitched seams, particularly under the armpits. Here, tiny holes and strains are in evidence, and repeated use of the arms, for example, stretches and exaggerates these vulnerabilities.

Perhaps of greater significance than these structural stresses, however, are the ways in which the characteristic elements which each interviewee has spoken about are clearly in operation whenever Aoyama is performing in the costume. The daylight and close proximity of the studio work exposes the difficult elements of the costume:

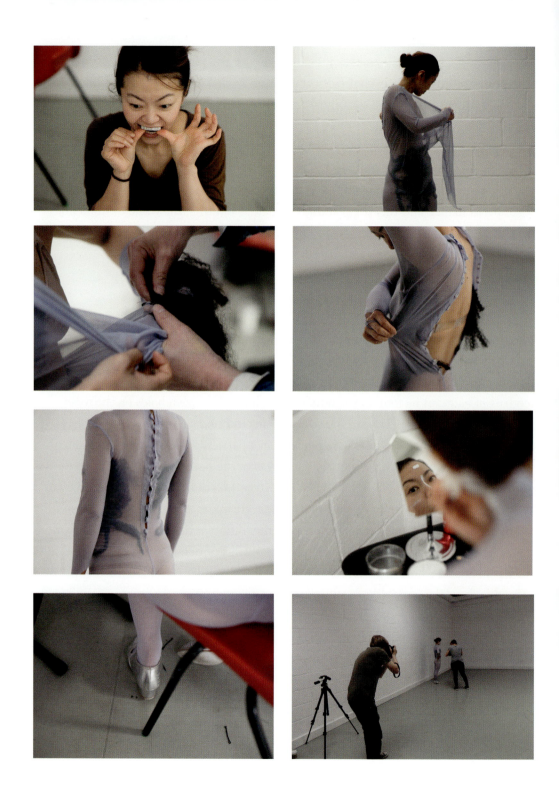

Makiko Aoyama preparing costume and makeup. Photos: Rik Pennington
Makiko Aoyama and camera crew. Photo: Mary Kate Connolly

the potential for discomfort, the strain of dancing to exertion in hard heeled shoes with prosthetic teeth and itchy pubic wigs. The exposure and nakedness of the costume is exaggerated by the setting (without the anonymity of distance and strong lighting which the theatre affords). Yet despite this, from the moment Aoyama is fully clothed in the costume, the fiction and strangeness of it holds up, creating a successful disappearance of her as performer. She is instead replaced by a hybrid creature of the chorus line – corpse like, beguiling, naked, yet genderless and somehow monstrous. The addition of metal teeth, the makeup and the postures of both face and body all conspire in this transformation. The effect is quite startling, even in the context of the casual studio atmosphere. All of a sudden Aoyama looks frightening and we joke that we can no longer locate the friendly dancer we had been speaking to minutes previously.

Throughout the day in the studio the aim is to make the Dead Skin *visible*, allowing it to transmit information about the choreography, the body of the dancer who inhabited it, and the creative processes involved in the making of *Yippeee!!!*, albeit through a process of translation and material destruction. If, as I have previously asserted, the materiality of the costume offers an actual physicality – a *body* of sorts, which persists in the face of performance's vanishing, then it seems crucial to give shape and voice to this costume body within a new framework (outside of the performance and the archive). This has been an intuitive process – constructing the framework in which the Dead Skin can perform, and then taking a position of active 'attending to' the garment – a creative attempt to transform it from its current material state to something other. The Dead Skins are garments which in fact already illuminated the archival work of time and disintegration as part of their live performance. Jay Cloth's description of them looking like 'they are on the verge of falling apart but they never do' (Jay Cloth 2017: n.pag.) is in step with their narrative language, and yet their material appearance belies their inherent resilience. These elements were at work during the performance life of the costume and therefore it seems fitting to exaggerate this, by attempting to speed up time in the studio intervention.

The 'success' of the costume in achieving a fragile appearance which masks an incredibly durable garment means that if one measured rate of disintegration as a criterion for success for the intervention, then it would be deemed to be only moderately successful. Through repeated performance of the choreography, the structural weaknesses of the garment become ever more exposed. Small holes and minor rips begin to stretch a little wider, a little deeper. Nearing the end of the intervention, we even seek to interrogate these physical stresses further by getting Aoyama to hold in stillness, the positions which stress the garment most, and tracking the tensions and damage to the garment. We even try tugging at the costume in these stress positions to see whether it will yield to the strain. Overall however, despite our attempts at disintegration, the garment remains intact – instead of disintegrating it becomes a document inscribed with more legible markings. The intangible forces of time and movement are rendered somewhat tangible or at least quantifiable, by the marks and etchings left by these stressors. Whilst we laughingly lament that we have failed to 'destroy' the garment during the intervention, on reflection I feel quite satisfied with how the degradation of the garment has played out. It has not been a vast acceleration of decay, but rather the illumination of the forces at work on the Dead Skin – both during performance and its long time in storage.

Finally, as Aoyama begins painstakingly to remove her makeup, unbuckle her shoes and peel off the Dead Skin, the footage is banked to await the film-editing process and the selection of photographs for exhibition. The costume has begun to shapeshift within these moving and still images, now held safe within the requisite storage hardware. A new after-life is beginning – as the physical costume is bundled back inside its packing box, its imagistic imprints travel elsewhere – onto my computer, into our memories to be rewritten. Waiting for further incarnation within a short film, on large mounted exhibition prints, in a book to be published. Across these new horizons, the costume holds its ground as a changeable trickster – glittering with silver and flesh yet mired in decay – which offers up the relationship between costume and body as an indecipherable tangle, bound together through mutual contagion. Many months later, the Dead Skin Disintegration short film is uploaded to a television screen which sits atop a wooden plinth to be viewed within the *Smithereens* exhibition. Headphones hang next to the screen, the soundtrack tinnily audible to the gallery visitors. This installation of film, the accompanying photos on the gallery walls, and the physical display of all of the Dead Skins hanging from the gallery ceiling does not mark the end of the after-life of these mercurial and resilient garments. It is the next step on their journey – one which aims to reveal their potency as archival ciphers, which cradle, within their fibres and outlines, a host of bodies and choreography now (not entirely) vanished.

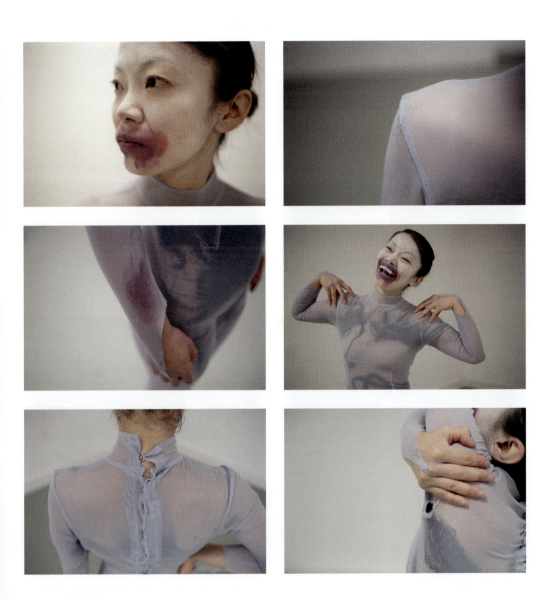

Makiko Aoyama in costume. Photos: Rik Pennington

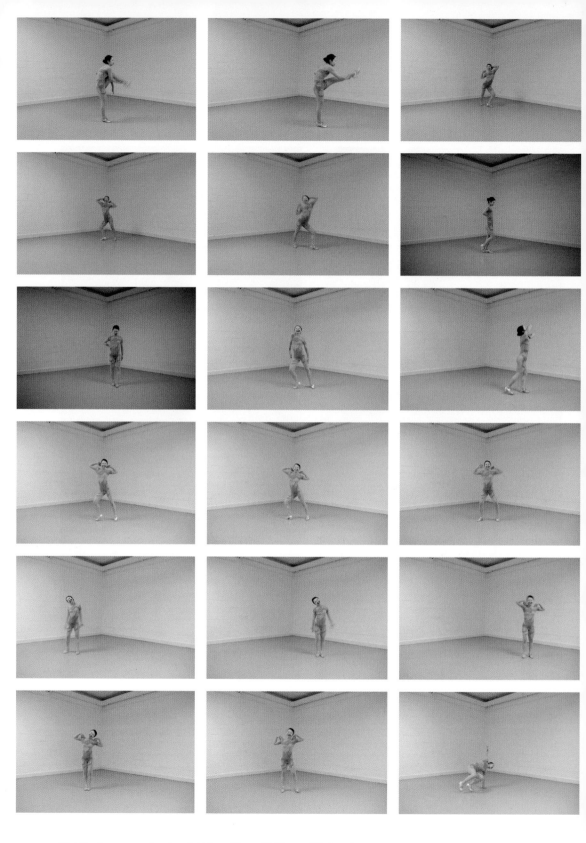

Makiko Aoyama performing *Grid* from *Yippeee!!!*. Photos: Rik Pennington

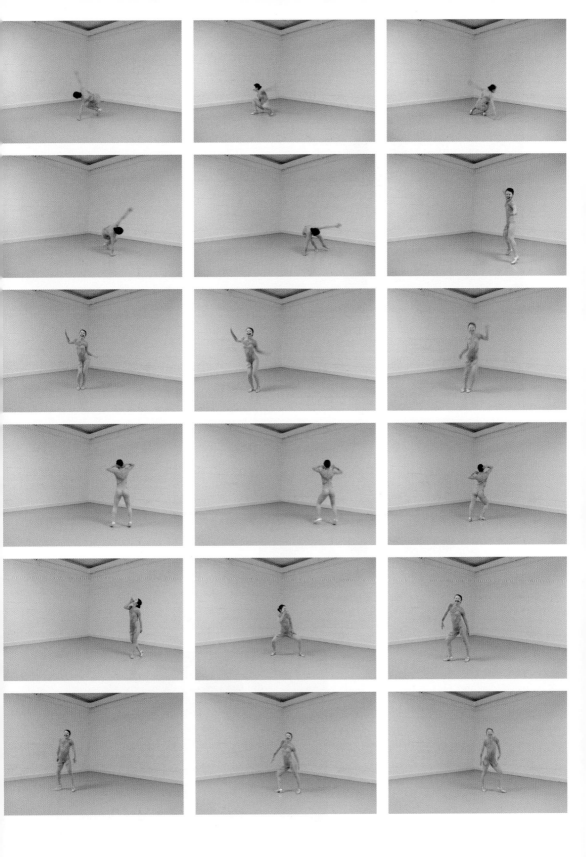

Notes

1. Mad Cow Disease is the common name for 'bovine spongiform encephalopathy' or BSE. It is a neurological disease which can affect cows, and be transmitted to humans (as the fatal Creutzfeldt-Jakob disease), via the consumption of contaminated beef (US Food and Drug Administration: n.pag.).

2. At time of writing this DVD can still be found in library holdings such as the LABAN library at Trinity Laban Conservatoire of Music and Dance, or acquired directly from Anderson herself.

3. In the creation and first tour the dancers were: Macarena Campbell, Anna Pons Carrera, Gary Clarke, Greig Cooke, Kath Duggan, Valentina Formenti, Maho Ihara, Tim Morris, Inn Pang Ooi, Ryen Perkins-Ganges, Frauke Requardt and Csongor Szabo. Jay Cloth was wardrobe mistress and Joanna Young was Wardrobe Mistress' assistant. In the second tour Kevin Muscat replaced Greig Cooke and Paul Wilkinson replaced Tim Morris. Roberto Sassi replaced Simon King during some performances in the second tour. Makiko Aoyama was understudy and Wardrobe Mistress' assistant. Annika Spampinato was rehearsal director for *Yippeee!!!*

4. For deeper analysis of Kracauer and contemporary consideration of social choreography, and the interrelations and aesthetics of social order and choreography see: Cvejić, B. and Vujanovjić, A. (2012), *Public Sphere by Performance*, Berlin: books.

Also: Cvejić, B. (2019), 'How does choreography think "through" society?' in M. Bleeker, A. Kear, J. Kelleher and H. Roms (eds) (2019), *Thinking Through Theatre and Performance*, London: Bloomsbury Methuen Drama, pp. 270–83.

5. The former home of the Laban centre, now still in use as supplementary studios to the main dance faculty building of Trinity Laban Conservatoire of Music and Dance at Creekside, Deptford, London.

Makiko Aoyama in costume. Photos: Rik Pennington
Overleaf: Green painted mask from *Smithereens*. Photo: Rik Pennington
Costume items from *Smithereens*. Photos: Pete Moss

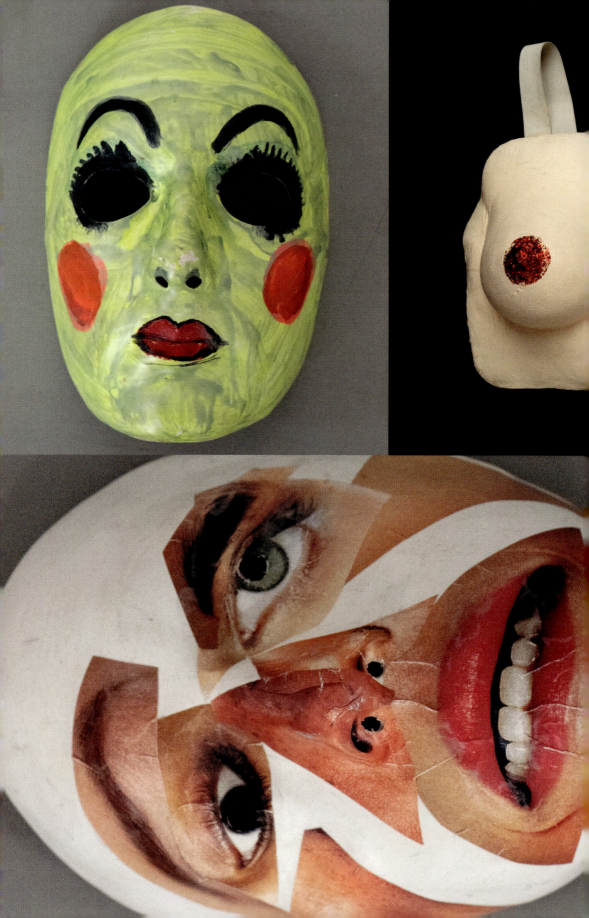

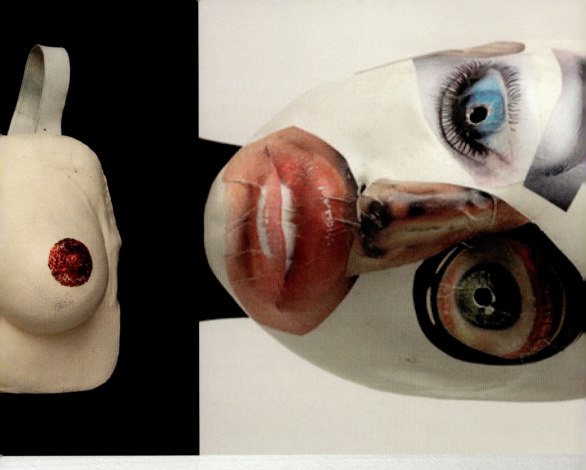

Preservation

Not for the first time, I become aware that I have forgotten to breathe. That by suspending my exhalation, so too am I hoping to ward against calamity. We are in the studio once again with a costume and a film crew. This time I am wielding a scalpel over one of the *Smithereens* masks. Today, after many months of preparation, I am attempting a physical gesture towards the preservation of these artefacts.

I am conscious that despite the breath-holding I am beginning to find within my hands, the 'steady does it', slow, reverent pace of the conservators whom I have watched work. The costume maker who taught me how to use a scalpel like this had been swifter and bolder in her movements. Her attitudes towards the costumes differed from those working in museum archives. As a pragmatist on the front lines within a prestigious Opera House, her concerns had been less with preserving relics for the ages, and more with creating workable, durable items which could be used to death. Due to my inexperience with conservation work and the definitive aim of preservation within this context, I opt for the hesitant, minimal-intervention strategy. Easy does it. Try not to shake.

After all this time living in their cold lockup, bumped around in vans, torn off and on in haste during performances, dropped on the floor in the white blindness of theatre lights, I don't wish to be responsible for their demise. A lurking terror besets me that after all this time I could singlehandedly enact their maiming or destruction. At each step I check in with Lea: 'Shall I scrape away a bit more of this adhesive? Shall I try to remove this makeup sponge?' With each step I require her consent, her blessing. The masks have by now very definitely transformed from objects of function into sacred artefacts for interpretation. This has happened gradually with each new step taken towards their cataloguing and preservation. They have morphed from a pile of old masks stacked together so tightly in a battered plastic box that they had to be roughly prised apart, to beautiful costume objects. Nestled in bespoke conservation-grade archive boxes, wrapped in silk and acid-free paper. Never touching one another or the edges of the boxes. Handled only by the edges, never cast face down on an abrasive surface. The masks themselves have not thus far physically changed – only our approach to them and our perspective.

Today Lea and I are taking actual steps towards the restoration and preservation of them – removing stuck in labels, makeup sponges which have become bonded to their surface, and visibly degrading masking tape. These will be minor alterations and we have debated long and hard over whether to leave them be, or take some steps toward cleaning them. Through these debates I have stumbled upon opposing philosophies; from conservation and museological agendas to the pragmatic perspectives of costume professionals, and finally, the personal wishes of Lea Anderson as the keeper of this archive. Never has stripping away some sticky tape felt like such a radical gesture. And yet here I am ... tentatively peeling ... gingerly paring away at the sticky residue left behind. Conscious at all points of the weight of thinking around the after-life of these strange little death masks.

In addition to trying to emulate the dependable hands of a conservator, my movements have the self-conscious slowness of one aware of being on camera. I am being filmed and photographed as I proceed. The need, in one action, to satisfy the demands of conservation, documentation and the aesthetics required to generate materials worthy of gallery exhibition adds peril to the whole endeavour. There is only one chance at this. Do not let the scalpel slip.

The masks from *Smithereens* (1999), have long stood out as significant objects demanding an after-life beyond that of their box in the lockup. The idea of allowing an artefact to speak back and influence its own after-life readily applies to the masks – they are performative in and of themselves in how they look and feel in the hand. It has also been apparent from the outset (in conversations with Anderson and her collaborators) that they are affectionately revered as totems of performance and beautiful design objects. On our first trip to the costume lockup Anderson addressed them as old friends as she lifted them out of their boxes. Holding each one up to the light to carefully survey the features of each face, she could identify every cast member. Dancer Luca Silvestrini's mask for instance, was instantly recognizable even to me, due to the characteristic outlines of his chin and cheekbones.

They were formed from plaster casts of the dancers' faces and as such, closely resemble death masks, suspending the image of each dancer in repose (as the casts were made with them sitting in a chair). They carry the imprints not only of the dancers themselves, but also the designers and makers who further transformed them (with various rudimentary materials) into individual artworks. Here we find ourselves not so much in the dominion of ghosts and haunting, but rather in the realm of the uncanny. Freud's conception of the uncanny does not uniformly relate to the masks (in for example his relating the uncanny to the return of repressed primitive beliefs,

Photos: Rik Pennington

or ideas of animism). He does, however, touch on the unsettling effect brought about when the viewer is unsure whether something seemingly animate is in fact inanimate, and vice versa (Freud [1919] 2003). He also draws a distinction between the operation of the uncanny within fiction and everyday life. Freud argues that paradoxically, 'many things that would be uncanny if they occurred in real life are not uncanny in literature, [and conversely] [...] in literature there are many opportunities to achieve uncanny effects that are absent in real life' (Freud [1919] (2003): 155–56). He cites fairy tales as a way of illustrating that in a constructed fictive world, occurrences such as Snow White opening her eyes in her glass coffin do not appear uncanny, whereas they would be deeply disturbing in 'real' life (Freud [1919] (2003): 155–56). This interplay between real or everyday life and a constructed fictitious (in this case performative) world seems important in how the *Smithereens* masks operate. They appear uncanny on a basic level due to their material likeness to an automaton or life-like doll, but moreover, they appear uncanny on a more profound level within the world of *Smithereens* (which riffs on recognizable tropes of cabaret and dance hall performances, creating certain visual expectations which the masks subsequently fail to meet). They not only bear the maker's marks and evidence of their past life, but their essential physicality as masks moulded from individual dancers' faces endows them with a further ghostly dimension. They are not simply an artefact now unworn or missing the body which once inhabited it (as with the Dead Skins), but crucially, they were originally forged with that self-same body. They could not have been made without it. Thus their involvement with the dancers who wore them predates the moment of rehearsal or performance – those individual faces have been there from the moment of their inception.

There are 36 masks in total – three complete sets of masks from the cast of ten dancers and two musicians. The first set of masks were kept in their original white plastic finish with no augmentation. The second set was collaged with magazine cuttings by designer Sandy Powell, and overlaid with a layer of translucent glue (Powell 2018). This set are reminiscent of the collages made by artists such as Hannah Höch (cited by Anderson and Powell as a strong influence in the work) (Anderson 2018a). The final set were hand-painted by artist David Hoyle (with water-based paint and glitter) in a similar style to how he used to wear his own makeup during his performances as the drag persona *The Divine David* during that time (Powell 2018).[1] Each performer had one plain white mask, one collaged mask and one painted mask. They were alternated for different chorus lines, worn on both the front and the back of the head.

The masks formed only one element of the costumes from *Smithereens* and yet despite their partial nature seen alone out of context of the performance, they remain individually performative due to their striking persistence as aesthetically arresting objects. The masks thus differ greatly to the Dead Skins from *Yippeee!!!* in the ways in which they remain post-performance. Whilst the Dead Skins are not particularly aesthetically pleasing and appear quite disconnected from their performance lives (in that they are unadorned aged garments), the masks are immediately eye-catching. In actuality, they (like the Dead Skins), are severed from their surrounding performance context and are only one item of a wider costume, yet their apparent completeness as visual and material objects obscures this reality. So too, the intervention and after-life which these objects demand contrasts dramatically to that of the Dead Skin. The guiding process is therefore less an interrogative mapping and questioning of the artefacts, but rather, has been about harnessing the acknowledged totemic and aesthetic nature of the masks as a jumping off point, leading to an intervention situated within the realms of *preservation* rather than disintegration. Here again the core methodology is borne out of my early conversation with Anderson about the several different avenues which could be explored in the context of the archive. Instead of 'burning' the Dead Skins, we have attempted a creative destruction. With the masks, instead of placing them with an institution such as the V&A for preservation (as Anderson has considered doing), we attempt to walk a path towards preservation – emulating as much as possible, the conditions of conservation and protected storage which a museum might provide. Due to my background (largely based in performance and dance research) this has inevitably required upskilling in a whole new area of research and conservation practice – I was wholly unfamiliar with the museological and conservation worlds which I was about to enter. This quest for preservation has also steered the nature of the interviews and my thinking around them. The research process has therefore been one of acquainting myself with unknown museological worlds – the technical and practical skills required to work with artefacts such as these, and furthermore, the overarching curatorial ethos which might govern their after-lives.

In their introduction to *The Explicit Material* (2019) the volume editors outline that they utilize the 'phrase "explicit material" [...] as a means of referencing the ways conservation explicates objects and artefacts in terms of relational and temporal materiality, thereby also reaching beyond the tangible sphere of the material' (Hölling et al. 2019: 4). This conception of conservation as a multidimensional practice of explication or illumination is one which resonates with my approach to the masks.

It speaks to the characteristics of the masks themselves alongside the wider aims of recuperation and representational repair which my archival work hopes to initiate. The masks seem to demand engagement on discreet levels – their materiality first and foremost, but perhaps more significantly, the entangled ethics of care in relation to any potential actions carried out on them under the guise of preservation or restoration. In my forays into these new museological worlds it has become apparent early on that an after-life of preservation would be informed by a variety of perspectives (some diametrically opposed), and that navigating this unfamiliar world must ultimately be done in close collaboration with Anderson, as holder of the archive. Furthermore, it can only approximate certain elements of what might be their reality if they were actually incorporated into a prestigious institution.

Hölling et al. (2019) state that the aim of their book is to work towards the confounding of 'continuing assumptions that artworks and artefacts are made of static, inert matter – inactive, stagnant and passive "objects" of investigation, subordinated to hygienic orders of museum vitrines or of preserved historical sites' (Hölling et al. 2019: 2). Rather, they argue, that artefacts 'exist as complex constructs of material relations' (Hölling et al. 2019: 2). The overarching aim of any gesture of preservation carried out in this intervention is less bound up with the (impossible) task of acquiring conservation levels on a par with a professional institution, and more specifically about utilizing a gesture of preservation as a means to unpack these material relations. To call attention to the relatedness of these artefacts – to the individuals and cultural worlds which are inextricably linked with their past and continued existence into the future. There has seemed an urgent need to do the masks justice somehow – to slow (if possible), the ravages of time and potentially damaging storage. Insurance policies, packing processes, conservation, restoration and (sustainable, undamaging) possibilities for exhibition have been the drivers of the methodology. These considerations sit in stark contrast to those influencing the Dead Skin intervention. The masks have begun to shape-shift within my thinking – it has become clear that they are now on a journey of transformation, or perhaps more accurately, one of recognition of their essential essence as precious relics, which had been somewhat eradicated by the physical realities of their inertia in the lockup.

Along this methodological journey perhaps most informative has been the conversations and encounters along the way – the contexts and frames of reference among conservators, performers, designers and insurers. Within each of these frameworks the objects reassert their totemic nature – gradually, the essence of these fabric remains accumulates at each new turn. My position as previously uninitiated novice in the world of conservation and curation has come to bear on the means by which knowledge has been gathered. It is beyond the scope of this project for me to become expert in physical conservation skills and fully conversant with the wide-range of relevant curatorial and conservation agendas. Nonetheless the encounters I have had with a variety of professionals (from costume professionals to curators and conservators), are hugely fruitful in building a preservation framework for the masks. Crucially, these conversations have also helped my understanding in my forays navigating technical preservation manuals and the writings of fashion history and curatorial scholars such as (among others), Schäffler (2019) and Taylor (2002). The eloquence of textile and costume objects have formed a key theme in the interviews I have carried out with conservators working at the V&A. The ways, for example, in which they can deduce historical information from the details of garments. Paul Ricoeur (1978) suggests that 'as soon as the idea of a debt to the dead, to people of flesh and blood [...] stops giving documentary research its highest end, history loses its meaning' (Ricoeur cited in Merewether 2006: 68). This primary function for documents to refer back to lived histories and communicate their experiences which Ricoeur speaks of, chimes with the conservators' assertion of the importance of tangible cultural heritage. Perhaps particularly so when their tangibility can serve as an interlocutor to otherwise archivally-sparse histories such as in the case of *Smithereens*.

These conversations have reinforced the usefulness of an after-life centred around preserving these particular masks. Their specificity as interlocutors of Anderson's legacy has been thus foregrounded, bound up with the need to stem or slow the inevitable decline of the objects due to age and unideal storage. It has also become clear that the means by which the 'explication' of material objects is carried out through conservation (as described by Hölling et al. [2019]) is always a negotiated process; tailor-made to the particular needs of each object and the purpose for which restoration or conservation is being carried out. Whether there is a particular curatorial aim at work for example (such as the work carried out by V&A conservators in preparation for an exhibition of fashion designer Balenciaga discussed later in this chapter), or whether it is just a means of 'stabilizing' an object in the archive to insure against its rapid decline. Whilst I have been able to glean specific technical advice from conservators in relation to the masks, the most valuable information has really come about through my burgeoning understanding of the ways in which a conservator might view an object as an embodiment of tangible cultural heritage.

The gesture of preservation which has been carried out attempts to serve both the material logistical needs of the aging objects and the rich histories embedded literally and metaphorically within them. The marks adorning the masks – from the brushstrokes of the artists to the makeup and sweat stains of the performers – point towards striations of performance history. These marks are left from the original run of performances, but also their post-*Smithereens* performance life when they have been used in student projects and performed exhibitions. The alterations made for example, in order to make a mask fit on a dancer not from the original cast (makeup sponges or polystyrene packing noodles glued roughly inside to prevent the mask slipping on a face it was not moulded from). The ways in which these objects are catalogued, stored and exhibited can either eradicate or emphasize these historical scars. The politics of preservation becomes thus apparent at every step. Rather than creating a visual dancing image as with the Dead Skin, the preservation intervention has become one of methodical care and a documentary approach that reveals each of these traces to the viewer or reader; peeling back the layers of performance history, and crucially, not attempting to fill these masks with bodies once more (as has been done with the Dead Skin). This chapter documents the historical details of *Smithereens* (1999) and seeks to provide an overview of the objects themselves. It charts some of the specific training and research practices undertaken in order to facilitate preservation strategies for the masks and how these have then been utilized within this project. In keeping with the particular way in which the methodology has been forged, through direct interaction and *doing*, the training and knowledge which forms the basis of the Preservation intervention is captured in a descriptive way, reflecting the gradual accumulation of knowledge and formative encounters which shaped the after-life of these masks.

Smithereens

Smithereens was originally named *The Cholmondeleys, The Featherstonehaughs and The Victims Of Death in Smithereens* (Watson 1999). Most works in Anderson's repertoire were initially titled with the full titles of all companies involved (the dance companies of *The Cholmondeleys* and/or *The Featherstonehaughs*, and usually a company name for the band of musicians who played the score). The musicians would create a band title specific to each work – in this case it was *The Victims Of Death*. The title of the work was later shortened for ease, to *Smithereens*. When the work was remounted by students (for example as part of the Trinity Laban Undergraduate Historical project, in 2003) (Bannerman 2017), it was always billed as *Smithereens* to signal that the original cast of *The Cholmondeleys* and *The Featherstonehaughs* were not performing it. *Smithereens* was choreographed in 1999 by Anderson with costume design by Sandy Powell, and stage and lighting design by Simon Corder. Music was composed by Steve Blake, who performed the score live with Dean Brodrick (billed as *The Victims Of Death*). Blake played soprano saxophone and keyboard with Brodrick playing accordion and keyboard. As with all Anderson's works, the collaboration with Blake and in particular the role of music is a significant element of *Smithereens*. The band was also incorporated as an important element of the performance and choreography of *Smithereens* – the musicians wore masks like the dancers and the instruments were sometimes moved around on the stage as part of the performance.

The cast was made up of *The Cholmondeleys*[2] and *The Featherstonehaughs*.[3] Detailed documentation on the work is now somewhat scant, but it premiered in late October 1999 before touring venues across the United Kingdom (including Lemon Tree – Aberdeen, Riverside Studios – London, Gardner Arts Centre – Brighton and Truro Hall – Cornwall). Since its original tour *Smithereens* has never been remounted in full, but excerpts have featured in student performances and were also performed as part of *Hand in Glove* (2016). *Smithereens* was described by Donald Hutera (2011: 33) as 'an intriguing coupling of a deliberate cookie-cutter uniformity of movement with seductively dark undertones of decadence'. Reviewing the work for *The Telegraph* newspaper at the time, Ismene Brown cited the impact of the costumes as a key component of the work, writing that 'Powell [...] has produced a Venice Carnival of costumes, masks, fetish-wear and superb tutus' (Brown 1999). As with *Yippeee!!!*, the significance of the costumes is illustrated in the critics' impressions of the work. Likewise, the operation of the chorus lines and the strangeness of the performative world which Anderson and her collaborators created. There are some apparent crossovers in the mechanics of costume and the (failed) uniformity of the chorus lines in *Yippeee!!!* and *Smithereens*. It is important to note however that the visual language of the two works is nonetheless quite different when considered on a deeper level (than as a work which uses bodysuits and accessories as part of the visual language). *Smithereens* predates *Yippeee!!!* by seven years and each reflect the styles of their designers (Powell and Vincenzi). *Smithereens* centred on the idea of a number of short 'turns' or acts. Anderson described her affection for 'short vignettes of separate things [...] singles records [...] acts [...] turns. With these, everything is about how you

Hand in Glove, V&A. Third Year Student Performers from London Contemporary Dance School. Photo: Pau Ros

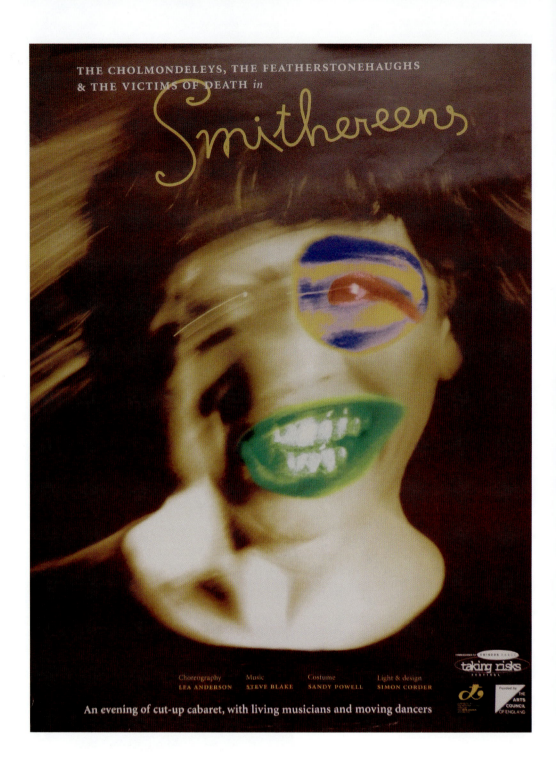

Playbill from *Smithereens* tour. Designed by Pep Sala. Image of Lea Anderson by Eddie Monsoon

put things together. How do you make lots of things into a show?' (Anderson cited in Connolly 2017: 17). Drawn from the heritage of cabaret and early twentieth-century performance, *Smithereens* featured a number of tropes of the dance stage, usually incorporating a failure to live up to the expectation set by the context of performance. A torch song singer who has lost her voice for instance, and whose exaggerated facial mime is accompanied by a second performer hidden behind her, using their gloved arms to provide the dramatic gestures for the singer. This also serves as an illustrative example of the operation of the uncanny within the performative world constructed in *Smithereens*.

Anderson cites significant influences for the work as including Weimar Republic performers such as Anita Berber and her associates[4] and the wider catalogue of iconic twentieth-century modern dance performance. The work draws from a somewhat similar vein of inspiration as that utilized in *Yippeee!!!* (in terms of early twentieth-century performance), but *Smithereens* employed more explicit references to particular artists, and the world of cabaret.

> With *Smithereens*, I was thinking about what contemporary dance had become, and I began to look at what we had started out with in its early origins: Bauhaus, Expressionism – all these interesting people. I had a big collection of images. Before the internet was such an easy tool, paper images were the thing. I would keep them for years and years and keep adding to them [...] I remember I had lots and lots of images of chorus lines, and early-twentieth-century performance by people like Claude Cahun (she was a kind of shaman for me). There were lots of strong images which she had made and one of them became *Music Box* (a performed vignette within *Smithereens*).
> (Anderson 2018a: n.pag.)

In addition to the visual influences of early twentieth-century performance, the structure of a cabaret (with a number of acts interspersed with chorus sections) formed the underlying framework of the work. *Smithereens*, the title, thus reflected Anderson's concept of numerous fragments of performances spliced together and punctuated by chorus lines.

> I had this idea of *Smithereens* having bits of stuff. And what is a bit? And what is an edge? Is it because somebody in a certain costume leaves the space and someone in a different costume enters – that makes an edge? Or is it when the music changes? So we had all these different ideas that I talked to about edges [...] it was 1999 and that century full of performance work had come [...] I wanted to make something that [...] [felt like] [...] looking through [...] a kind of an index drawer.
> (Anderson 2018: n.pag.)

Chorus lines (in which the masks predominantly featured, worn over black bodysuits) juxtaposed with small vignettes (such as the aforementioned Torch Song Singer) form the backbone of *Smithereens*. The exploration of 'edges' which Anderson references above is underpinned by the musical score, the variety of costumes, and the ways in which they were employed structurally within the work. There was a chorus line (named by Anderson as 'Bobblehead Chorus') made up of dancers wearing headdresses made out of black tulle which resembled the layers of a tutu or 'Bobblehead'. Other costume accessories included prosthetic breasts with sparkly red nipples and stockings worn over the face with red streamers cascading from the top (see accompanying images). Anderson credits Powell for the concept of having numerous accessories worn over a selection of black dance garments (different styles of leotards and bodysuits) to create an illusory effect.

> For the costume, Sandy said, 'well this is a bit mad but wouldn't it be marvellous if it looked like it was really simple – just black and black with these other little bits which are made up from the language of theatre (masks, tutus) – but that actually it's really difficult! Would you be up for it?' And of course I said 'yes, that would be brilliant!' Often I think I will easily manage something, with no sense of the reality of it when it becomes vastly complex!
> (Anderson cited in Connolly 2017: 18–19)

This utilization of costumes not only created the illusion of a far larger cast than the ten dancers performing, it also added a layer of complexity both visually and logistically (for the performers) which became crucial to the work itself. 'Costumes for each successive appearance of a chorus line', wrote Ramsay Burt in 2007, 'revealed an unexpected, new twist on the previous one' (Burt 2007a: 193–94).

Pages from Lea Anderson's notebooks. Photos: Mary Kate Connolly

Costume within the devising process

The costume changes (from one type of bodysuit to another, from masks to bobbleheads to fake breasts, etc.), became so convoluted within the work and were required to be executed at such speed, that part of the devising process of *Smithereens* involved choreographing costume changes in minute detail and timing them (Anderson 2018a). Simon Corder suggested partially revealing the costume changes on stage during the performance (by lifting the backdrop of the stage slightly) so that the audience could see the dancers changing behind it. The costume changes were not only therefore intricate and skilled, but in fact, became an intriguing visual component of the performance. Whilst in *Yippeee!!!* the costumes were wheeled around on rails and dancers changed in front of the audience, here there was only a partial view afforded of this 'performed backstage'. It was not an accurate view of backstage activity, but a choreographed one. Thus the costumes in *Smithereens* provided a referential framework of a never-ending chorus line which seamlessly shifted from one costume to another whilst the 'backstage' view intentionally complicated this framework. This is somewhat akin to the theatrical falsity laid bare in *Yippeee!!!* though the visual language of *Smithereens* is stylistically quite different. Viewed now in retrospect, this element of *Smithereens* can be regarded as a key moment within Anderson's working process – when the choreography of costuming (necessitated by logistical reasons) became an integral part of the overall performance.

> There was so much going on with the changes, that things needed to be choreographed. We realised that it would be much better, for example, to make a particular gesture rather than just sticking your leg up to get your tights off. We explored kicking it off, or using the hands in a certain way to create specific costume behaviour. So not only was it like in *Flesh & Blood* [1989] where we re-choreographed the danced movement [following the addition of costumes], now we had to perform the costume changes. Every night after the show we did more rehearsals of it! It was just us – there was no wardrobe mistress so we had to work out which dancer would be free at which moment to help another with their costume changes.
> (Anderson cited in Connolly 2017: 19)

Dancer Luca Silvestrini described the costumes as necessitating 'survival mechanisms [for each dancer] which [were] very individual' (Silvestrini 2018: n.pag.). He outlined

False breasts made by Robert Allsopp. Photos: Pete Moss

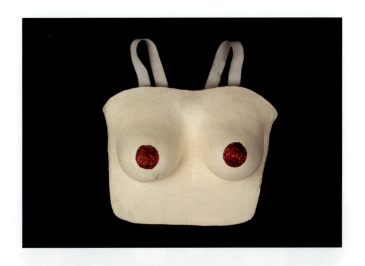
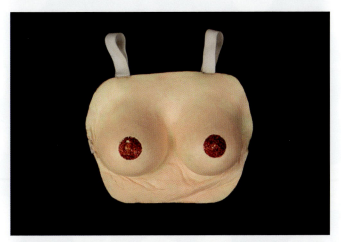
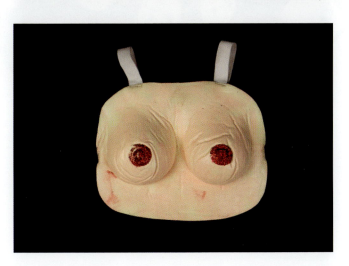

Doll head tutu. Photo: Pete Moss
Right: *Smithereens* costumes. Photos: Pete Moss

the physical set-up of costumes backstage with each dancer having their own table and chair next to one another with all of their costumes arranged on it.

> the masks, the gloves, the mouth, the tits, you name it. We had probably around thirty items each backstage [...] So there was a lot of people [...] there was a lack of space, lack of time, and you have to find your own discipline in a way [for] how to cope.
> (Silvestrini 2018: n.pag.)

Here perhaps we see a familiar dynamic at work – the welcome complications which arise in Anderson's work through the addition of costumes (particularly numerous and tricky ones). The 'edge' which these survival mechanisms of Silvestrini's inculcated in the dancers' performance appears to be a signature component, not only of *Smithereens*, but many of Anderson's works, including *Yippeee!!!*.

The rich quality of the costumes was cited as significant to the overall work by Anderson and dancer Anna Pons Carrera. Powell commissioned highly skilled costume makers and artists to make individual items – a tutu maker from the Royal Opera House (name unknown)[5] made the 'Bobbleheads' (head pieces made with black tulle as previously described) and the ballerina tutu overlaid with doll head images (see accompanying images) (Anderson 2018a). The masks and false breasts were cast and made by renowned props maker Robert Allsopp.[6] These high production values and the creation of beautiful costume objects also marked a turning point in the ways in which costumes influenced Anderson's working process.

> it was just so lovely to work with those people, and to get something freshly made. All the dancers had the masks made to fit their faces so they were very connected with the making of everything. I remember when the false breasts arrived how they were so beautifully crafted. There was a new relationship with the costumes and the objects which was very special.
> (Anderson 2018a: n.pag.)

Pons Carrera described how interacting with the costumes in this work felt distinctive due to the creative individuals involved:

> You did have the feeling with this piece that everything was just such good quality because we had costumes from Sandy, direction and movement from

> Lea, music from Steve, Divine David doing makeup [...] everything was just like 'wow!' We were parading these beautiful clothes and these crazy masks, it was a real privilege.
> (Pons Carrera 2018: n.pag.)

The quality of the costumes not only arguably enhanced the performers' experience of working with the costumes, but potentially also increased the resilience and longevity of the garments themselves. In the main, the *Smithereens* costumes remain in very good condition. The speed with which the performers carried out costume changes subjected the masks to potentially significant wear and tear (particularly so in remounting projects done subsequently with students). They are now (at the time of writing) well over 20 years old. Up until when I commenced my research the masks were stored in unideal conditions; nested together in boxes with no padding or protection. Taking these factors into consideration, the excellent quality in which the masks still remain is a testament to the craft which went into their production. Whilst there is some age-related degradation and small damage due to trauma (paint chips for example, where a mask might have been dropped accidentally), overall their material condition would be considered very good relative to their age and usage.

Encounter with the masks

The masks are made from acrylonitrile butadiene styrene ('ABS').[7] It is a stable, durable plastic material used in a variety of domestic and industrial products (including car bumpers). The process of making the masks began with a mould of each individual dancer's face. They each sat in a chair whilst alginate (a quick setting mould material, often used in the dentistry profession) was worked by hand, over their face, carefully leaving the nostrils free to allow breathing. The speed of hardening for this material depends on the temperature of the water used to dilute the mix (colder water speeds up the setting process). The whole process would have taken approximately fifteen minutes, before the mould could be removed from the face (Allsopp 2019). Luca Silvestrini recalled the somewhat claustrophobic sensations associated with the casting.

> I remember the sense of cold – it was very cold in your face [...] my god you feel like you were buried alive. It was awkward [...] it was extraordinary as an experience but it was also quite frightening [...] I do remember feeling particularly closed in and cold and unknowing. You stop sensing what's around

Above and below: Mask Photos by Rik Pennington. Middle: Robert Allsopp's workshop with Formech machine. Photos by Mary Kate Connolly

you and where you are. But still not frightened about the idea [itself] – actually feeling that this is such a contribution to the show.
(Silvestrini 2018: n.pag.)

Once removed, this impression was used to make a mid-strength 'Plaster of Paris'[8] mould. When this was fully hardened it was placed in a Manual Vacuum Forming Machine.[9] A sheet of ABS plastic would be placed in the upper compartment of the machine with the mould beneath. The vacuum machine would heat the plastic until sufficiently malleable and then raise up the Plaster of Paris underneath, bonding it to the plastic through the creation of a vacuum (sucking out all air surrounding the plastic). The finished product would be a sheet of ABS plastic with the outline of the face moulded into it. A scalpel would then be used to score lines for the rim of the mask and the plastic would be cracked manually along the scalpel lines. Small holes were drilled for the eyes. Elastics were subsequently fixed onto the masks, glued under leather patches to secure them in place (most likely by designer Powell – the details of this are forgotten).

At this point in the process, all 36 masks were unadorned plain white plastic. Twelve masks remained in this state. They were originally used in a scene of *Smithereens* featuring a tableau of performers on a platform. This scene was abandoned during rehearsal stages however, so the plain white masks were only utilized from time to time in the completed work, when certain dancers were required to move scenery around on stage or perform small functional duties in between scenes (Anderson 2018a). The second set of twelve masks were collaged by Powell, using clippings from magazines. The collaged faces which she created through the composites of different facial features drew on the images of artist Hannah Höch[10] for inspiration and she then worked 'instinctively' as to what she felt 'looked right' (Powell 2018: n.pag.). She described in interview the low-tech hands-on process which this entailed. 'I remembered [Höch] was one of her [Anderson's] references [...] it's just cut out magazines, and then glued on and then it must be a PVA glue over the top to hold it all on. It's really quite simple' (Powell 2018: n.pag.). Powell worked from her home at that time. She spoke in interview of the sharp contrasts between the gathering and utilization of imagery then (in 1999), and the time of interview (2018). Her description is evocative of the differences in working processes and the ways in which the masks remain as a historical testament to a particular pre-digital mode of design and making with specific materials involved.

> I would have made these here [at home]. I mean there's nowhere else to make them – I didn't have a work room or anything [...] You know really even now you wouldn't do this. You wouldn't be flicking through magazines [...] This [the imagery on the masks] was [clipped from] Sunday supplements and fashion magazines which actually [...] people don't buy magazines anymore. [Today] you'd be trawling through the internet, getting an image, printing it off onto paper that was too thick – because what's nice about this [collaging on the masks] is the quality of the paper as well.
> (Powell 2018: n.pag.)

The final set of masks were hand painted by David Hoyle. Powell had met him on the set of director Todd Haynes' film *Velvet Goldmine*[11] and also saw him perform regularly around that time at the Royal Vauxhall Tavern, London, as *The Divine David*. Powell was struck by the way in which Hoyle employed makeup as *The Divine David* and also by the portraits that he would sometimes paint live during his performances.

> his own treatment of makeup was extraordinary. It was different every week, every time. And it was just this mad anarchic [...] the lipstick went somewhere near his mouth and the nail polish went up to the knuckles and it was just incredible. And he did these amazing paintings every week in the show [...] usually of somebody in the audience and they were as mad and as free, and as anarchic as the way that he painted his own faces, so his actual paintings were very similar to how he painted his own face and body. I just thought that it would be really interesting to transform that into use within the costumes.
> (Powell 2018: n.pag.)

The masks were painted by Hoyle, most likely in an acrylic paint (the exact paint was not verifiable in interview), with additions of glitter. They were painted in a selection of colours, each mask featuring individual details and colour combinations.

Performative traces

As outlined, each performer had one plain white mask, one collaged mask and one painted mask. They were alternated for different chorus lines and worn on both the front and the back of the head. The plain white masks are perhaps the most ghostly looking in their acute resemblance to death masks. They accentuate the features of the dancers most distinctively – it is possible to trace the etched lines rendered from eyebrows, the indents of flesh and hollows beneath the cheekbones. They bear some scratches now, and have lost the glossy uniformity of unblemished white. Here and there the contours seem to be greying slightly, and scuffed. The interior of these white masks, like the other sets, are arguably as performative as the outside. Due to their plain white finish they offer up the imprints and smudges from the dancers' heavy makeup in minute detail, akin to etchings taken from a statue. The dark blemishes above the eyeholes conspire to create a surprised expression inside the masks. Smears around the lips form a somewhat comical moustache on the imprinted face. Strips of masking tape stuck inside the foreheads feature the names of both original cast members and new student casts. The 'T' in Teresa Barker's name is missing its vertical line, the elastic of Dean Brodrick's mask is tightly knotted to make the elastic shorter. Each of these details points towards traces of the performance life of *Smithereens* – the hasty scribbling of name tags to aid identification in the dark backstage, the restrictions of breathing and condensation build-up during strenuous sections of choreography.

The collaged masks enact a wholly different performative effect. Though they are overlaid on to the same contours of the moulded faces, their startlingly composite nature contrives to give a more 3D element to their presentation. The mismatched eyes, oversized teeth and sometimes partial collage (such as Rem Lee's mask which features cutouts of magazine pictures in striking diagonals, leaving large patches of the white plastic visible underneath in the spaces around it) create an unsettling, almost animated, effect. Hues range from purple, to Caucasian flesh-coloured, to vivid lipstick-red. Greig Cooke's mask features bright blue female eyes with lashes carefully layered with mascara. The eyes of Gabrielle McNaughton's mask are positioned vertically, reaching practically down the length of the collaged nose which sits in between. Yellow stains from glue can be observed on the insides, leaching out from behind the glued-on leather patches securing the elastics on certain masks such as Ragnhild Olsen's. At times the collaged paper cuttings peep over the rim of the mask into the inside, overlaid with PVA to keep them bonded to the plastic (seen in Luca Silvestrini's mask). Some mask interiors (such as Eddie Nixon's collaged mask) remain relatively unblemished from makeup stains, whilst others (including Greig Cooke's) appear almost to have been painted especially (with makeup) to render the impressions of the face. The outer surfaces of the collaged masks are perhaps the most fragile and visibly aging of all the sets of masks. The paper cuttings remain well bonded to the surface, however white creases are often in evidence, illuminating the edges where the paper has been folded down to cover a contoured surface. This can

Photos: Rik Pennington

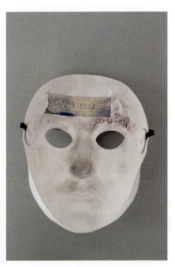

be seen for example, on the nose of Silvestrini's mask, where the folds are prominent and white in comparison to the coloured surface of the magazine cuttings.

The hand-painted masks operate on another distinct level – unlike the collaged masks, the features of the faces remain in proportion to that of a human face (eyes, nose and chin in the same location as those of the moulded facial contours). They also feature 'rouged' cheeks – circles or arcs of varying colours painted in the centre of the cheeks (and sometimes repeated on the chin). Eyelashes and arched eyebrows are painted over the eye holes. As such they create a somewhat 'flatter' effect (as opposed to the 3D sense of the collaged masks). Visually they operate more in the realm of a painted inanimate object (such as a doll's face or traditional theatrical mask). Their sometimes-lurid colour combinations however, render them equally striking as those that have been collaged. Some in rusty yellow with red cheeks, some with green faces daubed with pink. The brushwork on the masks is intentionally crude and asymmetrical. It is possible to see the lines from the brushstrokes and clumps of paint which have gathered in certain areas of the masks and dried (e.g. on the forehead area of Silvestrini's painted mask). Mouths are painted on – some with bared lips revealing painted teeth, some with pronounced cupid's bows or black lined lips. The painted masks are similarly fragile to the collaged ones due to the ways in which the paint has begun to chip off, especially on prominent areas such as noses or chins. This wear and tear can be observed on most of the masks in a minor way. Given they were painted over twenty years ago in acrylic (which might not remain particularly durable under stress such as abrasion and being knocked against surfaces or dropped onto the floor), the painted masks remain however, in good condition. The paint abrasions and chips in evidence are fairly minor and do not detract from the intended visual effect of the masks. Their rough, intentionally rudimentary paintwork aids in camouflaging the minor damage to them.

Masks in dialogue with the dancing body

The masks operated as a key facet of the visual language of the work, prompting a particular embodiment among the dancers in performance (due to the physical restrictions imposed by wearing a mask).[12] Facial features were obliterated and replaced with an altered hyper-theatrical image; one of a nonetheless somewhat recognizably *human* composite face. Doll-like paint or absurd facial collages reorder

Student Performer from Trinity Laban Conservatoire of Music and Dance. Photo: Lea Anderson

the facial structure, overlaying it with an entirely constructed image that operates within a theatrical frame of reference. The operation of the masks in this instance is perhaps more suitably situated within Freud's conception of the uncanny (as touched on earlier) rather than for example, the constructed nudity of the corpse-like Dead Skins. The masks succeed in appearing uncanny both on a fundamental aesthetic level and also more deeply within the visual language of *Smithereens* as a whole. The anonymizing effect of the masks along with the black bodysuits and other theatrical accessories enhanced the unsettling nature of the chorus lines and presented the dancers' bodies in an alternate light. As Anderson put it

> The faces painted or collaged onto the masks were far more disturbing and upsetting than the [dancers' own] faces, and also it made the chorus lines anonymous and strange. It's almost like 'these *creatures* – who are these people that is every man or every woman?'
> (Anderson 2018a: n.pag.)

Both Anderson herself, and writers who witnessed the performances, further unpicked this strangeness in relation to the presentation of gender among the chorus lines. Burt suggested that the combination of leotards and masks 'had the effect of blurring the outline of the buttocks, thus making the dancers' genders harder to determine. The identical masks and costumes, the unison movement, and the seemingly endless line of interchangeable dancers suggested an absence of individual identity' (2007a: 194). Anderson spoke of her surprise at realizing the neutralizing effect of the costumes, in particular, the masks:

> the masks [...] did a really weird thing in that I realised that it made this big statement [that] male and female are actually [...] almost the same thing. There's very little difference between the male body and the female body. There is if you accentuate it and you really go for it. But if you just play it down – you just dress everyone the same and you cover their face, its people. They're just humans, and it made no difference whatsoever [in *Smithereens*] if they were male or female. And that was really interesting for me [...] I really liked that the chorus were sort of unisex or sexless. And then the acts were performatively gendered in some way [through costume and gesture] [...] It was really interesting but I hadn't thought about that until Sandy brought the masks in.
> (Anderson 2018: n.pag.)

Perhaps the viewer here finds themselves once again in a spectacle of the 'Mass Ornament' as conceived by Kracauer (discussed in Disintegration). Certainly his assertion that the 'patterns seen in the [...] [1920s and 1930s] cabarets [...] are composed of elements that are mere building blocks and nothing more' (Kracauer 1995: 76) seems pertinent. 'The con-struction of the edifice', he continues,

> depends on the size of the stones and their number. It is the mass that is employed here. Only as parts of a mass, not as individuals who believe themselves to be formed from within, do people become fractions of a figure. (Kracauer 1995: 76)

The role of the masks in achieving this quasi erasure of individuality was profoundly effective. Not only did the masks and costumes produce a 'unisex' effect for those watching in the audience, it was true also for the dancers themselves that at times (in the dark backstage) they were unable to recognize each other and would need to whisper to one another in order to determine whether they were beside the correct person for the next entrance onstage. Pons Carrera laughingly described that despite the fact that Anderson could recognize each dancer individually onstage, it proved far more difficult mid-performance backstage.

> once we were backstage with the Bobble Heads [or masks] we're running as fast as we can and we're not standing upright showing our bodies – we're a bit [crouched] and so we were backstage going [mimes whispering] 'who are you? who are you?' 'I'm Anna!' [...] these memories make you laugh out loud!
> (Pons Carrera 2018: n.pag.)

Anderson and her collaborators seem to view this 'disappearance into costume' (effected by the masks) as having created dual, somewhat contradictory effects. On the one hand, anonymizing the dancers through the blurring of defining characteristics such as physical details of gender, but on the other, directing the focus towards the individuality of each dancer's physique as a reassertion of identity. The physiques of the dancers in *The Cholmondeleys* and *The Featherstonehaughs* varied greatly from one another in height and proportions. In a somewhat similar vein to the way in which the Dead Skin operated, the masks therefore suggested the exactitude of an endless chorus line whilst simultaneously drawing attention to the digressions from uniformity. In this way, the *Smithereens* masks diverge from

Kracauer's annihilation of individuality, instead directing the viewer's attention to the individual differences between dancers. Silvestrini and Pons Carrera seemed to experience this as a liberating element of performing with the masks. Silvestrini asserted that whilst directing a cast of varying heights and body shapes to do the same choreography might sound like a 'contradiction', that in fact the conflict which this engenders is where 'the speciality or artistry comes out' (Silvestrini 2018: n.pag.). Relating *Smithereens* to broader representations of the dancing body, Burt (2007) viewed the concealment created by the costumes as allowing a transgression; both of heteronormative presentations of gender, and normative behaviour more generally (societally and within the canon of dance performance).

> Through camouflaging themselves [through the use of masks and costumes] to blend in with their environment, they, thus escaped any censure they might otherwise have attracted for lack of conformity to ideologies of normative behaviour while publicly revealing possibilities for subversive, intersubjective relations.
> (Burt 2007a: 194)

Physical adaptations

The physical limitations imposed by the masks were undoubtedly held as a formative choreographic influence by Anderson and the dancers. Two inescapable realities of the masks were that they limited the dancers' visual field considerably and that they impelled the dancers to face forward at all times during the choreography (so as not to reveal the edges of the mask in profile). The eye-holes for the masks were very small circles meaning that the dancers had no peripheral vision. Like the Dead Skins in *Yippeee!!!*, the masks therefore possessed a somewhat adversarial quality. Silvestrini described the sensory deprivations as having contributed significantly to his performance: 'those restrictions psychologically, physically, emotionally, makes you a heightened being, which increases your performance energy, your performance focus, your intensity' (Silvestrini 2018: n.pag.). Interestingly, the sensation of wearing the masks registered quite differently for Pons Carrera and Silvestrini. Pons Carrera felt that because the mask was moulded for her face and fitted perfectly, it allowed her to relax her facial muscles and release tension in her upper body. She described it as 'almost like a massage, like a soothing thing, like a layer of soothing material

Smithereens cast member Ragnhild Olsen in costume. Photo: Chris Nash

that makes you keep your face as neutral as possible. You don't feel like laughing or changing the expression because it fits ideally, it fits perfectly' (Pons Carrera 2018: n.pag.). Donning the mask within the context of her interview she noted that

> I realised [wearing it just now] that it just makes all the muscles in your forehead relax, the muscles on your cheek relax [...] Because if you move them, they touch [the inside of the mask] in different ways and it doesn't feel so nice.
> (Carrera 2018: n.pag.)

Pons Carrera felt that in her case, this sense of relaxation 'helps the quality of the movement' (ibid.). Silvestrini had an entirely opposite perspective on the effect of the masks; outlining that

> you can't relax your face under a mask [...] you still have to offer some kind of expression, some kind of presence. Even if that mask has its own presence and light, you still have to energise that behind the mask.
> (Silvestrini 2018: n.pag.)

He felt that the mask is 'not cover – it actually brings life out [...] you feel the pressure, you feel the contact [of the mask]. So it's actually a presence that you can't ignore' (ibid.). The pressure of the mask, coupled with the heat and sweat inside and the resultant restrictions on breathing and vision all fed into the corporeal relationship with the masks, shaping the dancers' performances accordingly. This is where a dialogue between dancing body and masks comes to the fore – the unavoidable adaptations that the masks demanded of the performers. Despite the differences in their embodied experience of this, both dancers emphasized their perceived enhancement of their performance which the masks brought about. Sometimes this enhancement appeared due precisely to the disorientating impact which the masks had in restricting sight and breathing, and increasing body temperature. Silvestrini described the masks as thus 'both wonderful and claustrophobic' (Silvestrini 2018: n.pag.).

The physical adjustments which the masks engendered did not end with breathing and presentation – amendments to the choreography were also undertaken. Anderson's working process tends to embrace the influences and changes to choreography brought about by the addition of costumes (Connolly 2017). In

Smithereens this was no exception, and the introduction of the masks prompted various changes to the orientation of the movements. The prolonged process of casting, making and decorating the masks (involving numerous individuals) meant that it was quite late in the nine-week devising and rehearsal process of *Smithereens* when the masks finally arrived in the rehearsal room. Anderson amusedly described her initial revelations upon seeing the masks on the dancers: 'I realised there's a whole thing about masks and there's reasons for this! It's not just sort of history stuff, they actually only work in a particular way and if you ignore it, it looks like shit' (Anderson 2018a: n.pag.). Anderson was referring to instances in the choreography where dancers would turn their heads, and in doing so, reveal the edges of the mask in profile, shattering the illusion (of a painted face) brought about by seeing the masks front on. Anderson outlined that they had to make a number of adjustments to the choreography to prevent this happening. These adjustments were largely to do with avoiding movement which revealed the edges of the masks and finding strategies for the performers to preserve the integrity of the choreography (e.g. the correct spacing in chorus lines) despite the physical limitations which the masks imposed. The spacing of the chorus lines became particularly problematic as the dancers needed to be evenly spaced despite the physical disparities between them (with one dancer's gait being much longer than another's for example). Achieving this exact spacing without being able to rely on peripheral vision became exceptionally challenging and frustrating. Anderson outlined that in order to combat this, the dancers

> had to feel it, learn it, and get a muscle memory and do it that way. And then when they got off [the stage], they had to run like the clappers round the back to get back on. But you've [the dancer] got a mask on and you can't see the booms and there's all the costumes set out everywhere [...] all the costumes are black in the dark. It was really *really* challenging!
> (Anderson 2018a: n.pag., original emphasis.)

Despite the difficulties which performing in the masks provoked, Anderson also noted that visually, they worked extremely well and 'brought it [the chorus line] right into the world of [her] images' (Anderson 2018a: n.pag.). The fact that the expressions on the masks were unchanging also created the specific visual effect which she was searching for, in a way that could perhaps only be achieved with masks, rather than dancers attempting to maintain a contrived facial expression for a prolonged period of time. Anderson recalled that

the dancers hated it, and they couldn't see very well. It was difficult for them, and that's when I started thinking 'I'm really only interested in dancers who are willing to put up with really bad things and to be excited by it'.
(Anderson 2018a: n.pag.)

Despite the initial reservations of some dancers working with the masks, Anderson emphasized their transformational nature and the realm of the uncanny and ghostly which they conjured: 'Once you start following the rules of masks, it becomes apparent that what emerges is this whole ghostly other kind of thing and you realise where you're going [...] you are sort of dabbling in this *magic of the mask*' (Anderson 2018a: n.pag., original emphasis.)

Pons Carrera: 'gosh that changed the movement and kind of made it more interesting even – more quirky and weird' (Pons Carrera 2018: n.pag.). As with other works (such as *Yippeee!!!*), the masks solved certain choreographic issues for Anderson. In addition to the fixed unsettling facial image which they created, she described a scenario in which one chorus line did not seem to 'fit' with the flow of the overall work. It was essential however that it remain in the piece to facilitate the costume changes needed for the subsequent scene of *Smithereens*. Powell was present on many occasions in the rehearsal room during the making of *Smithereens*, collaborating on the placement and use of the masks. In this instance, she suggested that the dancers wear the masks on the back of their heads rather than the front. They then performed facing the back of the stage. Anderson described how the audience could 'just see their buttocks wiggling on the front and it was horrible [...] really disturbing!' (Anderson 2018a: n.pag.). In sequences such as this, the chorus lines oscillate between appearing to be made up of animate dancers, and automatons. Figures which bear recognizably human composite features (bone structure, muscles, contours) are re-arranged to be somehow monstrous – knowable, yet utterly strange and uncanny. A sense of the *unheimlich* pervades *Smithereens* as a whole – the possibility that the chorus are not *quite* human – appearing both inanimate and animate at the same time.

Remains of *Smithereens* and leaps of archival faith

There was no costume bible compiled for *Smithereens* (Powell 2018)[13] and very little documentation remains now concerning the production. There are a couple of poor-quality film clips of the work in performance (remaining in Anderson's personal archive)[14] and detailed photos of the costume items which Anderson subsequently commissioned in an effort to document her archive. There are also a few photographs of the original cast in costume (such as Chris Nash's photograph of Ragnhild Olsen, see accompanying images), playbill posters from the *Smithereens* tour, and a handful of press reviews (Watson 1999; Brennan 1999; Brown 1999; Leddy 1999). The *Smithereens* masks function as remains or traces of performance in a distinctly different way to that of the Dead Skin from *Yippeee!!!*. For *Yippeee!!!*, a good quality DVD film of the full work and multiple high resolution performance images exist, whereas the choreography and imagery of *Smithereens* in performance is for the most part no longer visible in any form outside of the costumes. Corresponding performance histories have therefore also been fractured due to the lack of contextual and photographic remains of the work.

The capacity for archival remnants to operate as historical documents has been explored in museological contexts, and also more broadly, the operations and failures of historical documents in enacting a retrieval of history. In his introduction to the edited volume *The Archive: Documents of Contemporary Art*, Charles Merewether outlines that the collected writings within the publication, question 'in what way is the document sufficient in representing [...] histories where there is [...] no longer a thread of continuity [...] but rather a fracture, a discontinuity, the mark of which is obliteration, erasure and amnesia?' (Merewether 2006: 12). If we are to look to the *Smithereens* masks as documents within this context, prolonging their survival and mapping the web of absences which they illuminate seems a prescient concern. Considered thus, the costume remains of *Smithereens* are rendered all the more significant as interlocutors of their past performances. *Smithereens* remains in physical form solely within these artefacts. Aesthetically and physically, the masks also present quite differently to the Dead Skin in their current state in that they successfully function as highly crafted design artefacts, albeit severed from their original performance life. It is possible to look to these masks both as prompts and conduits for memory (seen in the ways in which handling and looking at the masks by the dancers and makers provoked remembrance of numerous details), but also as vessels of a haunted nature. This is true to a certain extent with each of the costumes within this research. Makiko Aoyama for example, alluded to the fact that trying on the Dead Skin at different times over the years since her first performances reveals the ways in which her body has changed in the intervening time (Aoyama 2017). The fact that the *Smithereens* masks were moulded to the faces of the dancers however,

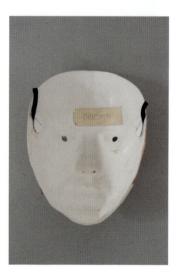
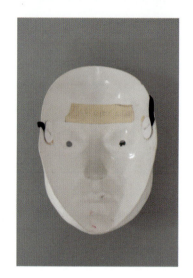
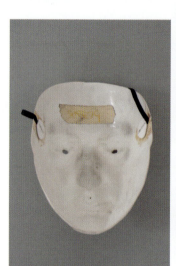

Photos: Rik Pennington

 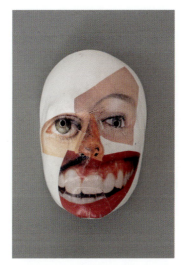 
 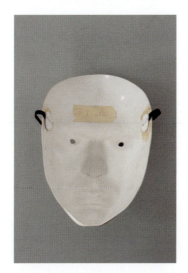 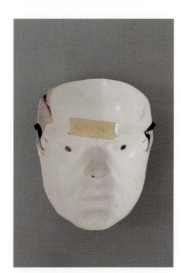

renders this dynamic particularly acute. At first glance, the masks may trick the uninitiated viewer who encounters them now alone in the archive into thinking that they are a 'whole' object (as opposed to one item which made up a larger costume, within a wider performance work). In a first encounter, the masks' partial reality is perhaps rendered less visible than that of the lifeless Dead Skin (which by its aged nature and plain design makes it obvious that it was a base layer that is now missing other crucial elements of costume). Closer consideration of the masks' performative remains, however, reveals the loss of many other presences, movements and images: choreographies vanished, embodied memories forgotten, makers' marks rendered indecipherable.

Jackie Peterson, a conservator (undertaking an internship at the V&A) spoke in interview of her work with everyday clothing in collections from the early 1900s, and in particular, dating from the Cambodian genocide (1975–79) under the Khmer Rouge regime. She remarked that 'It's one thing to see photographs and they tell quite a story, but tangible cultural heritage is really [something unique]' (Peterson 2018: n.pag.). She asserted that

> for the most part the [textile] objects are documents [...] And the thing that I find really attractive about textiles is that [...] maybe more than any other material, they speak to their relationship with people [...] [Sometimes] garments are [...] all that remain and they serve as documents [...] for something that was quite a difficult period in human history. When you see those objects now, decades removed from whatever that event was, I think it really communicates what the experiences of those people were.
> (Peterson 2018: n.pag.)

This observation is in line with Hölling et al. in their conceptualization of artefacts as 'complex constructs of material relations' (2019: 2). In attempting a physical 'restoration' of the masks, there is a broader aspiration to restore some elements of the aforementioned embodied memories, historical details and choreographic moments of *Smithereens*. The goal is to reveal some of these complex material relations and to allow the masks to function as interlocutors of lost histories. The process of researching conservation and museum techniques has been shot through at all times by vivid recollections from the individuals who designed, made and performed with the masks. Observing the power of the masks to unlock discarded memories and encounters has reinforced the sense of presence of performances now vanished. These aims, for preservation as a means of interlocution for the masks, are also inherently entangled with a sense of precarity of the objects. There is a perception of the process being somehow a leap of faith, or rather a testament of belief in the artefacts. The faith at the heart of any preservation endeavour (for the protection of artefacts for the future) is a topic explored by Hannah Hölling in conversation with curator and historian Jorge Otero-Pailos (Hölling and Otero-Pailos 2019). Otero-Pailos puts forward the idea of material objects facilitating cultural transitions. Highlighting that it is impossible to guarantee the imagined future for which we preserve artefacts, he argues that '[i]nescapably, we can only act in the present […] the claim that we are preserving for the future is actually misleading in terms of what we actually do' (Hölling and Otero-Pailos 2019: 262). Rather, he suggests,

> a […] more nuanced way to say that would be that we are testing our ability to believe in the reality of a temporality we call the future or to believe in the reality of a temporality we call the past.
> (Hölling and Otero-Pailos 2019: 262)

To enter into a quest for preservation is thus unavoidably one of faith; one which strives towards an imagined future whilst acknowledging both the inscrutability of that future and the eventual decline of all material artefacts. For Otero-Pailos, the curation and preservation of objects is a way to 'test our ability to conceive or to experience reality as temporal and not simply as instantaneous' (Hölling and Otero-Pailos 2019: 262). Whilst the Dead Skin journey towards disintegration has sought to highlight the unavoidable degradation of material objects, so too, the preservation intervention must acknowledge that selfsame inevitable decline, whilst also attempting to place the masks in relation to their imagined future, and taking steps to allow them to prevail a little longer, as intact materials in that imagined time.

Journey towards transformation

Gordon, describing the presence of (metaphorical) ghosts, cites the 'special instance of the merging of the visible and the invisible, the dead and the living, the past and the present – into the making of worldly relations and into the making of our accounts of the world' (2008: 120). Such merging of past and present resonates strongly within the context of the museological world. Acknowledging the totemic nature of the masks and therefore the urgent need for their preservation, directs the research process towards logistical and philosophical ideas concerning the conservation and display of objects in museums. The training and research I have carried out in this vein has been guided by a largely intuitive process based on which particular institutions and individuals it has been possible to gain access to. There is no attempt here to provide certifiable museum-standard levels of conservation and storage for the masks, but nonetheless the aim is to emulate such (as is feasible), using the facilities and materials to hand, whilst remaining in step with Anderson's wishes for her archive.

The conservation and protective storage of the masks is something which Anderson has long welcomed, but the attendant requirements of the masks as working, functional, objects have necessarily been factored into consideration. The dimensions of the space which is available in Anderson's lockup for example, determines the total number of storage boxes possible (and therefore the number of masks stored per box). The masks also need the accessibility and flexibility of short-term storage (to enable them to be transported at short notice) alongside the sustainability of long-term conservation. Ultimately they are stored, not in environmentally controlled archive conditions, but rather, in a costume lockup as before, and the overall aim is therefore to secure the best conditions possible for the masks within their logistical, economical and functional confines.

The information-gathering, upskilling in practical conservation-related skills, and interviews relating to the masks has fallen into two phases – that of initially becoming acquainted with museum and material culture archival practices in a general context, and then incorporating the masks more specifically into interview content to garner advice on their particular requirements in terms of preservation. As with each of the costumes within this book, the 'doing' of these practical gestures sits at the heart of the intervention. Like the attempt at creative destruction of the Dead Skin, it is only possible to test the feasibility of a strategy centred on preservation by actually attempting a physical intervention which might approximate essential elements of preservation and museological conservation and storage. Through each interaction with the masks, they evolve a little further towards being conceptualized as the totemic remains which my research has deemed them (and how, anecdotally, they had already been regarded by Anderson for some time). This in turn spurs these artefacts further along the path towards a physical display in exhibition which progresses their alternative after-life. Once again the aim here is to journey down this path as far as is possible. To see what happens.

An early influential encounter with the world of prestigious museum archives comes with a guided tour of the textile conservation workrooms at the V&A, during a conference in January 2017.[15] Snow fell as I walked to the museum and my research journal entry from that day details my self-conscious efforts to stem the flow of muddy droplets from my clothes onto the floors of the spotless, environmentally-controlled work rooms. Even at this early stage the prestige of the museum and the economic outlay required to sustain a high-status institution such as this was in evidence. We, the conference delegates, were privy to a 'behind the scenes' view of the museum not usually afforded to members of the public. The conservators we witnessed were working on a selection of hats designed by fashion designer Cristóbal Balenciaga in preparation for an upcoming retrospective exhibition. Being briefed on the processes carried out to ready the objects for exhibition, it was striking to see the ways in which conservators were striving to make their repairs/augmentations to the objects invisible to the viewer. In the context of the Balenciaga exhibition, their chief concern was the display of the garment or object in its best possible condition, as opposed to rendering obvious their repairs and changes (which would highlight a historical account of the garment). This particular curatorial and conservation approach is something I explored in more detail during subsequent interviews with conservators Susana Fajardo and Jackie Peterson, both of whom were working at the V&A at that time. These impressions of the archival and museological worlds within a prestigious cultural institution inform my instincts regarding the masks. It affirms the need to view them as artefacts to be preserved, and raises questions of how these operational practices might be employed outside of prominent museums. For the Dead Skin, it has seemed that a strategy of acknowledging and accelerating a process of degradation is in fact the most appropriate way of 'caring' for the object, and revealing its essential nature as it progresses towards an alternative after-life. With the masks however, the opposite seems true. Revealing the hidden histories within the artefacts and gesturing towards the haunting which they can enact seems best served by explicating a framework of care in relation to them. Explicitly framing them as valued totemic objects which ought to be preserved for as long as possible.

Specialist training

It has been essential for me to garner basic skills and specialist knowledge in conservation practices (and attendant museological philosophical perspectives towards artefacts). I have been lucky to attend workshops on 'Dress Handling' (delivered in partnership by London College of Fashion and the V&A).[16] This has involved presentations from dress historians, curators and conservation specialists. It has also comprised a visit to The Clothworkers Centre for the Study and Conservation of Textiles and Fashion, then located at Blythe House.[17] Many of the V&A's textile collections are stored here and conservation work is also carried out. Events such as these have been formative in the research process, both in advancing my practical skills and knowledge, and also in terms of revealing the overarching contexts within which these professionals operate.

My role as researcher in this aspect of the project has been (and largely remains) that of the uninitiated amateur. The intervention carried out for the *Smithereens* masks is therefore based on the best-practice and accessible techniques which can be successfully acquired and carried out within the budget and timeframe available. This is in step with the realistic conditions of the masks (in a personal archive outside of institutional support with no funding to sustain it beyond the individuals closely associated with Anderson). These objects, like many others, exist outside the provisions and protections of the museum. This chapter does not attempt to provide a specialist treatise on the care and conservation of masks and costume. It merely hopes to unfold some of the upskilling process, the rationale behind any decisions taken with the masks, and to provide signposts towards repositories of expert knowledge. It is worth noting that the specialist reading and research which I diligently carried out has only become legible in a practical sense during the conversations and encounters I have had with expert professionals. They alone hold the requisite expertise to translate the literature into pragmatic and viable strategies for the storage and protection of the masks.

Object interpretation and handling

One workshop finds me confronted with an aged pair of brown corduroy trousers. We are learning about object interpretation in museums. Curator and historian Amy De La Haye (drawing from Susan Pearce on the interpretation of objects in museums [Pearce 1994]), instructs us to deduce ten facts and ten speculations from a detailed appraisal of the garment before us. A survey of the labels, makers' marks and wear and tear of the garment throws up a surprising amount of concrete information and there are many plausible speculations about them which taking an approach of 'informed assumption', affords. The amateur garment sleuth in me is delighted to find secrets within the trousers become legible through careful examination. It is worth noting here that there are various distinct frameworks for object and material analysis put forward within material culture scholarship. These range from practical methods, to philosophical approaches in the interpretation of objects (Pearce 1994; Prown 1994; Elliot 1994; Mida and Kim 2015). During the course of my research a number of the methodological tools and aide memoires advocated by specialists (such as noting the material, function and provenance of a garment, alongside detailed descriptions, historical research, deduction and consideration of my own sensorial and emotional responses) have been of significant use. These strategies have not been utilized in a formal way as they would be by a museum specialist. Instead, they are valuable as a kind of check list, providing a framework to consider the costumes and their surrounding context.

Back to the corduroy trousers and I am learning how to handle and fold garments, particularly fragile ones. There are discussions on scrupulous hand hygiene and the need for nitrile or cotton gloves depending on the materials being handled. I begin the journey of learning how to embody the physical touch of the conservator; handling with confidence, and slowly, mapping handling protocols for every garment before I touch them. I learn how to investigate the condition and structure of garments, to be alert to their inherent weaknesses – areas that usually rip for example, and the ways in which linings are usually more fragile than outer layers. Assessment procedures (taking measurements, photographs, writing brief descriptions) are also outlined. I encounter the shattered fragments of a silk blouse and the sad faded grandeur of misshapen felt hats with ragged adornments. In addition to these deductive and handling processes, the logistics of storage are touched upon. The packing and storage of items is particularly pertinent to the masks, as aside from basic restoration or cleaning that might be carried out, the correct packing and storage of these items are the single most crucial elements which could prolong their life and protect their condition. Mercifully this aspect of protection is also fully within the capabilities of this research.

I learn that storage boxes should be suitably sized to 'just' fit the object and surrounding padding. The boxes should be made of conservation quality corrugated cardboard (free of acid and potentially corrosive materials). The box should be lined with acid-free paper and packed with 'wads' and 'sausages' (colloquial terms employed by conservators to describe the protective shapes they form from tissue paper before packing them around the objects). The objects should then be overlaid with paper, and potentially a layer of silk, as a way of protecting them from any long-term abrasion from the tissue paper. As part of the workshop, we are taught how to form these wads and sausages from sheets of tissue, how to handle and move textile objects (such as hats), and how to pack them safely and sustainably. Further training is provided in the moving of larger objects, and the transfer to display for exhibition. Mounting for exhibition is also touched upon and we are signposted towards manufacturers and suppliers of conservation grade materials such as plastazote foam, acid-free paper and bespoke archive boxes.

The second day of the workshop finds me at Blythe House witnessing the work of archivists and conservators – the usually unseen elements of the museum. Here we are educated on the processes of acquisition, restoration and storage of textiles within the V&A. One example is the quarantine period, when new items are placed in giant freezers in order to kill any potential pests harboured within the textiles. Detailed precautions against pests, water and fire damage are outlined – my research notes become cluttered with specifics on blunder traps, pheromone patches, conservation-grade fabric coverings, elevated storage and transit areas.[18] This registers with me once again on two levels – garnering practical knowledge as an amateur, but also intuiting the wider institutional mechanics and significant overheads governing these processes. Subsequent to the training I have followed up with the professionals involved, who have been hugely helpful in providing specific advice pertaining to the packing and transport of the masks themselves. Through these interactions it has become feasible to devise a protocol for the packing and storage of the masks and to forge plans for further interviews and a final gesture towards preservation of the masks.

Thinking around objects in the archive

Aside from the practical hands-on knowledge that has been gleaned through this training, it has been significantly influential in shaping the ways in which the masks are conceptualized within my research. De La Haye was keen to emphasize during her workshop, that 'when the object enters the museum, it changes from an object of consumption to an object of interpretation'. This is clearly in evidence, not only in the reverence and rigour of conservation practices in the V&A archives at Blythe House, but also in the small incidental details which I have observed. The casual anecdote told, for example, that some museum professionals would regard the wearing of vintage fashion in their everyday lives as taboo, as it doesn't treat the vintage item as an historical object which should no longer be worn, but only preserved. I have been struck too by the way in which some of the conservators visibly recoil at my description of the storage arrangement for the masks (being at that time, still in their plastic boxes in the lockup). The genuine reverence for historical objects as ciphers for the past is acutely evident in these encounters. Here I become distinctly aware of my position in this project as being decidedly outside of the traditional museological world. The care and skill of the textile specialists and curators towards precious objects cannot but be admired, and viewed within such a context, the approaches towards costume within my research (including the Disintegration intervention) begin to appear somewhat radical and drastic. It becomes essential to reconsider my ground in terms of the roles of the archive in the after-life of objects. I do not wish to demonise the museological approach unintentionally. Rather, the aim is to concede the value of object preservation for the ages, whilst also reasserting the possibility for an alternative approach for certain costume artefacts. Furthermore, the intention is to foreground a specificity in approach to archival objects and to allow the methodological strategies arising from their material, economic and cultural realities to enjoy equal prominence. This strategy feels in step with Anderson's personal perspective on the objects in her archive, and indeed the playfully subversive nature of her choreography more generally.

Viewing items from the archives in Blythe House is an undeniably seductive experience and it casts the time frame within which this research is operating, as extremely short in comparison to many of the historical objects housed in the archives. The standard protocol for some items of particular age and fragility is such that if exhibited, they will automatically go back into storage for ten years, before *possibly* being authorized for exhibition again. I could not help but be moved by the story of an Icelandic bridal dress which survived fire and shipwreck in the 1800s, only to resurface and be donated to the V&A in the early 1900s by the grandson of the explorer who had sought to bring it to England in the first place many years previously. Witnessing items such as this, replete with sublime craft and the fragility of great age, is humbling. The operation of the totemic and veneration of relics is clear to behold in this context. The wider surroundings of Blythe House too are awe-inspiring – unadorned mannequins awaiting garments, the ghostly outlines of dresses on stands beneath plain cotton coverings. Endless rows of hanging garments obscured by their protective coverings, and pull-out drawers housing unknown gems secreted beneath white tissue paper. The exclusivity of this environment is also keenly felt. Buzzing the intercom to gain entrance at the vast entrance gateway, packing away all belongings barring a pencil and notebook in lockers before admittance.

An institution such as the V&A represents the pinnacle of museums in terms of the resources available and the facility for public access to collections. It is notable that the professionals at Blythe House lamented the unfortunate reality that many textile collections are held in private archives and therefore not accessible to a wider public (research journal notes, 30 November 2017).

The transition from functional textile to revered artefact seems to occur at the moment in which the item crosses the threshold of the museum or archive. As Pearce summarizes '[w]hat distinguishes the "discrete lumps" from the rest [...] is the cultural value it is given, and not primarily the technology which has been used to give it form or content, although this is an important mode of value creation' (Pearce 1994: 10). It is not only these factors which render an object into a prized artefact, argues Pearce, but furthermore 'it is the act of selection which turns a part of the natural world into an object and a museum piece' (Pearce 1994: 10). The 'discrete lumps' which Pearce is referring to here are rocks and elements of the natural world incorporated into museum collections, but these sentiments appear equally prescient when applied to costume and dress. Here I am conscious of my conception of acquisition as being a kind of vanishing point – a mummification and silencing of the item (following museum acquisition). The vast size of some museum holdings means that a large percentage of their collections may seldom, if ever, achieve public visibility in exhibition. From previous conversations, it was clear that Anderson sought to avoid such a disappearance for the *Smithereens* masks and severance from their original purpose (despite the lure of storage in a prestigious cultural institution).

Steps towards preservation

Following the initial phase of appraising the masks, and developing basic knowledge and skills to aid their preservation, the first steps in progressing the Preservation intervention have been bound up with insuring, transporting and sourcing suitable interim storage for the masks, prior to any preservation intervention being carried out. The masks thus become temporarily housed within the costume department of a London performance conservatoire (in a secure locked studio with no public access and minimal risk of theft or damage). As an interim measure, readymade cardboard boxes of appropriate diameter are purchased to house the masks comfortably – lined with acid-free tissue paper, cushioned and packed as per the conservators' careful instructions.

An insurance policy is secured with Hencilla Camworth insurance Group.[19] The masks become categorized as exhibition materials, and I, an artist, whose artistic practice 'involves the creation of alternative remnants of performance from previously worn dance costumes and performance ephemera' (Insurance Policy document). Under this policy, the masks are regarded as 'Goods in Trust'. The question of what sum to insure the masks for, becomes a thought-provoking one. Describing the objects in phone conversations with the insurers and their underwriting staff highlights both the difficulty in communicating accurately the nature of the items, and the variability in their worth. In purely monetary terms, the masks would not be deemed particularly valuable (as remnants of a contemporary dance work), yet within the context of Anderson's archive and the central themes of this research, they are deemed highly valuable – priceless almost (due to their irreplaceability). Finally, it is agreed in consultation with Anderson that they are to be insured for the sum of 5000 pounds (with an excess of 100 pounds on the policy).

I employ a bespoke conservation-grade box-making service run by Lancashire County Council to make boxes for the long-term storage of the masks. Six boxes of identical dimensions are made, each designed to hold six masks, layered two upon two (allowing space for sufficient tissue paper padding). On the advice of conservator Susana Fajardo, sheets of silk are sourced from Pongees London[20] to lay over the top of each mask to prevent abrasion from tissue paper during long term storage. The masks are repacked into the conservation grade boxes in Spring 2018. I devise protocols for the storage of them in transit (using a hard-shell suitcase and extra wadded packing) in order to facilitate the occasional transport of several masks to the interviews I am carrying out (with the designers and makers involved in the work) at that time. Once the masks are securely stored, more concrete plans for a filmed gesture towards Preservation begin to take shape. This plan is forged through interviews undertaken with the conservators at the V&A, Sandy Powell and Janet Steiner (Head of Hats and Accessories in the costume department of Royal Opera House, London), and Lea Anderson herself.

Strategies for intervention

Anderson initially wishes to clean away all marks from the inside of the masks – to remove all name labels and rid them of all makeup stains. This impulse is echoed by Steiner, who confirms that as a costume maker within the opera house, her instinct

 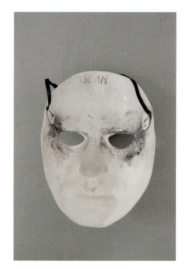 

Photos: Rik Pennington

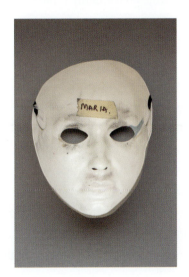
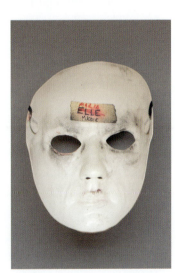

for the maintenance of costumes would dictate that she clean away all such marks and stains (Steiner 2018). She advocates using a wool detergent such as Stergene[21], heavily diluted with water to clean them and suggests that remaining adhesives (left from sticky tape or glue) could be carefully removed using a scalpel (Steiner 2018: n.pag.). The conservators' approach to the masks differs greatly however. They feel that from a historical point of view, the incidental marks and stains are incredibly valuable in highlighting the realities of the performance life of these objects. To obliterate these traces and embedded histories (from an archival perspective) would be to erase essential facets of the masks as historical objects, and (in their view), should only be considered if the overall stability of the object is threatened or affected by them. Speaking in particular with regard to her work with theatre costumes, Fajardo argues that

> because these are performance masks, the dirt and the makeup is important – it's part of the way it was worn [...] the 'travelling troop', you know, they didn't store things in acid free boxes. I work a lot with the theatre and performance collection, and I have costumes with many repairs [...] And I love all the repairs. They tell me a lot.
> (Fajardo 2018: n.pag.)

In addition to the trace histories which the marks and additions illuminate, close consideration needs to be given to stabilizing the objects. Whether, for example, the masking tape labels, makeup sponges and packing noodles (stuck inside several of the masks) might pose a threat of damage in the longer term, is deliberated at length. On the one hand, it could be prudent to remove the masking tape as it will most probably yellow the surface of the mask over time. Given the length of time that the tape and adhesives have been in place however, there is a significant risk that they could prove very difficult to remove, and leave sticky residue behind. This risk needs to be weighed against the desire to remove the tape. Jackie Peterson cautions that (if removed)

> you would have quite a lot of residue left and with tapes with poor quality adhesives, they become very difficult to remove. So you'd have to resort to chemical cleaning to get that residue off, and then you don't know what the chemical is doing to the plastic underneath. But then, if you leave it, there's a good chance that the adhesive will eventually fail and you'll end up losing the carrier and you'll be left with the residue [...] I mean, tapes are hard! [laughs].
> (Peterson 2018: n.pag.)

The complexity of whether to intervene physically with the masks unfolds throughout the course of this particular interview, with both conservators debating back and forth as to what might prove the safest course of action. It is agreed that without doubt, any knots in the elastics should be loosened so as to prevent stress on the structure of the item. The risk with leaving the makeup sponges and packing noodles is that over time these materials themselves will degrade, drying into abrasive grit and dust which could damage the surface of the masks. In summary, a gentle approach is advocated – perhaps attempting to remove the sponges or tape with tweezers or carefully by hand. If residue does get left behind, a sparing use of isopropyl alcohol or surgical methylated spirits (which are non-toxic) can be employed to remove the residue. Fajardo advocates a minimal intervention approach explaining that

> sometimes minimal intervention is sounder […] because whatever you do with the best intentions and all the testing, is an intervention, and you're going to inevitably affect the original, to carry out your treatment. So you really need to wait and think 'well do I really need to do it?'
> (Fajardo 2018: n.pag.)

This seems a sensible approach in the context of the masks. These considerations surrounding the provenance, aesthetics and after-life of the object inform the final decision making, taken in consultation with Anderson, as to what she wishes to do with the masks. We decide to remove the glued-in sponges and packing noodles and some masking tape labels (which bear the names, not of original cast members, but re-casts involving performance students). For Anderson, these labels don't feel in keeping with the original performance lives of the objects. For original cast members however, the masking tape will be left in place. These sentiments surrounding the performance lives of the masks are echoed by Powell in interview when she alludes to the fact that if she sees the masks used in student remounts or for performed excerpts (such as in *Hand in Glove* [2016]), that whilst it is nice to see the costumes, she feels that these remounts have 'nothing to do with me [Powell]' (Powell 2018: n.pag.). She considers that these performances are not in the context of how the costumes were originally designed (as part of the complete work of *Smithereens*, performed by the original cast). They are therefore viewed as separate entities, distinct from the specific performance history of *Smithereens*.

Anderson and I deem it necessary to remove the sponges and packing noodles (held in by sellotape) in order to mitigate against longer term damage from their degradation. The risk of residue or discolouration arising from this process is one that Anderson is prepared to accept as a better alternative to long-term abrasion. Carrying out removal on only a select number of masks also allows the possibility of tracking their progress after the intervention, and assessing if there has been any damage arising from it, before carrying out removal on any other masks in the future. These strategies represent an attempt to reach a middle ground – satisfying the needs for preservation of the artefacts long term, minimizing damage and the loss of trace histories within the masks, whilst also satisfying Anderson's wishes for the masks in their after-life.

A filmed gesture of preservation

The filmed element of the Preservation intervention is carried out in the same studio at Trinity Laban Conservatoire (Laurie Grove Studios, New Cross, London), where the Disintegration intervention has taken place. It is a functional well-lit space in which we can set up the necessary equipment and carry out basic conservation processes. Time and resource constraints are such that it is necessary to transport the masks, carry out the filming and photo documentation, attempt to achieve minor conservation alterations to the masks and repack them correctly, all within the space of five hours. It is not possible to coordinate the masks, equipment, film crew, Anderson, myself and the studio hire, for any longer. This means that the day has been meticulously planned in terms of timing, but also has a fluid intuitive flow between the collaborators. There is simply no time to lose.

An air of hushed reverence pervades the studio. The continual shutter clicks from the camera, the rustling of white tissue as each mask is liberated from its nest to be photographed and then returned once more. I have instructed Rik [Pennington] to take portraits of each mask inside and out for cataloguing purposes, before progressing on to stylistic images of the small details – the tiny fractures on the surfaces, the contours of a chin, a cheekbone. I have spoken to him of ghosts, of death masks, of the way in which the performance lives on somehow within the performative surfaces of these totems. It is his job to find them – to alert the viewer to their traces. Anne [Verheij] has improvised a film tripod out of a scooter and is attempting panning shots of the collaged masks lined up together like an identity parade along the back wall. The reverential handling and conduct around the masks is in stark contrast to the hurried grunt work which propels the day's tasks forward – hefting of chairs, moving tripods, adjusting a ladder to take the perfect photo, chasing the light as it pools in alternating corners of the studio. I dash between boxes of masks – to photographer, to filmmaker, and back. Checking images, issuing instructions for the next phase of filming, pointing out the significant masks, reminding everyone of the need to keep on track and on time. Lea and I chat about the masks and their provenance. She expresses joy at seeing them so revered in their sleek archive boxes. Meanwhile, a row of by now somewhat familiar equipment, is lined up expectantly. Acid-free tissue covers the work surface, there are bottles of surgical spirits, and scalpels, resting together, stuck in a bottle cork for safety. Lint-free cotton fabric, nitrile gloves, bowls for the liquids, a notebook to jot down observations.

When we come to the moment of carrying out some basic restoration of the masks, I am apprehensive. Of it all. I am acutely aware of the need to succeed in not damaging these precious artefacts which I have insisted on casting as relics. Of the need for the film footage to be translatable into a gallery space. Of the need to honour these articulate items – to communicate the ways in which they vibrate with after-life. We begin with Matthew Dalby's painted mask. It is pink, and inside it holds both a makeup sponge bonded tightly to its surface, and a masking-tape nametag bearing the name 'Alice'. It must be 'Alice' who required the makeup sponge to keep this mask anchored to her face – a man's features covering a woman's. Gloves prove too clumsy for the task required so I opt (with Lea's approval) to work with freshly washed hands. The sponge gives way without requiring mechanical tugging. Slowly it peels away from the surface, taking the masking tape along with it. Once the sponge is in my hand it is apparent that it is indeed beginning to degrade into hard sandy grit. The risk associated with its removal seems to have been vindicated. A small lump of grit is left behind inside the mask. Careful use of the scalpel pares it slowly away. The final hardened glue visible on the surface appears bonded entirely to the inside of the mask so I proceed no further. The mask is now as stable as possible, there is no more need to intervene.

And so it progresses. I peel away the sponge and masking tape from Matthew's white mask – presumably utilized for the student dancer 'Alice' once again. It comes away easily but leaves an inky blue residue from biro stains sweated onto the plastic through the masking tape label. A daub of isopropyl alcohol removes this. I scrape away some further residue but proceed only to the point that I am sure it is safe to do so without abrading and scraping the surface of the mask. Finally, the packing noodles sellotaped inside the forehead of the mask which once belonged to Steve Blake. These peel away immediately but leave a more problematic glue residue than the masking tape. When I feel more liberal application of the spirits is required to remove this I defer to Lea, and it is she who carries out the final cleaning of this mask.

We come to the elastics. By now we have released all the knots that we can find to allow the elastic to slacken and prevent stress to the masks. The elastic on Blake's mask has perished. We begin a conversation as to whether we should cut all the elastics off so as to protect the masks from the degrading elastic. Lea feels this might be 'handy' as it means that they can no longer 'just be put on. We need to reconsider who/how and why these would be worn', she says. It is at this moment that I realize that the masks have crossed a conceptual threshold. That the physical actions we have carried out in their cataloguing, storing, packing and cleaning has indeed transformed them. Their after-life, whilst not entirely severed from performance use, is now chiefly one of interpretation.

Film editing and preparation for exhibition

It is perhaps only after the frenetic activity of the intervention day is behind me and I am faced once again with the task of film editing, that I have the space to contemplate the transformation of the objects described above. It is a bittersweet contemplation to realize that the preservation has successfully transformed them from objects of function to objects of interpretation – relics to be preserved and venerated. It feels entirely fitting for these totemic objects to have attained such a status, but there is an inescapable sense of loss too in this transformation. Somehow their age and severance from performance is marked more indelibly by their new archival splendour. Despite being stored outside of a museum, they are nonetheless operating within an archival, museological realm. In editing the film, I find the writing of conservation and curatorial scholar Anna Schäffler, of particular resonance. Discussing the preservation of installation art as being reliant on its own exhibition, Schäffler suggests that '[w]hen presentation is a condition for the preservation of installation art, then formerly distinct curatorial tasks like arranging and contextualizing also become part of conservation practice' (Schäffler 2019: 169). She goes on to propose a re-imagining of traditional curation and presentation of installation art as one which instead makes explicit for the viewer, the traditionally unseen decisions and processes carried out by curators and conservators:

Only if the modes of interpretation are accessible and become explicit can the preserved artwork be fully understood in the state of its actual existence. The interpretive act and the forms of its transmission need to be taken into account as constituting the work's characteristics [...] Beyond the conservation discourse this fact is mostly overlooked – not only because art historians, critics, or visitors hardly experience artistic and preservation practices themselves but also because it is not recorded or indicated in the display of a work.
(Schäffler 2019: 169)

This seems a thought-provoking approach in the context of the film of the Preservation intervention. If I am aiming to reveal the layers of constructed relations entangled with these masks through a methodological and documentary approach, the process of preservation itself becomes a way of illuminating the totemic aspect of these artefacts. The framework of painstaking care and repacking of the objects renders the intangible conception of these masks-as-relics, somewhat more tangible. The gesture of preservation, then becomes the means of illuminating the status of these particular artefacts. As Schäffler argues 'only [...] if the act of interpretation [...] [and] preservation approaches are made transparent can the viewer's reception take the "preserved status" into account during the process of aesthetic reception' (Schäffler 2019: 169). As I did with the Dead Skin, I find the process of editing the raw film footage revelatory in terms of clarifying my perspective on the masks and their defining features. Attempting to create a suitable film document for exhibition brings all the key concerns of the research intervention to bear on each editorial decision. Likewise, the limitations which the research conditions imposed on the final film output with the Disintegration intervention are at work here too. Whilst the Disintegration film places the costume at its centre and does not elucidate particularly the intervention carried out, the Preservation film is much more concerned with explicating the process of transformation which the masks have undergone.

Steps towards exhibition

For curator Otero-Pailos (2019: 258),

> [o]bjects are a way for us to establish a kind of continuity that is artificial – it has necessarily to be artificially constructed because in reality our experience is of radical discontinuity. Our mind is constantly forgetting what happened before and constantly not grasping the experience that we're moving through.

When the planned exhibition and display of the *Smithereens* masks becomes stalled by the coronavirus pandemic in Spring 2020, this constructed continuity comes unavoidably to the fore, alongside the impossibility to imagine the future for which we preserve artefacts. The after-life of display in exhibition becomes stalled, held ransom to the pandemic. The masks must wait a little longer, nestled in their conservation boxes. In place of continuity, once again there is a fracture. The temporal realities of objects preserved for the ages becomes thus ever clearer to see. Whilst in many ways this merely serves to reinforce the precarity of the masks, and so too, any after-life which they could hope to enjoy, the rationale for their preservation (for as long as might be possible) is equally affirmed. As Hölling and Otero-Pailos suggest, '[o]bjects change [over time] because their constitutive material parts change, and nothing in this system inherits a fixed identity. It is an ecology of sorts that is full of intrinsic interdependencies and relations' (2019: 256). In light of such inescapable material reality, they propose that it is possible to 'think of objects as temporal-material forms' (2019: 256). The process of cataloguing, discussing, preserving and storing the masks has enacted a transition – a fundamental crossing of threshold in how these artefacts are regarded. Illuminating these steps becomes a process of 'explication' of the object as a gesture in and of itself, towards the temporal and material histories of the objects. Interlocution for the masks remains somewhat at the mercy of visibility however, and the 'interdependencies' and mechanics of institutions such as the gallery, to realize it. Archival leaps of faith are at work once again it seems – preserving artefacts in the hope of a largely imaginal future where we hope to meet them again. Where they might tell us things from 'then' and 'there' which speak to our 'here' and 'now'. Discontinuity. Fracture. But still *here*.

Notes

1. David Hoyle is a performance artist, avant-garde cabaret artist, singer, actor, comedian and film director. During the 1990s he performed under the drag persona *The Divine David* in venues such as The Royal Vauxhall Tavern. He also produced two shows for Channel 4 television *The Divine David Presents* (1998) and *The Divine David Heals* (2000), which starred the character.

2. Teresa Barker, Anna Pons Carrera, Maho Ihara, Gabrielle McNaughton and Ragnhild Olsen.

3. Greig Cooke, Matthew Dalby, Rem Lee, Eddie Nixon and Luca Silvestrini.

4. Anita Berber (1899–1928) was a German dancer, performer and writer, immortalized in the 1925 portrait of her painted by renowned artist Otto Dix (1891–1969), entitled *The Dancer Anita Berber*. Her associates included Sebastien Droste (1898–1927), a Weimar Republic performer and poet who collaborated with Berber through performance and writing, and was also her romantic partner.

5. No 'costume bible' (record book) was made for this work and therefore many costume details are not recorded. Some names and locations have been forgotten by those interviewed. Details have been pieced together here from reminiscences of the interviewees who were involved in the production.

6. Robert Allsopp & Associates are based in South East London at time of writing. They make props for a range of theatrical and film productions nationally and internationally. Credits include props and costumes for Hollywood Films such as *Notting Hill* (1999) and *Gladiator* (2000).

7. The following information is taken from interviews with Robert Allsopp who made the masks. As part of our interview he demonstrated how the masks were made, showing me the raw materials and machinery involved in his workshop. As with the conservation processes, this description is adapted from research notes and reflects the 'uninitiated' position of the research methodology in relation to the expertise employed in these processes. For further information on the composition of ABS, refer to the British Plastics Federation online resources: https://www.bpf.co.uk/plastipedia/polymers/ABS_and_Other_Specialist_Styrenics.aspx. Accessed 12 January 2024.

8. A quick-setting gypsum plaster consisting of a fine white powder (calcium sulfate hemihydrate), which hardens when moistened and allowed to dry.

9. The brand of machine used in Robert Allsopp's workshop at the time of interview (2019) was a Formech 450. Formech are a British company supplying vac-form machines to clients internationally.

10. German artist (1889–1978), known for politically provocative photomontages and collages, using appropriated imagery.

11. *Velvet Goldmine* is a 1998 film written and directed by Todd Haynes from a story by Haynes and James Lyons. It is set in Britain during the early 1970s. It was distributed by Film Four and Miramax. Sandy Powell was the costume designer and Lea Anderson was the choreographer for the production.

12. For a detailed discussion on the varying effects of masks in relation to suppressing or transforming the performer's body in early twentieth-century performance, see Monks (2010: 66–69).

13. As outlined in Disintegration, there was a costume bible compiled for *Yippeee!!!* which has since been lost. Powell stated in interview that at the time of making *Smithereens*, there was no costume bible created as she did not employ that as part of her practice at that time. Anderson did keep many notebooks with images of her choreographic influences, etc. which remain as the chief documentary evidence of the work in creation.

14. The term 'personal archive' is used here to denote the images, video footage, paper materials and textiles which Anderson keeps pertaining to her company. These are catalogued and archived solely according to Anderson's personal storage preferences, and kept within her home and rented storage facilities.

15. This was the *AHRC Techne Annual Student Congress*, held on 12 and 13 January 2017 at Imperial College, London, part of which included a visit to the V&A.

16. Training delivered by UAL and V&A as part of the AHRC TECHNE research training programme for Ph.D. students (28 and 30 November 2017). It took place in the London College of Fashion John Princes Street campus in central London and at The Clothworkers Centre for the Study and Conservation of Textiles and Fashion, Blythe House, London.

17. In late 2022, the V&A undertook a vast relocation of their archives from Blythe House to a new home in *Here East*, in Stratford, East London. https://www.theartnewspaper.com/2019/12/26/sent-packing-vanda-mission-to-empty-250000-objects-from-blythe-house-is-on-target. Accessed 12 January 2024.

18. These represent a selection of the technical steps which museums employ in their archive facilities. Simple adjustments such as storage being elevated slightly above the ground to protect against flooding, or the use of pheromone patches (sticky patches impregnated with a pheromone which attracts moths, or blunder traps which are traps to collect insects/pests). Conservation grade fabrics are fabrics usually of a natural material, which are considered stable and protective, and not likely to damage or interact with the objects in storage. Examples of these would be unbleached cotton, silk and acid-free tissue paper.

19. An independent insurance intermediary registered in England who have a specialist division for performing arts.

20. A renowned silk supplier based in central London who supply silk to fashion houses and museums such as the V&A, among other clients.

21. A brand of clothes detergent available to buy in supermarkets.

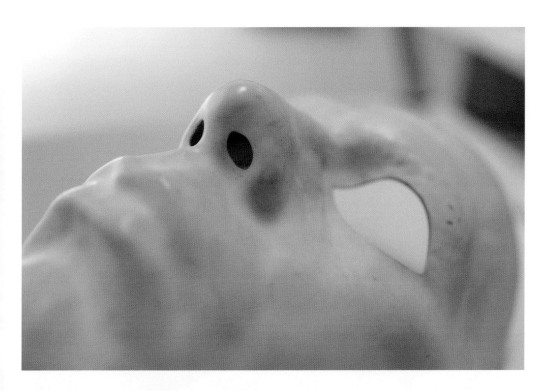

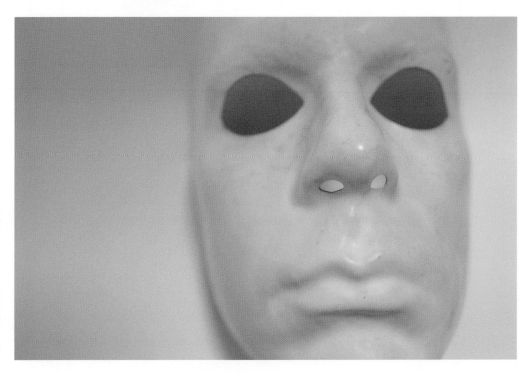

Photos: Rik Pennington

Photos: Rik Pennington

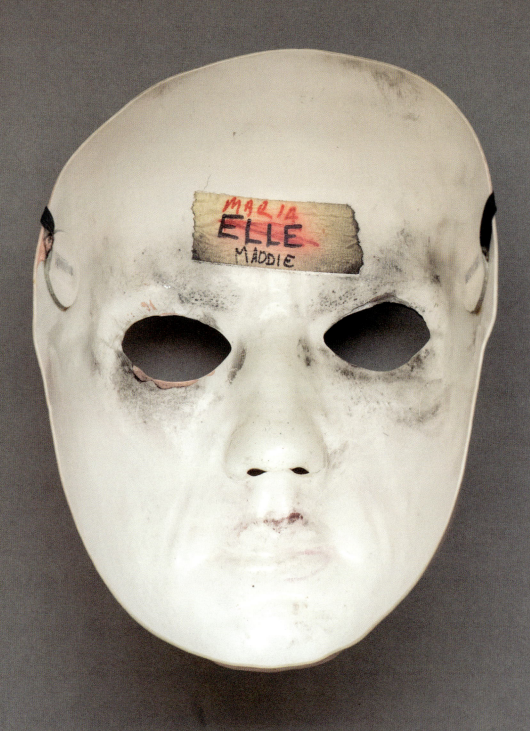

Photos: Rik Pennington

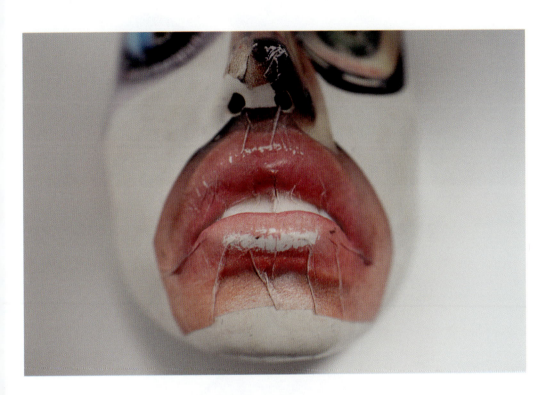

Photos: Rik Pennington

Photos: Rik Pennington

Photo: Rik Pennington
Overleaf: Suit from *The Featherstonehaughs Draw on the Sketchbooks of Egon Schiele*. Photos: Rik Pennington

Transaction

It is in the mental rehearsal for my first phone call to Sotheby's that it all becomes clear. I have spent weeks and months now, interacting with the painted suit from *The Featherstonehaughs Draw on the Sketchbooks of Egon Schiele* – having it photographed and tracing its provenance. This has seen me traipsing to a tailor's shop in Soho, speaking with designer Sandy Powell, listening to dancers' performance anecdotes – how it felt to move in it, how the colours of each suit interacted with one another, how the spirit of Egon Schiele's sketches seeped through choreography and design alike. But it is *now*, in the act of gathering my thoughts and practicing my 'pitch' to Sotheby's auction house, that the heart of this Transaction intervention becomes apparent, and the ways in which the suit operates (or fails to), within this framework.

I have been careful to come to the conversation armed with a glossy provenance brochure featuring all the necessary historical information and imagery of the suit.[1] In the design of this I have consciously chosen images which showcase the 'spectacular' elements of the suit and its sumptuously painted canvas surface. I have selected images which frame it as both aesthetically pleasing and in excellent material condition, deliberately avoiding photographs which betray the odd signs of wear – a ripped seam or a hanging thread. I have found myself employing, not the language of academia, in its measured and quantifiable statements, but rather, the terms of promotion and sale. I have highlighted the starry film associations which surround Mr Eddie's Soho establishment and Sandy Powell's blockbuster CV complete with collection of Oscars – the network of creative individuals from London's late twentieth-century performance 'scene' which is woven together in the fabric of this suit. Lea Anderson's MBE features prominently in the blurb. With each step I have been reminded that the trace histories of the garments and the functions of ghosts will not be of use here. I begin to view the suit through the eyes of a valuations expert and I find it becomes somehow lessened. Reduced to the metrics of saleability, market comparables and indices of utterly subjective values – mired in sentimentality and performance lore.

The difficulty in describing the garment also becomes evident; am I positioning it as memorabilia of performance (and risking the anonymity of the catch all term 'ephemera')? Should I, instead, try and pitch it as an artwork in itself – a beautifully rendered wearable canvas? It is a costume,

Handpainted Suit from
The Featherstonehaughs Draw on the Sketchbooks of Egon Schiele

The garment is a three-piece suit, with single breasted jacket, waistcoat, and high waisted trousers with button fly. It is a simple cut, with 1930s detailing to evoke the period in which Egon Schiele lived and worked. These details can be seen in the cut away nature of the front of the jacket (with the side and front cut from one panel of fabric, rather than with a central insert as is common from suits dating from the 1960s onwards). The high waisted button-fly trousers with four pleats and turn-ups at the bottom of the legs also evoke the period style of the costume. The suit is cut from hard wearing cotton canvas fabric and is in excellent condition. Both the stitching and the exquisite hand-painting have been preserved fully and show only minimal signs of wear.

The history of this suit is embedded in a rich heritage of contemporary dance, costume design, film, and tailoring in the UK. The suits formed the central costume of *The Featherstonehaughs Draw on the Sketchbooks of Egon Schiele*, a seminal work from renowned company The Featherstonehaughs, founded in 1988 by choreographer Lea Anderson. Along with their companion company The Cholmondeleys (founded 1984), The Featherstonehaughs were a key feature of the landscape of contemporary dance in Britain across a lifespan of over twenty years. They garnered a loyal following in dance and performance circles, and their extensive press coverage is indicative of the high esteem in which they were held, both in theatre and performance circles, and among the wider public.

Suit photographed by Rik Pennington

Suit photographed by Rik Pennington

Provenance brochure for Sotheby's. Photos: Rik Pennington

175

undeniably, and at the same time, save for the minor modifications in cut, it is a traditional tailored suit – potentially wearable as a functional personal garment. It is historical, in having featured in a dance piece now no longer performed and of an early twentieth-century style in tailoring. And yet it is not *that* old – a relatively modern garment in the context of historical costume. In its recognizably 'everyday' cut as a three-piece suit and its otherworldly painted nature, the costume seems to straddle numerous worlds from fashion to costume and visual art. It speaks to all of these contexts, but I wonder if from an auctioneer's point of view, this polyvocality is in fact a disadvantage... The horrid phrase 'Unique Selling Point' begins to haunt me.

Finally, I pick up the phone. I feel the impostor rise up inside me as I style myself as a dance historian and scholar working in collaboration with seminal artist Lea Anderson MBE, and her vast costume archive designed by stars of the film world such as the award-winning Sandy Powell. The Sotheby's valuations expert is polite but noncommittal: 'if you could send some photos please?'. If it is not something within the remit of Sotheby's, they might perhaps be able to direct me elsewhere to somewhere more appropriate. I thank her profusely; I send on the glossy brochure with photographs. I follow up with a polite e-mail a week later, and a phone message a week after that. I never hear from her again.

The suits from *The Featherstonehaughs Draw on the Sketchbooks of Egon Schiele* (1998 and 2010) are beguiling to look at, rendered as they are in the painted style of Egon Schiele.[2] They possess a '2D'-animated effect even when lying flat on a surface or hanging on a rail. The thick coating of paint on the cotton canvas surface, juxtaposed with meticulously tailored lines and button holes, creates a palette of ordered style and painterly chaos all at once. To move the suit even solely in the hand, let alone on a dancing body, causes the canvas to shape shift. It appears as if a painting has been given life and motion. In addition to the aesthetic qualities of the suits they are each readable or accessible on a number of levels – as a remnant of a very particular dance work, as a visual reference within the art world and as a functional three-piece fashion garment. Unlike the overtly theatrical nature of the masks or the Dead Skin, the suits could potentially sit astride the worlds of performance and fashion.[3] With the Schiele suits there is also a precedent of previous sale (with the successful auction of a 'spare' suit from the collection in 2016). This was a suit which was rendered surplus to the costumes due to cast changes in a remount of the work in 2010. The suit was sold as part of a crowdfunding campaign to raise funds for the mounting of Anderson's 2016 performed exhibition *Hand in Glove* at the V&A. The campaign was listed on the crowdfunding platform Kickstarter, with pledges of funding being rewarded with items commensurate with the amount pledged (£10 donors received a *Cholmondeleys* and *Featherstonehaughs* tote archive bag, £50 donors received a Constructivist style flag designed by Jay Cloth, £70 donors received a specially commissioned Sandy Powell design print, and so on) (Kickstarter n.d.). The suit was advertised as requiring a pledge of £1000 or more. It was listed as:

Pledge £1000 or more

Costume from The Featherstonehaughs Draw on The Sketchbooks of Egon Schiele designed by Sandy Powell. The costume was made for dancer Gary Clarke for the production in 2010 and consists of a jacket, waistcoat and trousers in shades of blue, hand-painted to resemble a work by Egon Schiele. Your name will be listed in the Exhibition Sponsor's panel at the Victoria & Albert Museum.

This suit was successfully sold to an overseas bidder, Deborah Nadoolman Landis, a renowned costume designer and historian based in the United States, for £1000. Her particular interest in the suit was linked to the fact it had been designed by Sandy Powell and was acquired for her personal collection.

The chosen suit

The Schiele Suits were designed by Powell for Anderson's 1998 production *The Featherstonehaughs Draw on The Sketchbooks of Egon Schiele*. The *Featherstonehaughs* had often been costumed in tailored suits for previous works. For this production they also wore painted bodysuits (made to look like naked bodies as painted on canvas). The suits were tailored to Powell's specifications by Soho-based tailor Eddie Kerr (known as 'Mr Eddie'). They were then hand-painted by set painter, the late Mathilde Sandberg, to resemble the colours and style of Schiele's paintings. Each suit was in a

Jacob Ingram-Dodd and Ronny Ming-hei Wong in costume. Photos: Matilda Temperley

distinct colour range or combination, such as blues, oranges or greens. The suit chosen for this research is rendered in shades of purples. It was originally worn by dancer Luca Silvestrini.

The makeup for the performance was designed by David Hoyle (who also painted one set of *Smithereens* masks). The makeup formed an integral part of the costume, continuing the colours and effects of the suits to render the dancers' faces otherworldly and painterly. In addition to the makeup sitting stylistically within the Schiele production, there are also echoes of the makeup and painted masks of *Smithereens* (in the sense of exaggeration and vividity of colour) which themselves bear similarities to Hoyle's own makeup during his drag performances. Hoyle also carried out minor retouching to the painted suits when the work was remounted in 2010.

The suit, like its counterparts, is a three-piece suit with a single-breasted jacket, waistcoat and high-waisted trousers with button fly. It is a simple cut with specific detailing (such as turn-ups at the end of the trousers and button fly) to evoke the early twentieth-century period in which Schiele lived and worked. The suit is made from a hard-wearing cotton canvas fabric. Considering its age and the wear it has endured, it is in remarkable material condition. The paintwork is for the most part completely preserved, with only an odd thread hanging here and there, and minor fraying of the fabric betraying the heavy use it has seen in its performance life. The suits formed the core costume of the work. They not only matched with the aesthetic of former *Featherstonehaughs* costumes, but evoked historical detailing and formed the key colour and thematic references of the work.

The notion of value pertaining to Anderson's costumes considered within a framework of transaction (particularly financial transaction), is at once problematic. To begin to ascribe monetary value to a costume object catapults the garment into a field of economic, museological and sociocultural forces which seem somewhat distant from the realities of these items as they are in the hand, nestled in the archive, or worn on the dancing body. It forces a garment designed and produced for dance performance within a very specific (or some might argue, 'niche') cultural context, into an arena of the wider competitive art market. Here it is compelled to navigate a market place dominated by high-end production values, the prestige attached to famed

Photos: Rik Pennington

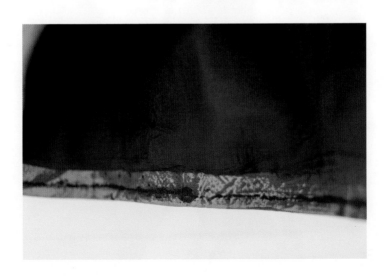

artists, and mechanisms for financial transaction (institutions such as auction houses and art fairs) which do not cater for artefacts such as these costumes.

Despite the knotty implications of considering a costume after-life in terms of sale and monetary worth, it seems imperative that some consideration of these elements be attempted as a means of assessing the 'value' of costumes such as Anderson's. To disregard the market and cultural forces at work in the plight of costumes post-performance would be to naïvely turn away from the very real logistical and economic challenges at work in the archive. The key concerns of enabling visibility and determining whether the plight of entombed and invisible costumes can potentially be altered through further exchange and circulation can only be investigated through actually attempting monetary valuation and exchange. The 'Schiele suit' becomes a testbed for the viability of sale or transaction as potentially providing an alternative after-life to the anonymity of the storage lockup. This strategy is also forged by Anderson's previous assertion that she might try to auction off some costumes in order to generate funds to make future works. The afterlife we encounter with the suit is not aiming therefore, to create an after-life solely for the garment itself, but rather, to potentially transform the suit from material object in the archive to be maintained and cared for, to solid capital which can be used in the creation of new performances and the sustaining of Anderson's companies. This endeavour differs greatly from that of the careful preservation and attempted destruction found in the preceding interventions.

Of the intervention strategies within the project so far, in ways this has been the most unpredictable and the most subject to external forces outside of my control. The unavoidable influences of sale and valuation have come to shape the intervention from the earliest point. An inevitable vanishing point comes on the horizon here – if successfully sold, the suit disappears into a private collection just like the one before it did. Not a museological disappearance into storage (as discussed in the previous intervention chapters), but rather a disappearance full stop. An after-life solely at the mercy of whoever pays the highest price. Journeying out on this quest with the suit has felt, in ways, anathema to the careful documenting and physical gestures of conservation that have gone before. Yet it is also a potent reminder of the financial and

Neil Callaghan in costume. Photo: Matilda Temperley

transactional precarities which govern this archive and its keeper. The creative output of choreographers such as Anderson – the creation of new performance works, the sustainability of performers' careers – none of these exist in a vacuum outside the economic world. They are each subject to the forces which shape conceptions of value, metrics of sale and judgements of worth. Perhaps the sacrifice of one costume in the service of sustainability isn't so divorced from ethics of care after all. The care of a whole body of work which is subject to erasures and ruptures – the fractures already disrupting this archive.

This chapter begins by detailing the performance histories and creative processes involved with the suit and outlining considerations of monetary value and transaction within the arena of performance ephemera and visual art. It goes on to chart the steps taken in appraising the suit within a realm of transaction and the potential for monetary exchange. Whilst this intervention has not required the level of upskilling in areas such as filmmaking or preservation processes found in the Disintegration and Preservation interventions, I was nonetheless equally unacquainted with the worlds of auction, valuation and collecting. As with the other interventions, the most striking elements of the research are found in the incidental details of the unfamiliar worlds which I have been entering into and the conversations with valuation experts and creative professionals associated with the suit. Step by step, the suit begins to take shape within this alien context, testing the possibilities for an alternative, transactional after-life.

The Featherstonehaughs Draw on the Sketchbooks of Egon Schiele

The Featherstonehaughs Draw on the Sketchbooks of Egon Schiele was choreographed by Anderson in 1998 and toured to venues across the United Kingdom. Music was by Drostan Madden with stage design by Simon Corder and costume design by Sandy Powell. The original cast was made up of Luca Silvestrini, Eddie Nixon, Frank Bock, Steve Kirkham, Rem Lee and Dan O' Neill. It was reimagined as a short (ten minute) film *The Lost Dances of Egon Schiele* in 2000, directed by Lea Anderson and Kevin McKiernan. This was a production for BBC and Arts Council England. The film is (at the time of writing) still accessible to watch online.[4] The purple suit worn by Silvestrini features prominently in this film especially in the opening scenes. The film

Neil Callaghan, Ryen Perkins-Gangnes and Ronny Ming-hei Wong.
Background: Jacob Ingram-Dodd. Photo: Pau Ros
Ronny Ming-hei Wong and Ryen Perkins-Gangnes. Photo: Pau Ros

also showcases the complex makeup and heavily stylistic choreography and use of gesture from the full-length production. The performance was reworked for stage and performed live in 2010, featuring a new cast and music by Steve Blake and Will Saunders.[5] Critical reception to the work whilst mostly positive, was varied and sometimes even varied between the original production and the subsequent 2010 remounting of the work (one critic writing that whilst they had really enjoyed the first production, they felt differently viewing it again over a decade later) (Brown 2010). It was classified by writer Emma Manning as 'the most imaginative piece Anderson has produced for some years' (Manning 2010: n.pag.). Writing in 2011, at the end of the 2010 remounting, and after Arts Council funding for *The Featherstonehaughs* had been withdrawn, critic Sarah Wilkinson described the work as 'a marathon of iconic poses with seamless interludes', arguing that she could 'think of no company more suited to bringing Schiele's sketches to life than *The Featherstonehaughs* and [...] the genius of this piece makes the recent 100% cut to their funding from Arts Council England seem criminal' (Wilkinson 2011: n.pag.).

'To convincingly bring such idiosyncratic and often paradoxical qualities to life is a remarkable feat', suggested Wilkinson, 'yet *The Featherstonehaughs* succeed with astonishing panache. From the dandyish, dishevelled suits by Oscar-winning Sandy Powell through to the grotesque, clownish make-up and invasive rock music, every detail announces Schiele's uncompromising attitude and disturbing allure' (Wilkinson 2011: n.pag.). *The Independent* newspaper critic Zoë Anderson described the costumes as 'smudged suits, cloudy as a painter's colour wash. Their faces are painted to give the same effect, their hair teased into wild shapes. They stroll and pose like zombie fashion plates, all fierce eyes and languid attitudes' (Anderson 2010: n.pag.). As with *Smithereens* and *Yippeee!!!*, these descriptions of the work foreground costume and the constructed visual landscape as transmitting the essence of the work, and the potential thematic dichotomies which Anderson explores. The vacillations between life and death, youthful beauty and decay, and the construction of a dancing body which defies easy categorization. The use of the words 'zombies' and the 'grotesque' in these reviews places *The Featherstonehaughs Draw on the Sketchbooks of Egon Schiele* in territory similar to that of *Yippeee!!!* and *Smithereens* in the liminal aspects of presentation which it gestures towards. The human faces rendered somewhat

Foreground: Ryen Perkins-Gangnes. Background: Sebastian Elias Kurth, Jacob Ingram-Dodd and Neil Callaghan. Photo: Pau Ros

Ryen Perkins-Gangnes. Photo: Pau Ros

unrecognizable (in this case disappearing into a constructed painterly visual spectacle) and the elements of the uncanny – that uneasiness engendered in an encounter with bodies seemingly both animate and inanimate at the same time (as discussed in Preservation).

Describing the suits in further detail, critic Terry O' Donovan suggested that the suits created 'a powerful image of the constructed male':

> They appear to have been painted with layers and layers of colour, melting into the dancer's painted face. In a mesmerising sequence in which three dancers slither along the floor and recreate the semi-erotic poses of Schiele's sketches they are dressed in skin-tight body suits with anatomically correct sketches notating abdominals, calf muscles and genitalia. It cleverly reflects the vulnerability of the artist creating nude drawings, with just the right amount of distance from reality to allow us to safely see ourselves in the depiction onstage.
> (2010: n.pag.)

This constructed nudity seen in the other costumes from the work (sheer body suits painted as anatomically correct sketches emulating Schiele's nude portraits) operates on a similar level to the nudity of the Dead Skin (as discussed in Disintegration). The body suits represent a stylistic representation of nudity – what Sparshott (1995: 306) perhaps meant when he argued that 'the medium [of dance] calls rather for suggestion or symbolism'. There is a doubleness at work in these 'naked' bodysuits in that they align with Sparshott's symbolism (in terms of symbolically representing a naked body), but they also sit firmly within a specific visual art frame of reference, in being easily recognizable as representations or stand-ins for Schiele's sketches. Arguably the three-piece suit operates in a similar vein in the slippage of imagery which it suggests – the swagger of a gentleman of the early twentieth-century dressed in an everyday suit, merged somehow into the landscape of Schiele's canvases. There are several layers of separation, then, between the dancing body in a suit, and the way this image is transmitted to the audience – the dancing body becomes (like the masked figures of *Smithereens* and the metal-toothed chorus girls in *Yippeee!!!*) somewhat remote and unknowable.

Ryen Perkins-Gangnes. Photo: Pau Ros

I would further argue that in this place of liminality it is possible to locate the traces of ghostliness in the work's thematic matter (in addition to the physical traces within the suit itself). Many of the real-life subjects of Schiele's sketches suffered from poverty and illness. There is an unmistakable hauntedness found in the original images of the figures who stare back at Schiele, malnourished or ailing. The makeup of the dancers echoed these representations, making the performers look similarly haunted too. Not quite human, or perhaps more accurately, figures who occupy the thin spaces between life and death, youth and decay, vitality and decline. They hold these contesting elements together, and in doing so, they are rendered inherently ghostly or liminal.

In addition to initial critical reception of the work, *The Featherstonehaughs Draw on the Sketchbooks of Egon Schiele* has remained a focus for exploration within dance and performance studies. Scholars have continued exploring various elements of the work (more so than with *Smithereens* or *Yippeee!!!*), ranging from critical readings of the hybrid relationships between painting and dancing bodies (Rottenberg 2004) to the potentially radical interplays between spectator and performer which it offers up (Stewart 2019).

Choreographic and design influences

The premise of the work was to reimagine a sketchbook of the Viennese artist Egon Schiele, not as a sketchbook, but as a notebook of choreographic notation. Thus his sketched portraits were used as a template to 'reconstruct' the lost dances of the 'choreographer' Egon Schiele. The sketches served as primary inspiration for choreography, costume design and staging. Each of the cast of six dancers wore a hand-painted suit in a specific colourway. The colours, textures and painted style echoed the work of Schiele, rendering the suits and the dancing figures, almost 2D in nature. The overall effect was to make the dancers themselves look like painted images, with their heavy face makeup continuing as an extension of the painted surface of the suits. As Anderson describes 'the concept is that we're pretending that this is not a work of art [...] we're reconstructing the notebooks [...] and we're working our way through them literally [and] [...] reconstructing it as Laban notation' (Anderson 2018a: n.pag.). Poses, postures and arrangements of bodies were painstakingly reconstructed to create choreographic tableaux and sequences.

Anderson notes that the early twentieth-century time in which Schiele was working coincided with the era of expressionist German dance (which featured as a key inspirational influence in the creation of other works such as *Smithereens*) and so the idea of conjuring up the figure of Schiele as a choreographer, akin to say, Rudolf Laban, felt in keeping historically with the timeframe and style of the work. Anderson also spoke of the concept of a 'colour narrative' as something which featured, not only in this work, but, as a strategy, in other works of hers:

> the colour narrative thing is a way to deal with not having a story and making the story be something different to 'and then this happened' etc [...] [Sandy Powell] had done different colourways way [in] *Cold Sweat* [1990] and *Walky Talky* [1992] [...] We grouped the Egon Schiele paintings [...] so that if you have a red and a blue person together, that would have a different feel from an orange and a red person together or whatever. So it would change the dynamic [...] I didn't want to imply certain characters or story. And so we did that. [Powell] had a whole set of colour references from each painting, like for orange and for red and for green and brushstrokes and lines.
> (Anderson 2018a: n.pag.)

Colours formed a key thematic anchor within design and choreography, and so the painted surface of the suits was a formative element of the overall work. Anderson went on to describe the ways in which colour can imply things in a narrative, rather than literal, fashion.

> A green and a blue person dance together and it gives you a certain kind of tension in the colour. Similarly, this describes what might happen in a relationship without saying 'this is the mother and this is the kid' [...] green and blue – bit of a mm-hmm [mimes an expression of uncertainty or unease]. Red and green – it's a whole different thing and you just see it really differently. So you're bringing ideas of dislocation or clashing or sympathetic values without actually having to spell it out.
> (Anderson 2018a: n.pag.)

Powell cited the specificity of the sketchbooks as providing a clear thematic vision for the work:

It was a lot easier [than *Smithereens* (1999)] in terms of a concept because it was very specifically about the sketches of Egon Schiele. So we had definite things to look at, which were images of men. Drawings of men and different kinds of drawings and paintings of men and that was it, and then the choreography was going to be very much obviously based on the angularity and the sort of essence of those drawings. And so for me it was all there. I didn't really have to search far and wide [...] All we had was the books, the images, and that's all we looked at. We [Anderson and Powell] looked at the same images but then I [also] looked at the rest of his work – you know not just the drawings of the men. I looked at the paintings and the style of painting and the colours that he would use. So we sort of went beyond the very specific drawings but it was just absolutely all Egon Schiele and really nothing else.
(Powell 2018: n.pag.)

The requirements for tailoring suits for dancers is, as Powell explained,

totally different to doing suits for actors who are playing characters, because suits for dancers have to work when they have to be danced in [...] But you know, you've still got tailoring and you've still got fittings and you've still got different silhouettes and different kinds of suits.
(Powell 2018: n.pag.)

Powell explained the choice to costume the dancers in suits as being a tradition.

It was what we always put *The Featherstonehaughs* in. *The Featherstonehaughs* always wore suits. I don't know how that happened. It's in the first shows we did and then it just was more suits and more suits. When we did the shows with *The Featherstonehaughs* and *The Cholmondeleys* combined that was when it was different, that's when they might be wearing different things [...] When *The Featherstonehaughs* were just *The Featherstonehaughs*, again it was men in suits and then naked men. Men in clothes and men not in clothes – so treated in exactly the same way.
(Powell 2018: n.pag.)

Ryen Perkins-Gangnes. Photo: Pau Ros
Sebastian Elias Kurth and Jacob Ingram-Dodd. Photo: Pau Ros

Chris Kerr with Schiele suit. Photo: Mary Kate Connolly

Despite the physical flexibility required in the cut of the suit there were minimal adaptations in terms of fit and material. The historical 'look' of the suit was prioritized. Powell cited the need to be able to move in the suits as paramount – the trousers were never tight and were made strong so that they wouldn't split along any seams. Powell said that whilst a few had perhaps split in places and needed mending, that she couldn't 'recall any major disasters. I don't recall doing anything specifically other than making the clothes that the guys could move in' (Powell 2018: n.pag.).

The Schiele suits were tailored by Soho tailor Eddie Kerr at 52 Berwick Street, London. Powell knew him as a contact through her film work and he tailored suits for many of *The Featherstonehaughs* productions. All of the dancers travelled to his shop in Berwick St with Powell for fittings. 'Mr Eddie', as he was known, had long been associated with the pop and fashion culture which emerged around the Carnaby St area of London during the 1960s, making bespoke suits for music industry and film stars. He was frequently commissioned to create suits for films, famously tailoring blazers for the 1981 film *Chariots of Fire* and 'lemon suits' for the band U2, which they wore on their 1992–93 *Zooropa* tour (*Chris Kerr* Soho n.d.). The business remains in the family as the longest running bespoke tailor in Soho and is now run by his son, tailor Chris Kerr.[6] I was able to interview Chris Kerr, discussing the Schiele suit – the particular details he could observe in the tailoring and the process of how fittings would have taken place.

Kerr noted the historical details of the suit seen in the cut-away nature of the front of the jacket (with the side and front cut from one panel of fabric, rather than with a central insert as is common from suits dating from the 1960s onwards). The high-waisted button fly trousers with four pleats and turn-ups at the bottom of the legs, also evoke the period style of the costume. Kerr observed that whilst many costume designers would choose to use a zip fly (despite the historical inaccuracy for a period suit), that the Schiele suits maintain the button fly. He highlighted the extra room built in around the shoulder area to allow the dancers to raise their arms without the suit slipping from their shoulders or splitting along a seam. He also drew attention to the hard-wearing nature of the suit and commented on how hot it would be to perform in, especially layered with paint (Kerr 2018).

Once tailored, the suits were brought to renowned theatrical painter and dyer, artist Mathilde Sandberg. Sandberg worked on a number of feature films during her career, including *Elizabeth* (1998), *Orlando* (1992) and *Braveheart* (1995). She taught at Wimbledon School of Art, training textile painters such as John Cowell and is described in an article by the Victoria & Albert Museum as 'the finest theatrical painter and dyer of her day' (V&A interview with John Cowell 1998). Sandberg's brief from Powell for the suits was to paint them (each in their own distinctive colourway) to look as if they were a painting by Schiele. Powell explained that

> it was just the sort of quality of the line or the strokes – whether it was painting or a pencil line or a crayon line or a pastel line, it was the *quality* of the painting which we really wanted to capture, which I think was successful.
> (Powell 2018: n.pag.)

The purple suit is a striking example of Sandberg's talent as a textile painter – the textures and painterly contours on the suit render it uncannily like the works of Schiele and create the optical illusion of the suit being a painted object. Powell described the process of working with Sandberg:

> I must have picked particular images and pictures and we looked at all of those together. And then to differentiate between the guys I did each one in a different colour scheme. The suits were made in a canvas – in a sort of heavy cotton calico like a canvas so that it would be a good background to be painted on, like paper, and she painted the suits as if they had been painted by Egon Schiele. And that was when we had the idea that if they're gonna be wearing these suits that are so stylised and so painted, and looked like 2D paintings […] what on earth do you do with the faces? You can't just have the faces [unadorned]. The idea was to treat the faces in exactly the same way as the costumes. I loved it.
> (Powell 2018: n.pag.)

This realization that the makeup would need to continue in the vein of the painted suits, led Powell to commission David Hoyle to design the makeup. He devised a makeup style which continued the hues of the suits and Schiele's

Neil Callaghan in costume. Photo: Chris Nash

Neil Callaghan, Ronny Ming-hei Wong, Ryen Perkins-Gangnes, Jacob Ingram-Dodd, Sebastian Elias Kurth and Inn Pang Ooi. Photo: Pau Ros

 Inn Pang Ooi, Ronny Ming-hei Wong, Ryen Perkins-Gangnes and Sebastian Elias Kurth. Photo: Pau Ros

use of paint, rendering the dancers strange and ghost like. Dark circles around the eyes and lurid colours evoked the tones of Schiele's paintings and also the aesthetic of the sketches – the raw way in which Schiele would render the faces of his (sometimes undernourished or ill) sitters. When the dancers first wore their newly painted suits, Hoyle came into rehearsal and did their makeup so they could then learn how to do it themselves.

Powell estimated that the suits were painted with fabric paint and then heat set.[7] Due to this they could not be washed but would have been dry cleaned which led to the paint fading over time. As a result of this, minor paint touch-ups were carried out initially by Sandberg and her assistants, and then in later years, by Hoyle. Powell mentioned that this had a slight stylistic impact on the suits:

> they were dry cleaned and then they'd fade and that's why the costumes every now and then, after every run, they'd be painted over – just touched up. Like you'd touch up make up that's come off – put it back on over the top [...] The last time I remember, it was about 2000 or 2001, I was working in Italy and the costumes were sent to Italy and David was there and John (Cowell). He helped Mathilde with the original costumes painting them [...] so then he took over and repainted, and then David helped him. And it is interesting because when David started you can see that there is a difference, because he has a different style of painting. It kind of got a bit more like David's painting than Mathilde's and Schiele's so I had to [...] try and control that a little [...] I had to stop him turning them into his paintings as opposed to Egon Schiele's painting.
> (Powell 2018: n.pag.)

The make-up too had stylistic changes as time went on, depending on the cast and how they did their makeup. Powell:

> that changed over the years, and from person to person. Because then of course they had to do their own make up. They had to learn how to do it [...] so everybody sort of develops their own technique for doing it. It's difficult, and of course during the performance itself, it changes.
> (Powell 2018: n.pag.)

The heat from the lights combined with exertion in the heavy fabric of the three-piece suits meant that the dancers sweated profusely which streaked their makeup. For dancer Luca Silvestrini, makeup is always an important 'feature of not looking yourself' (Silvestrini 2018: n.pag.) and of being 'a canvas yourself – you're a surface to draw on as a performer' (Silvestrini 2018: n.pag.). He explained that he is 'someone who sweats a lot onstage, with all the lights and everything […] I mean your face was not the same from when you started this show to the end. It was completely different' (Silvestrini 2018: n.pag.).

The dancers were trained to do their makeup and had photographs to copy from. Despite this however, at times the makeup would not look correct and Silvestrini described how he would sometimes need to reapply it all over again. This level of preparation was cited by him as a useful process in honing his performance and achieving the necessary characterization (Silvestrini 2018: n.pag.). In a somewhat similar vein to the (more dramatic) restrictions brought about by the Dead Skins in *Yippeee!!!* (2006) and the masks of *Smithereens* (1999), he outlined the adaptations demanded by the suits and the ways in which they influenced movement and posture. He noted the transition from rehearsing in practice clothes to wearing the suits and boots as having a

> completely different feeling. You have to adapt and inhabit somehow, the sequences and movement and the connections with the other dancers because of the limitation of the suit […] you became more like a sense of […] character or a drawing […] you became more of a drawing in this instance.
> (Silvestrini 2018: n.pag.)

He continued:

> having that suit as well made us feel part of that world of sketches and also the relationship between the artist and the model. Because naturally that section was all about pretending or assuming that there was someone else outside taking us as a model – you know, someone drawing – almost like the audience was the artist making drawings and we were just moving from position to position, bringing life to these sketches […] Basically it was a really strong landmark in the way we

embodied the movement because of the restrictions and because of the quality of the actual fabric and the texture of the painting on them. And so it made a very strong sort of impact.
(Silvestrini 2018: n.pag.)

Silvestrini described the suits as a 'bit rigid [...] comparing to a normal suit, because of the paint' (Silvestrini 2018: n.pag.). He also recalled that he felt very hot on stage. In light of these sensorial challenges, he was keen to stress a key element in working with Anderson, for him as a dancer:

> I need to point out something: What I am particularly fond of with Lea's art, and having worked with her, is this sense that it's not easy. As a performer you actually feel on your body a sense of, almost sacrifice [...] you have to give away some of your freedom or some of your individuality or some of your desire. Something of yourself, to become someone else. So you are serving an idea – in the best possible way you're serving it, and you give your body, soul, mind, emotions, to a vision which is quite totalising and which is wonderful for a performer – to accomplish that idea you actually give flesh and blood to it. And the costumes and the props are so important for Lea's work. That's one of the most important parts in her work. You feel you are embodying all that through becoming [...] it becomes almost your second skin, if not your skin. I had to say that because it wasn't just about wearing a suit, it was more than that. The actual fabric, the trousers (which were quite big), the braces [...] the jacket (which was quite thick) – you were very hot and forced into this sort of 'shell'. It made you a *specific* performer, not a generic one.
> (Silvestrini 2018: n.pag.)

Once again the sometimes adversarial nature of the costumes and props in Anderson's works arises. Akin to the difficulties experienced by dancer Makiko Aoyama in coping with the prosthetic teeth and tongues of *Yippeee!!!*, Silvestrini outlined the productive ways in which challenging costumes can spur on the performers. The costume as adversary or trickster is something which appears across many of Anderson's works. Even with a superficially 'uncomplicated' costume such as the painted suit (as opposed to prosthetic tongues or masks with limited peripheral vision), the specificities of the fabric, the painting and the ways in which the dancers were required to navigate the choreography of costume rendered it a significant challenge. Silvestrini related these challenges with costume as key to characterization in Anderson's works:

> Some people work with characterization from an emotional point of view, or from a story point of view. With Lea, the characterization comes through the limitations she offers you – through costumes, props, staging. So it's a process; you go through a process of feeling comfortable, feeling that you know there is a challenge. You need to go from here to there – it's not just given, you've got to find it, you've got to adapt, you've got to surrender bit by bit to whatever limitations are offered to you. But that becomes part of the performance. That becomes part of your subtext and your reason to be onstage.
> (Silvestrini 2018: n.pag.)

A consideration of value

The after-lives chosen for each garment in this research have emerged from direct interaction with the costumes in the archive and in dialogue with Anderson's original musings on potential futures for her costumes. With this intervention the attributes of the garment (as aesthetically pleasing and expertly crafted) coalesce with wider considerations of the economics of costumes post-performance. As previously mentioned, a 'spare' suit from the work (rendered surplus due to casting changes in remounts) has already been sold by Anderson in a crowdfunding auction to raise funds for the V&A performed exhibition *Hand in Glove* (2016). There is therefore directly comparable economic provenance for the item. Moreover, the idea of transaction chimes with Anderson's early assertions to me that in addition to considering 'burning' the costumes or giving some over to a museum archive, that from time to time, she wonders about auctioning off some pieces through an establishment like Sotheby's, in order to generate income for her companies (Anderson 2016: n.pag.). Here, the motive for transaction is both to facilitate an after-life for the costume sold, but furthermore, to generate funds for future costumes. Sacrificing one item signifies the hope of creating new work for the future (which might ultimately lead to the creation of more, archive-worthy, costumes).

The contextual framework and thinking around value supporting this intervention is drawn largely from theorists, critics and artists writing about visual art (Degen 2013; Grampp 1989; Wilson 2001). The decision to situate perspectives of value in this way has been made for several reasons. First, the context of writing on costumes tends to be largely situated in perspectives outside of direct monetary exchange. There is a far longer history of valuation, sale and the influence of capitalism and market forces within visual art than there is in the collecting or sale of costume artefacts. Second, the creation of indices of value in relation to artworks and auction sales is greater in visual art contexts than it is in costume. Finally, the costumes chosen for this research are considered as works of art specific to unique dance performances (with their performance life being firmly situated in the past). This marks them out as different to, for example, the collection or sale of design objects, historical utilitarian items or decorative artefacts (such as textiles or ceramics). Whilst scholarship does indeed exist on the collection and value of objects such as these (Stapleton 2012; Hooper et al. 2005), the material instabilities of Anderson's costumes, and the ways in which they straddle performance, craftsmanship, historical significance and potential for exhibition render these writings less relevant than those pertaining to visual and site-specific art. The vagaries of the 'art market', the politics of visibility and attention regarding the artist, and the fashions of taste among collectors and viewers appear relevant in the context of the valuation and worth of the Schiele suit (which was of course painted in the style of a famed visual artist).

In her introduction to *The Market*, editor Natasha Degen asserts that 'to consider a work of art in economic terms is to invite accusations of pragmatic instrumentality and crass materialism' (Degen 2013: 13). She goes on to highlight however that 'to exclude economics from this discourse is to obscure the dynamics of value' (Degen 2013: 13). In sketching out the wider context of the costumes in this book there is a significant temptation to shy away from economic considerations. Particularly as the somewhat unquantifiable values of history, memory and trace significance often seem to overshadow the pragmatics of money or transaction. Yet Anderson's impulses to auction costume items arise solely out of pragmatism and at the acknowledged cost of sacrificing other metrics of intrinsic or symbolic value. They come from the necessity to sustain a company; to make new work, to free up physical space and alleviate the logistical restraints of insurance costs, storage and so forth.

Sociologist and philosopher Georg Simmel's musings on value and money (first published in 1900), weave together ideas of aesthetic value and monetary value. Despite writing at a distance of over a century ago, the basic tenets of Simmel's arguments nonetheless hold true in relation to the Schiele suits. For Simmel, 'Even though aesthetic value, like any other value, is not an integral part of the object, but is rather a projection of our feeling, it has the peculiarity that the projection is complete' (Simmel [1900] 2004: 73). He continues: 'the content of the feeling is [...] absorbed by the object and confronts the subject as something which has autonomous significance, which is inherent in the object' (Simmel [1900] 2004: 73). Unpicking the dynamics of this absorption, Simmel suggests that 'If an object of any kind provides us with great pleasure or advantage, we experience a feeling of joy at every later viewing of this object, even if any use or enjoyment is now out of the question' (Simmel [1900] 2004: 73). He likens this joy as being akin to an 'echo' (Simmel [1900] 2004: 73). The sense of it being an echo relates to the fact that the object is now solely being *contemplated* rather than consumed or utilized in any way. 'Echoes' can be related both to the concept of costume after-lives in this book, and also the transition of garments within a museum (from objects of consumption to objects of interpretation, as discussed in Preservation). The trace histories held within the garments arguably operate like echoes – ones which relate to a specific network of individuals who designed, made and performed in them. If knowledge of this link between the costume's performance history and its current material state has been fractured (i.e. the costume is being appraised by someone unfamiliar with the original performance in which it featured), it becomes questionable whether the aesthetic properties which Simmel identifies, can operate. The valuations expert at Sotheby's whom I initially consulted for appraisal for example, was not familiar with the work of Anderson, and it is likely that many of the attendees of auctions within a visual art context would not have direct links with, or personal memories of these specific dance performances either. The aesthetic 'value' of the garment is therefore potentially lowered in this context, and so too, its monetary value and appeal. This narrows the potential aesthetic resonance for the object (as Simmel would regard it) to a narrow demographic of individuals. Aesthetic regard in relation to objects is, according to Simmel, vital in terms of increasing its economic mobility:

When I call an object beautiful, its quality and significance become much more independent of the arrangements and the needs of the subject than if it is merely useful. So long as objects are merely useful, they are interchangeable, and everything can be replaced by anything else that performs the same service. But when they are beautiful, they have a unique individual existence, and the value of one cannot be replaced by another, even though it may be just as beautiful in its own way.
(Simmel [1900] 2004: 74–75)

If, as Simmel suggests, aesthetic values are influenced by our relationship to an object (and knowledge of, or involvement in its past life), and classifications of beauty and rarity are also directly tied to the economic value of an object, the (monetary) value of the Schiele suit becomes quite limited. Despite the fact that Simmel was writing well over a hundred years ago, these assertions resonate with sentiments expressed by the auctioneers of film and theatre costume and memorabilia whom I interviewed (Hodgson 2019; Lane 2020). The rarity of an object (and resultant difficulty in acquiring it) can directly influence monetary value at auction; usually the rarer the item, the more valuable. Yet in the case of Anderson's costumes it seems that perhaps they are *too* rare and outside of mainstream cultural visibility to be highly valued (as opposed to costumes from the *Ballets Russes* or contemporary companies such as *The Royal Ballet*, for example). As previously discussed, Anderson does not currently benefit from the prominence afforded to contemporaries such as choreographers Matthew Bourne or Wayne MacGregor. Thus her name and reputation are not as well-known outside of a dedicated contemporary dance audience.

In his 1989 publication *Pricing the Priceless*, William Grampp reinforces the argument that (in the context of visual art) the assertion of aesthetic value (as attributed by museum professionals, curators, etc.) impacts positively on the monetary worth of a painting (Grampp 1989). He also highlights other significant drivers of price, including the standing and visibility of the artist (in particular in the context of living artists). Drawing on research carried out by the late Willi Bongard (economist) during the 1970s, which attempted to quantify the value and standing of living artists, Grampp sought to assess whether there was a direct link between an artist's eminence and the financial worth of their paintings. Bongard's original research had assigned numerical values to living artists by assessing the 'recognition the artist received in such ways as being in the permanent collections of museums, by one-man shows, group shows, by the notice received in periodicals and television and by other marks of esteem' (Grampp 1989: 33). Grampp (with the aid of a colleague), then 'did a regression analysis of the information in order to see if the price of a painter's work was consistent with the points assigned to him [by Bongard] and I [Grampp] found that it was' (Grampp 1989: 33).

It is of course important to consider that the ways in which artists can now present their work (outside of mainstream gallery contexts/art publications) have been utterly transformed by the digital age and social media, which did not exist at the time of Bongard's or Grampp's research. Arguably, however, many of the constraints and indices of visibility which these writers describe as impacting on economic value still operate in the context of Anderson's work and legacy. The performance works dealt with in this book were made during the rise of digitalization (films were made of *Yippeee!!!* and *The Featherstonehaughs Draw on the Sketchbooks of Egon Schiele* and uploaded online) yet they were made before the meteoric rise of social media as a promotional tool. Even though the tools of social media are now available to Anderson for promotion, maintaining a significant and successful online presence requires funding and resources, as do the programming and mounting of performance works and exhibitions. Thus, if the 'capital' of mainstream esteem of the creator is regarded as crucial to the sale value of their art (or costumes from their work), the Schiele suit is once again maligned – deemed not substantially valuable in financial terms. The plight of artists who may suffer as a result of the interrelations between the esteem and visibility which an artist has among high profile galleries or theatres and their monetary worth, is touched upon in the 'tenth commandment' of the feminist artist cooperative *Guerilla Girls*[8] 'Code of Ethics for Art Museums' (1989):

> X Thou shalt admit to the Public that words such as genius, masterpiece, priceless, seminal, potent, tough, gritty and powerful are used solely to prop up the Myth and inflate the Market Value of White Male Artists. (Guerilla Girls: 1989: 63)

Mainstream accessibility, institutional validation (through critical and museological esteem) and visibility, as contributing directly to the price of artworks are seemingly inescapable requirements for the majority of artworks to achieve significant market value. 'Business art', wrote Andy Warhol in 1975, is 'the step that comes after Art' (88). The concept of business art or the artist-entrepreneur (as used to describe Warhol's commercial ventures and the evolution of figures such as British artist Damien Hirst) is by now, very familiar. Warhol argued that 'making money is art and working is art and good business is the best art' (1975: 88). Large-scale artist brands (such as Hirst's or Jeff Koons') appear to successfully capitalize on the elements of accessibility and institutional validation; consequently appealing to both the discerning, and the newly wealthy, collector. This feeds in to the idea of collecting both as a status symbol and also as a worthwhile monetary investment. Summarizing the success of business art 'brands' and their appeal to collectors, Degen suggests that 'the monumental scale of a Koons, the opulent materiality of a Hirst and the detached, god-like perspective of a Gursky embellish collectors' egos' (Degen 2013: 19). It is perhaps noteworthy that each of the examples Degen has selected are white male artists (as were Grampp's and Bongard's), conceivably chiming with the Guerilla Girls critique of museums' role in influencing the price of art. What Degen is speaking to here however is the sense of certain artists being a 'safe bet' both for financial investment and prestige. Once again, the ability for costume items from Anderson's archive to reach large sums at auction seems greatly compromised by the failure of them to operate within these metrics. Collecting items for prestige and the assurance of financial appreciation simply do not apply to these fabric remains.

Discussing contingencies in relation to value, Barbara Herrnstein Smith argues that viewing the intrinsic and financial values of an object as being distinct from one another (as favoured traditionally in economic and aesthetic theories) neglects to account for the shifts and fluctuations in 'personal economy' as well as financial economies (Herrnstein Smith 1988: 30). She suggests that 'the value of an entity to an individual subject is also the product of the dynamics of an economic system', and that

[l]ike any other economy [...] this too is a continuously fluctuating or shifting system, for our individual needs, interests and resources are themselves functions of our continuously changing states in relation to an environment that may be relatively stable but is never absolutely fixed. (Herrnstein Smith 1988: 30)

Herrnstein Smith goes on to unpick the variables in this complex interplay in far more detail, but for the purpose of this research, the sense of flux that she conveys in terms of cultural 'worth' or intrinsic value being subject to changes over time is of most significance. It is also conversant with the views of valuations experts and auctioneers whom I have interviewed, who emphasize that the appetite for collecting cultural objects not only relies on accessibility and visibility of the individuals associated with the item, but is also highly dependent on fashions of taste and wider economic conditions. Memorabilia expert Sarah Hodgson outlined for example, that the increase in value and interest in memorabilia from the *Star Wars* film franchise[9] coincides not only with the release of recent sequels, but more especially with the growth of a demographic of (mostly male) collectors for whom the original *Star Wars* films featured significantly in childhood, and who are now reaching an age and financial status which enables them to invest in collecting the memorabilia (Hodgson 2019). It would appear that the elements of mainstream acclaim or fame, personal economies of intrinsic value and seemingly secure financial investment are at work together in this example.

Despite all the ways in which it becomes clear that the Schiele suit fails to operate successfully within these wider measures of value (in the way that a Hirst artwork or *Star Wars* costume might), these contexts nonetheless remain the only viable ones in which to test the value of Anderson's costumes realistically. Placing the suit in this context provides a jumping off point to consider in detail how it might succeed or fail in attaining concrete monetary value. There are undoubtedly 'fans' of Anderson's work for whom the fabric remains of her performance are of great intrinsic value. For these individuals the costumes could successfully operate in the manner of Simmel's 'echo' in the recall they bring of performances now gone (which gave great joy and intrinsic personal value). There are also students/former students who have trained with Anderson and performed in remounts of her works and worn some of the costumes. Additionally, there are the dancers who have performed in her works and the critics and scholars who have written about it. There are individuals who would be particularly appreciative of the work of Sandy Powell (who enjoys mainstream visibility due to her costume design for films).[10] It is somewhat impossible to determine the detailed economic particulars of these demographics. It is perhaps not unreasonable to estimate however, that a majority of them (given their career profiles and attendant salaries) would lack the funds available to collectors of valuable visual art or famous film memorabilia such as from the *Star Wars* franchise. Lastly there are cultural establishments and museums such as the V&A who look to acquire costume items for their collections via auction purchases. From my conversations with museum professionals such as Susana Fajardo (conservator at the V&A) however, it appears that restricted funding and the financial burden of sustaining collections means that museums are highly selective of what items they acquire and would only look to purchase an item that had featured in an iconic performance, was worn by a world famous dancer (such as Vaslav Nijinsky or Margot Fonteyn), or was designed by a particularly famous fashion or costume designer (Coco Chanel, for example).[11]

Steps towards valuation

Through each of my interactions with the network of individuals who were involved in designing, creating and performing in the suit, the historical and reconstitutive value of the garment was clear to see, just as with the Dead Skin and the *Smithereens* masks. The challenges of translating these abstract values into monetary value however, became excruciatingly clear with my first pitch to Sotheby's (as described in the opening of this chapter). Attempting financial valuation of the suit shone a wholly different light on all of the garments in the archive, and in many ways, came to reinforce their isolation as being cultural ephemera existing outside of dominant structures of value, heritage and monetary worth. It is misleading of me to suggest that Sotheby's auction house did not engage with my enquiry at all. Following a long period of no further contact from them (twelve months which coincided with a planned hiatus during the research project), I re-contacted them afresh and began the process once again. This time my enquiries proved more fruitful. Once again the valuations expert whom I initially spoke to over the phone was courteous but non-committal. Following further discussion, she went on to explain via e-mail that Sotheby's would be unable to assist in the sale of Anderson's archive:

I understand the broad scope of the collection, which is fully encapsulated by this painted suit. The collection straddles various auction categories i.e. textiles, contemporary art, modern design, and culture. Unfortunately, however, the multifaceted nature of the archive makes it difficult to align it with a particular sale department. We have checked with our colleagues in the Contemporary Art department and, unfortunately, they have confirmed they cannot assist. Furthermore, we no longer have a Textiles or Popular Culture department at Sotheby's, and our design sales now take place in Paris and are focused on high end mid-century decorative art.

Our fashion and textiles consultant [...] does not feel her sales are the right platform for you either.

I am sorry for this disappointing outcome.
(Excerpt from author's correspondence)

Whilst this response is disappointing, it is nonetheless greatly informative in illustrating how the Schiele suit would be appraised from an auctioneer's perspective. It is starkly illustrative of the fact that within a framework of monetary exchange the suit would fail to compete in value or align sympathetically with other auction categories. The move towards larger auction houses such as Sotheby's no longer operating a Popular Culture department is also a significant element.[12] According to valuations and auction specialists Sarah Hodgson (of Wallace and Hodgson) and Stephen Lane (specialist in the sale of film props), this has been much influenced by the growth in recent decades of online selling platforms such as eBay.[13] Such a development has both driven many lesser valued items to be sold on online auction sites as opposed to through auction houses, and has equally opened an opportunity for more bespoke services (such as which Hodgson and Lane provide) to deal with the valuation and sale of valuable Popular Culture memorabilia items such as props, costumes, musical instruments and manuscript material.

Following Sotheby's response I approach Wallace and Hodgson, experts in valuation and sale of Rock and Roll and Film memorabilia, for advice on how to proceed. The company was founded by Carey Wallace and Sarah Hodgson in 2009 (both former employees of the auction house Christie's). Wallace founded Christie's Popular Culture Department in 1985. Both Wallace and Hodgson have served time as Heads of the Department during their tenure at Christie's auction house. Wallace and Hodgson have dealt with a number of high-profile valuations, auctions and private sales. Their projects have included insurance valuations of Marilyn Monroe costumes (2012), the Stanley Kubrick Archive (2023), memorabilia pertaining to bands such as The Beatles and The Rolling Stones, Eric Clapton's auctions of guitars and amps (Christie's 1999 and 2004 and Bonhams 2011) and the auction of the Dame Margot Fonteyn Collection in 2000 (Christie's).

Hodgson's initial response is that the archive would, as Sotheby's have outlined, fall outside of categories for auction and would not merit an auction solely devoted to Anderson's archive due to the low monetary worth of her costumes. Hodgson is also keen to highlight that theatre and dance costumes tend not to be considered valuable in comparison to film costumes (which have been worn by iconic film stars for example). This seems a significant point – the low yield which theatre and dance costumes habitually fetch at auction render them in general, an unappealing proposition for any major auction house. Whilst Hodgson appreciates the worth of Anderson's costumes within a contemporary dance context, she emphasizes that the main obstacle to valuation would be the difficulty in acquiring market comparables (similar items that had previously sold and their value).

Rather than commissioning her to undertake the market comparable research, she suggests ways in which I can research the market comparables myself. The fact that one Schiele suit has already sold, Hodgson explains, is a very useful indicator for value and demonstrates that it could potentially mean a sale price for another suit as being in excess of £1000 – perhaps £1500. She suggests that I look at the online archives of auction houses such as Bonhams, Christie's or Sotheby's (which list auction lot items, their reserve price and the sum which they were sold for). Given the potential financial value of the suit might be approximately £1500 (and certainly unlikely to be over £2000), it becomes clear that the fees associated with valuation services and the percentage of profit needed at auction in order to be financially viable for the valuation experts and auction house, renders the suit highly unsuitable for sale through an established auction house. Its maximum worth would simply not be lucrative for an auction house to consider managing its sale.

Meeting with Hodgson is highly informative and unpicks the various elements which influence the value of an object, highlighting by comparison how the Schiele suit would fail to garner much monetary value. Whilst much of the interview covers anecdotal accounts of her work as a valuations expert, each anecdote nonetheless speaks to the wider economic and aesthetic considerations considered earlier in this chapter. The worth of visual art in light of the visibility of an artist, the fashions of taste more generally, and the knowledge and provenance of the object's former life (as a costume in a film for instance), all chime with the specific examples which Hodgson describes. The transformation for example, of *Star Wars* film memorabilia – from discarded merchandising to collector's items, has emerged in direct relationship with the demands of the market. Thus, a Stormtrooper's helmet, originally salvaged from a *Star Wars*[14] film and used for many years as a child's dressing up prop, was eventually sold at auction for a considerable sum (Hodgson 2019). This metamorphosis from an object of consumption or leftover detritus to an auction lot of great worth, reflects similar transitions enacted when a costume object crosses the threshold of a museum into protective storage or display, never to be worn again. I am curious whether, in the context of purchase by collectors, a costume item would ever be worn or used by the collector, or alternatively be treated with the protective and restrictive reverence of a conservation expert. Hodgson says that she has not been aware of collectors wearing or 'using' the objects they buy – generally they would be revered as objects for aesthetic and totemic appreciation. It is common nonetheless that objects might not enjoy anything like the level of care in handling and storage, that a museum-archived costume would. Hodgson explains that very often collectors display their memorabilia or costumes in their own homes (without any environmental regulation or protection) (Hodgson 2019).

During the course of our interview Hodgson suggests that I contact Stephen Lane, of Prop Store London regarding my research on the valuation of performance artefacts. Props maker Robert Allsopp (whom I interviewed regarding the masks he made for *Smithereens*) had also suggested to me that Lane would be a useful source of insider industry information concerning the auction and sale of performance memorabilia. Prop Store was founded by Lane in 1998 and the company has offices in London and Los Angeles. They specialize in the acquisition and sale of film costumes and memorabilia from a range of blockbuster films (including a large array of *Star Wars* memorabilia alongside props and costumes from other iconic franchises such as the James Bond and Batman films). Some months after my interview with Hodgson, I interview Lane and the Head of Client Services for Prop Store, Tim Lawes. Their collection spans 25,000 square feet of archived props and costumes. Chiefly operating as an auction service (they host online and large-scale live auctions), Lawes is also keen to stress to me that they aim to provide best possible storage conditions for the costumes (akin to that of a museum archive), and that they also have a significant network of specialists who carry out conservation work when needed (Lawes 2020). Much of Lane's and Lawes' observations echo those of Hodgson in terms of the demographics and market/cultural forces which drive indices of value within sale and collection of memorabilia. Lane cites the current decline in value of Elvis[15] memorabilia for example, as a result of the advanced age that original Elvis fans would now be. He confirms that memorabilia from *Star Wars* and franchises such as *Batman* are currently popular, and muses on whether the value of Harry Potter costumes and props might begin to soar as the fans of the films reach middle age (Lane 2020).[16] There were some differences in anecdotes however – whilst Hodgson had not experienced collectors using the items they collected, Lane relays anecdotes in which film costumes have been purchased in order to be worn to fancy dress parties[17] (Lane 2020). In these examples it is clear to see that the impulses for the sale and collecting of costume and memorabilia items operate in a different vein to that of acquisitions policies for museum curators or conservators. Hodgson (2019) outlines that in general, theatre ephemera would not be as financially valuable as that pertaining to film, and that for a costume to be of substantial monetary worth, the costume designer or dancer who wore the costume would need to enjoy significant acclaim and mainstream visibility, particularly so in the case of living dancers or designers. Within this context, the costumes of Sandy Powell (as a famous living designer) would not currently be as financially valuable as those designed by a now deceased designer such as Edith Head.[18] The need for mainstream visibility is again highlighted by this example and demonstrates once more that even if a costume artefact of Anderson's could successfully switch context from theatre into an art or memorabilia auction, it would still be held as too niche to be of monetary worth. It simply could not compete with artefacts which enjoy mainstream visibility due to their associations.

In the case of film costumes, the provenance of the item is also of great importance – whether it is the specific costume worn within a film scene, or in publicity materials, for example, or a spare costume. A gingham dress worn by Judy Garland in the 1939 film *The Wizard of Oz* which was sold at Bonhams auction house in New York in 2015 (for USD 1.56 million) was one of ten identical dresses made for the actress. It was believed however, to be one of only two dresses that Garland actually wore. In this case, the provenance of the garment was verified by the sweat stains still in evidence, as being a costume which was actually worn for the production (*The Guardian* 2015). In this vein, the importance of provenance is somewhat similar to the importance given to the verification of provenance in the visual art world (establishing whether for instance, the painter him/herself painted a painting, or whether an apprentice or protégé close to the artist may have contributed to the artwork which historically was commonplace practice).[19]

Within the framework of film and theatre costume, provenance appears to be tied most significantly to the bodies who did or did not inhabit the garment, and whether there are embodied traces of their presence still left behind. Whilst Hodgson's main experience is with film and popular culture memorabilia, she was closely involved with the auction of the Margot Fonteyn Collection – a collection of personal garments, artworks, letters and costumes from the dancer's estate, which was auctioned at Christie's London in late 2000 (Christie's n.d.). Conducting research of my own as advised on the auction records of Bonhams, Sotheby's and Christie's, this particular auction seems to be of closest relevance. As costumes and memorabilia of a famed British dancer auctioned through a renowned auction house, the details of this archive sale provide a relatively comparable framework to that of the costume archive of Lea Anderson. Whilst the costumes were from ballet productions and Margot Fonteyn would have enjoyed greater fame during her career than Anderson, these items are nonetheless probably the most similar that it has been possible to research. At the time of the 2000 auction, the press noted that members of the ballet community had reacted in distress to the sale of the archive. The ballet director Peter Wright expressed concern at the fracturing of the archive which comes with sale when it is broken down into single lots for auction. Speaking to *The Guardian* newspaper journalist John Ezard at the time he said that

'[i]t breaks my heart to think that these things may be hidden away in some collection in the US or South America' (Ezard 2000: n.pag.).

The collection contained a number of ball gowns and evening wear designed by fashion designer Yves Saint Laurent, alongside costume items from Fonteyn's ballet roles such as Odile in *Swan Lake*, Princess Aurora in *The Sleeping Beauty* and Juliet in *Romeo and Juliet*. The records of the sale of the costume lots records the names of the costume designers under the details of ballet productions and locations of performance premieres. In the case of the fashion clothing items from Fonteyn's personal wardrobe, the lot item is generally titled by the name of the fashion designer – e.g. Yves Saint Laurent. This detail is perhaps indicative in and of itself, of the differing indices of value between high-fashion garments and costumes. This difference in esteem is also reflected in the guide price and achieved price of most items. Despite the fact that Fonteyn's fame was derived from her dance career, her dance costumes and shoes on the whole, failed to match the monetary value attributed to the couture items from her personal wardrobe.

The costume item sold for the highest price for example, was Lot 198, a black velvet tutu decorated with gilt braid and rhinestones which had a guide price of £3000–£5000 and was sold for £64,250. By comparison, the highest price for personal wardrobe was Lot 19, an haute couture evening ensemble from Yves Saint Laurent's African inspired Spring collection, 1967, estimate £800–1200, sold for £91,750. It is also striking to see that some smaller costume items such as headdresses worn by Fonteyn in performance reached relatively low prices. Lot 159, a beaded headdress from the ballet *Le Corsaire* had an estimate of £400–£600 and sold for £588 (Christie's n.d.). These figures seem quite low when compared to the vast sums which costume items from film achieve at auction. One of the dresses made for Audrey Hepburn in the 1961 film *Breakfast at Tiffany's*, designed by Givenchy, was auctioned at Christie's

London in 2006, and despite an estimate of £50,00–£70,000, it achieved a sale price of £467,200 (Carter 2006). Sarah Hodgson was personally involved with this auction; she stressed the difficulty at times, in predicting the actual price that an iconic item such as this might achieve at auction (Hodgson 2019).

In the face of all these considerations – the wider context of auction and sale, the social and economic predictors of value and esteem and the seemingly prerequisite fame and mainstream visibility necessary for successful auction, the Schiele suit shrinks ever further, in monetary value. It fails to perform within any of these contexts other than that of the realm of historic, totemic ghost. Whilst on the one hand, a potential estimated value of £1500 appears favourable when compared to a surprisingly low £588 sale price of one of the headdresses worn by Margot Fonteyn (many others sold for much higher sums), the suit nonetheless fails to operate within a wider framework of saleability. There is no suitable auction lot to place it within and such a low (individual) sale value renders it totally unfeasible for a prestigious auction house to consider. Items from the Fonteyn collection were bought by a variety of personal collectors and also for costume museums and collections. Arguably, an equivalent bank of would-be collectors willing to purchase items from Anderson's archive does not exist.

Steps towards an after-life

In light of the knowledge I have gleaned on the wider context of auction and transaction, I begin to turn once again to the specifics of the Schiele suit in the archive. To research other avenues and potential for auction. I attempt to garner further information regarding the purchase of the other Schiele suit via online auction in 2016. I wish to gain more information on the reasons for its purchase and to attempt to trace the after-life of this other suit. Where is it being stored? Is it visible to anyone other than the keeper of the archive it has been placed in? Unfortunately, it is not possible to find out any further information and this trail of enquiry, like so many others with the Schiele suit, runs cold. Once again, the after-life of transaction for the suit seems unfeasible, inappropriate, impossible.

In addition to my concerns around the inability for the Schiele suit to 'perform' in the wider contexts of auction and transactional institutions, I become increasingly aware of the potential risks to the suit if auctioned. The more my concerns become bound up with valuation, financial worth and successful sale, the greater the capacity for an irreversible loss of context for the Schiele suit. I become painfully aware of the eradication of performance histories and embodied traces that could come with a sale which would complete a total severance of the costume from its performance life. There would no longer be a complete set of suits in Anderson's archive, and the links between the suit and its performance histories would potentially be forgotten or disregarded (depending on who might buy the suit and for what purpose). Renowned visual artist Fred Wilson[20] has written of the strange fates of his works of art when they have been sold to collectors, and of the distortions of meaning which can occur by their placement in new domestic contexts outside that of the gallery or museum. Wilson describes that

> I have at times come across my work at parties in the homes of wealthy people; misplaced and mute as a stuffed bird or bear, it seems to function there as a trophy acquired in a foreign land, as if it has been bagged during an art safari.
> (Wilson cited in Cohen 2001: 54)

What of Anderson's costumes in the face of what Wilson describes? Perhaps the attempts to create an alternative after-life through transaction would merely confirm the anonymity of the object and reinforce its disappearance. Cut off from the performances in which it lived, the surrounding associated objects (other costumes and props from the production) and dancer's bodies, perhaps the Schiele suit would be further devalued, both monetarily and associatively. The suit would be rendered mute. Whilst this anonymous after-life might be somehow justifiable to Anderson as an unavoidable sacrifice in order to generate significant revenue for the sustainability of her work as a whole, such justification does not hold up if the income generated is so meagre as to be totally insignificant. This plight of severance and lack of appropriate context for sale informs the final attempt at Transaction which Anderson and myself sketch out for the Schiele suit.

It has become increasingly evident during the avenues of research described, that in the end on a very fundamental level, it is only possible to value an item by assessing the sum that someone would be willing to part with, to purchase it. Whilst this is an extremely basic consideration, it nonetheless emerges as an inescapable endpoint when considering all the elements which might feed into, or equally devalue, the worth or sale price of the Schiele suit. It is clear that ascertaining this specific knowledge would not be possible through a mainstream auction house and it has already been somewhat tested via an online auction platform with the previous sale of the surplus suit. The question of 'what next?' thus presents itself.

Anderson and I turn over the potential further steps we could take, going back and forth over the pros and cons of sale, and what the eventual fate of the Schiele suit might be. Eventually we reach the decision to test the financial viability of the suit through facilitating a silent auction during the upcoming gallery exhibition which I have planned. It seems the most appropriate way of conveying the knotty questions around the worth of costumes post performance within the gallery exhibition, whilst also showcasing the suit itself. This after-life appears to be the only one that seems viable for the suit – one that would allow us to discover how the garment could perform in terms of sale. This would be explored, quite literally, in the eyes of the beholder – those who came to see the exhibition and who arguably might be the closest equivalent in demographic, to that of *Star Wars* fans now purchasing 'Stormtrooper' helmets for vast sums. Up until this point it has appeared the Schiele suit is unsellable from the auction houses' perspective. In addition to providing an alternative space and way to experience costumes outside performance or museum contexts, perhaps so too, the exhibition might provide a favourable environment for the conditions of sale.

Revision of plans

As preparation for the originally planned *Smithereens* exhibition (scheduled for May 2020) gains momentum, the challenge of how to display the suit safely and attractively and include accompanying interpretative text come to the fore. In consultation with production technician Karsten Tinapp, I design a suspension frame with wire cabling that will act as a mannequin but allow the suit to be displayed in a non-symmetrical way, in broad reference to the postures which Silvestrini would have adopted when he wore the suit in performance. I also begin to sift through the performance images and photographs of the suit. These photographs have served as documentation, but more crucially, have formed the central element of the provenance brochure I compiled and sent to Sotheby's and Wallace and Hodgson in my initial attempts at valuation.

These plans, along with all others, come to an abrupt halt in March 2020 with the outbreak of the Coronavirus pandemic. Plans for the auction of the suit become thus imperilled. At this time, myself and Anderson also brainstorm ideas of whether there could be other ways in which we could auction the suit, or include it as part of an additional event (aside from the *Smithereens* exhibition). The conclusion we reach, is no, this would simply not be possible. It would be impossible to achieve satisfactory conditions for auction which could maximize the sale potential for the suit outside of a live exhibition. The design of the silent auction, as something encountered in the live moment of the exhibition visit within an ideal contextual backdrop cannot be replicated in an online forum. Whilst the suit photographs well and appears attractive in film footage, these elements are poor substitutes for encountering the suit 'in the flesh' so to speak. An online catalogue or solely static photos would not do it justice, and would ultimately fail to conjure the sense of theatre and excitement required for a successful silent auction. When the *Smithereens* exhibition finally does happen (in late 2021), ongoing pandemic restrictions on exhibition conditions make it impossible to execute a silent auction within the restricted gallery space. The suit is exhibited as planned in terms of its structure and accompanying photographs, but it stands purely as a costume on display, and not as an item for auction.

This is perhaps a disappointing outcome for our diligent attempts at transaction, but it helpfully reinforces the findings of the Transaction intervention as a whole. It illustrates that a satisfactory and context-specific mechanism for the auction of items from archives such as Anderson's simply does not currently exist. To attempt to sell off the suit in an online auction forum such as eBay or a crowdfunding platform (as was previously done), would be to do it an injustice. Such a sale would sever it from its appropriate context, and thus disembodied, the suit would be at the mercy of the financial and aesthetic metrics of the arts and memorabilia market. These are not favourable metrics for this costume archive. Whilst this conclusion might feel unfortunate, given the 'value' which this book places on these eloquent costume artefacts, it remains an inescapable reality of market and societal conditions. If mainstream indices of monetary value render the costumes mute, it becomes ever more important to craft an alternative frame of reference. Transaction becomes an interlocutionary exchange – money doesn't change hands, but memories, residues and echoes do, instead.[21]

Sebastian Elias Kurth, Neil Callaghan and Jacob Ingram-Dodd. Photo: Pau Ros

Suit photos: Rik Pennington

Handpainted Suit from
The Featherstonehaughs Draw on the Sketchbooks of Egon Schiele

The garment is a three-piece suit, with single breasted jacket, waistcoat, and high waisted trousers with button fly. It is a simple cut, with 1930s detailing to evoke the period in which Egon Schiele lived and worked. These details can be seen in the cut away nature of the front of the jacket (with the side and front cut from one panel of fabric, rather than with a central insert as is common from suits dating from the 1960s onwards). The high waisted button-fly trousers with four pleats and turn-ups at the bottom of the legs also evoke the period style of the costume. The suit is cut from hard wearing cotton canvas fabric and is in excellent condition. Both the stitching and the exquisite hand-painting have been preserved fully and show only minimal signs of wear.

The history of this suit is embedded in a rich heritage of contemporary dance, costume design, film, and tailoring in the UK. The suits formed the central costume of *The Featherstonehaughs Draw on the Sketchbooks of Egon Schiele*, a seminal work from renowned company The Featherstonehaughs, founded in 1988 by choreographer Lea Anderson. Along with their companion company *The Cholmondeleys* (founded 1984), The Featherstonehaughs were a key feature of the landscape of contemporary dance in Britain across a lifespan of over twenty years. They garnered a loyal following in dance and performance circles, and their extensive press coverage is indicative of the high esteem in which they were held, both in theatre and performance circles, and among the wider public.

Suit photographed by Rik Pennington

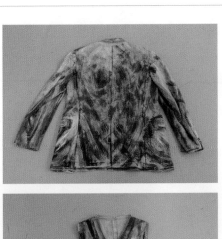

Suit photographed by Rik Pennington

Overleaf: Sebastian Elias Kurth and Neil Callaghan. Photo: Pau Ros

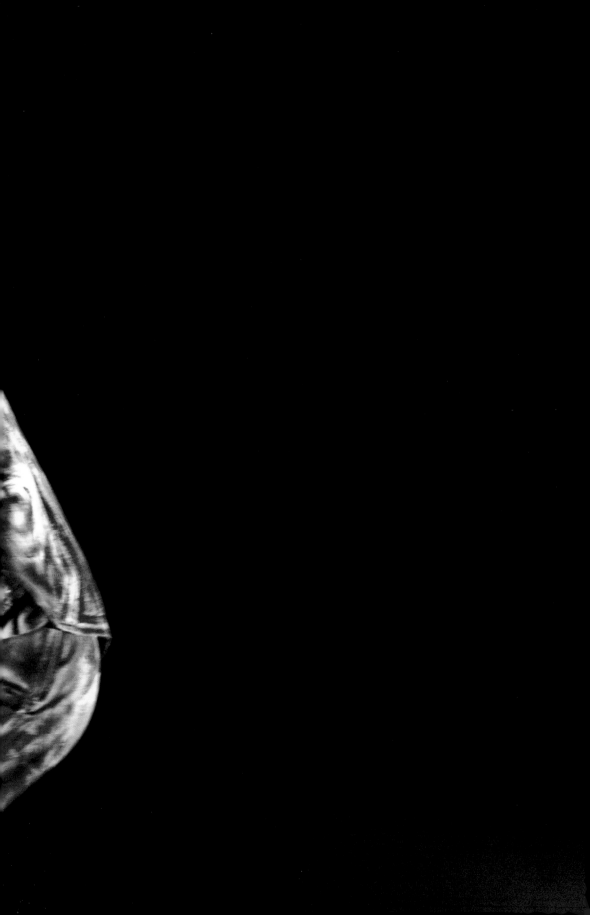

Details of the show for which the suit was designed and made

The Featherstonehaughs Draw on the Sketchbooks of Egon Schiele

First Choreographed and Performed live: 1998
(toured to venues across the UK)
Choreography: Lea Anderson
Music: Drostan Madden
Stage Design: Simon Corder
Costume Design: Sandy Powell
Original Cast:
Luca Silvestrini
Eddie Nixon
Frank Bock
Stephen Kirkham
Rem Lee
Dan O'Neill

Reimagined for film as *The Lost Dances of Egon Schiele* (2000) directed by Lea Anderson & Kevin McKiernan

Reworked for Stage and performed live: 2010 (with new cast and music by Steve Blake and Will Saunders)

The Featherstonehaughs Draw on The Sketchbooks of Egon Schiele was a dance work which reimagined a sketchbook of Schiele's early twentieth century portraits as choreographic notation, painstakingly reproducing poses, postures and movements drawn from the sketchbooks. The sketches served as primary inspiration for choreography, costume design and staging. There was a cast of 6 male dancers, each wearing a handpainted suit in a specific colour. The colours, textures and painted style echoed the work of Schiele, with the effect of rendering the suits and therefore the dancing figures, almost 2D in nature. The overall effect was to make the dancers themselves look like painted images. They had heavy face makeup which served as an extension of the painted surface of the suits.

The suit was designed by multiple Oscar-winning designer Sandy Powell, tailored by Eddie Kerr (famously known as Mr Eddie) of Soho, and hand-painted by acclaimed theatrical textile painter, the late Mathilde Sandberg. Subsequent paint repairs and accompanying makeup was designed by radical performance artist David Hoyle (then known as *The Divine David*). It was worn and performed in by Luca Silvestrini, now artistic director of *Protein Dance* and internationally respected choreographer.

Thus the provenance of this suit is formed by an interlinked web of significant individuals across the theatre, performance and film sector (Mr Eddie's clients included a host of film stars and music icons). As part of a wider doctoral research project, the history of the suit and of the people who designed, made and wore it has been mapped. As such, this suit is a rich living archive in and of itself, displaying exquisite craftsmanship and artistry, and stands as an important relic of performance history.

Suit photographed by Rik Pennington

Choreographer and Founder member of *The Featherstonehaughs*

Lea Anderson MBE is a founder member and Artistic Director of *The Cholmondeleys* and *Featherstonehaughs*, two of the foremost contemporary dance companies in the UK. Notable works include *Flag* (1988/2006/2017), *Flesh and Blood* (1989/1997) *Birthday* (1992), *Car* (1995/96), *The Featherstonehaughs Draw On The Sketchbooks Of Egon Schiele* (1998), *Smithereens* (1998), *3* (2003), *Double Take* (2004), *Yippeee!!!* (2006) *Russian Roulette* (2008) and *Edits* (2010).

Anderson also created works for television, video and film. These include *Tights, Camera, Action* (Channel 4) which she wrote and presented, choreography for Todd Haynes' feature film *Velvet Goldmine* (1997) and choreography for the 2018 feature film *How to Talk to Girls at Parties*, directed by John Cameron Mitchell and starring Nicole Kidman and Elle Fanning.

In 2002 Lea Anderson was awarded an MBE for her services to dance, and in 2006 was awarded an Honorary Doctorate of Arts from Dartington College of Arts. Her films *Flesh and Blood* and *Cross Channel* were designated set texts for GCSE and A' level Dance and Performance Studies in the UK for a number of years.

In autumn 2014 Lea was appointed Regents Professor at the University of California in Los Angeles, and has served as Artist in Residence at the Southbank Centre. Her latest works include a performed exhibition of choreography and costume at The V&A museum in London, in which costumes from *The Featherstonehaughs Draw on the Sketchbooks of Egon Schiele* featured. A selected list of press and academic articles on the work of Lea Anderson and *The Featherstonehaughs* can be found as an appendix.

Lea Anderson

Sandy Powell

Tailor Chris Kerr with the suit   Photo: Mary Kate Connolly

Costume Designer

The costumes for the work were designed by acclaimed costume designer, Sandy Powell. Born in London, Powell studied at Saint Martin's School of Art, where she met Lea Anderson and went on to collaborate with her numerous times. She left St Martin's and began working on costume design for theatre companies and shortly afterwards, on Derek Jarman's *Caravaggio* (1986). She has designed costumes for countless feature films, including six by Martin Scorsese and three by Todd Haynes, notably *Velvet Goldmine* (with choreography by Lea Anderson and featuring performance artist David Hoyle) and *Carol*.

Powell has been nominated for an Oscar numerous times, including for *The Crying Game* (1992), *Gangs of New York* (2002), *The Departed* (2006), *Hugo* (2011) and *The Wolf of Wall Street* (2013), and to date has won three Oscars, for *Shakespeare in Love* (1998), *The Aviator* (2004) and *The Young Victoria* (2009). She also won Baftas for *Velvet Goldmine* and *The Young Victoria*. In 2011, she was awarded an OBE for services to costume design and the film industry.

Selected Press Coverage of Sandy Powell from *Vanity Fair* magazine and *The Guardian*.

https://www.vanityfair.com/hollywood/2017/11/wonderstruck-sandy-powell

https://www.theguardian.com/culture/2016/jul/17/on-my-radar-sandy-powell-costume-designer

Tailor

The suit was tailored by Soho tailor Eddie Kerr at 52 Berwick Street, London. The business remains in the family as the longest running bespoke tailor in Soho, and is now run by his son, tailor Chris Kerr. It was established in 1960 as Len Wilton at 82 Berwick Street, London, where it remained for 50 years (eventually moving to 31 Berwick Street in 2010). In 1963 Eddie Kerr joined as an assistant cutter and by 1970 had been made partner, eventually buying the business in 1990.

In the early 1960s 'Mr Eddie' as he became known by customers began to make bespoke suits for the new pop & fashion scene emerging around Carnaby Street including stars like Matt Monroe, Procol Harem & The Swinging Blue Jeans. Over the next 4 decades, Mr Eddie continued to build on his reputation as the 'go to' bespoke tailor for creative people including many in the film and TV business. Some of his more famous commissions include blazers for the film *Chariots of Fire* (1981), cutting the coat worn by Richard E Grant in the film *Withnail & I* (1987), and band U2's 'lemon suits' for their *Zooropa* tour (1992-93).

In 1997 Mr Eddie's son, Chris Kerr joined the business as an apprentice cutter under his father's tutelage and took over the business when he retired in 2002. Continuing in the showbiz tailor tradition, Chris Kerr has cut suits for such stars as Brad Pitt, Johnny Depp & Nick Cave.

Mr Eddie cut suits for many of *The Featherstonehaughs* productions. Their suits were viewed as an iconic element of their look as performers, wearing suits and heavy boots in almost all of their works performed as *The Featherstonehaughs*. For the suits cut for *The Featherstonehaughs Draw on the Sketchbooks of Egon Schiele*, all of *The Featherstonehaughs* travelled to the Berwick St tailor shop along with Sandy Powell for all fittings.

Selected press on Mr Eddie's tailors, now known as Chris Kerr tailors:

https://www.huffingtonpost.co.uk/jason-holmes/chris-kerr-making-clothes_b_1922152.html

https://www.esquire.com/uk/food-drink/restaurants/news/a3139/the-bespokesman-meet-the-tailor/

Lea Anderson. Photo: Margaret Williams

Hand Painting

The suit was handpainted by the late Mathilde Sandberg, a renowned textile theatrical painter. She worked on a number of feature films, including *Elizabeth* (1998), *Orlando* (1992), and *Braveheart* (1995). She taught at Wimbledon School of Art, training famed textile painters such as John Cowell, and is described in an article by the Victoria & Albert Museum as "the finest theatrical painter and dyer of her day" (V&A Interview with John Cowell, 1998, online).

Her painting brief from designer Sandy Powell for the suits was to paint them, each in their own distinctive colourway, to look as if they were a painting by Egon Schiele. The purple suit is a striking example of Sandberg's talent as a textile painter – the textures and painterly contours on the suit render it uncannily like the sketches of Schiele himself, and give the optical illusion of the suit being a painted object, creating an almost 2D visual image.

Sandberg's profile on the Internet Movie Database (IMDB) and reference article:

https://www.imdb.com/name/nm0761287/

http://www.vam.ac.uk/content/articles/t/the-textile-painter-john-cowell/

Makeup design and Suit retouching

The makeup design for the work, which formed an integral part of the costume was designed by performance artist and painter, David Hoyle. Hoyle also carried out minor retouching to the painted suits when the work was remounted in 2010.

Hoyle is an English performance artist, avant-garde cabaret artist, singer, actor, comedian and film director. His performances are known to combine many disparate elements, from satirical comedy to painting, surrealism and striptease. Hoyle came to prominence in the 1990s as *The Divine David*, a kind of anti-drag queen who combined wit and lacerating social commentary, targeting both bourgeois Britain and the materialistic-hedonistic gay scene. *The Divine David* featured in a series of outré late-night Channel 4 shows and a cameo in *Todd Haynes' Velvet Goldmine*, before Hoyle killed *The Divine David* off during a spectacular show at the Streatham Ice Arena in 2000. As well as the Royal Vauxhall Tavern (RVT), with which he is most closely associated, he's performed at the Soho Theatre, Chelsea Theatre, Battersea Arts Centre, National Portrait Gallery, Tate Britain and Bethnal Green Working Men's Club. Hoyle has also made a return to the world of cinema with the award winning film *Uncle David* (2010) (as director), and *Set the Thames on Fire* (2016) as actor. A limited edition book of photographs and artworks produced from a collaboration between Hoyle and photographer Holly Revell, *David Hoyle: Parallel Universe*, was launched in 2017.

David Hoyle was commissioned by Sandy Powell to design the makeup for the performers in *The Featherstonehaughs Draw on the Sketchbooks of Egon Schiele* which he did in response to the Egon Schiele sketchbooks, and the painted suits themselves. The makeup completed the surrealistic painterly nature of the dancing figures in the work. Hoyle subsequently also carried out retouching to the suits when they had become worn, echoing Sandberg's original work.

David Hoyle

Dancer Luca Silvestrini (right) in the press cutting

Dancer who wore the suit

The suit was originally tailored for and worn by *Featherstonehaughs* company member Luca Silvestrini. Born in Italy, Silvestrini graduated in Performing Arts at Bologna University in 1995, and moved to London to complete his dance training at Laban. Silvestrini has worked with a range of choreographers in the UK as a performer, including Maxine Doyle's First Person, Catherine Seymour Dance Company, Lea Anderson, Bock & Vincenzi, Sarah Rubidge, Joanna Portolou and Aletta Collins.

He co-founded Protein Dance in 1997, and became widely known for his choreography - idiosyncratic dance theatre work provoked by deep connections with the everyday. He has worked on large-scale cross-generational and participatory events, including the world record-breaking *Big Dance Class, Eat London* (which won a Visit London Gold Award) and *Big World Dance 2010*, which took place in Trafalgar Square. He has created full-length intergenerational productions in Valenciennes, Athens, Barcelona, London, Turin, Kinosaki (Japan) and Wadebridge (Cornwall); and has taught and presented Protein's participatory work at schools and conferences in Singapore, Spain, Italy and Canada.

In addition to his work for Protein, Luca Silvestrini has created work for the Royal Opera House, Transitions Dance Company, CandoCo, Bare Bones, Intoto, From Here To Maturity, Company of Elders at Sadler's Wells, Sankalpam, HeadSpace Dance, Verge and Sardoville. Theatre and opera credits include work for English National Opera, Theatre Rites, Royal Court Theatre, Duckie and Youth Music Theatre UK. He has won a Jerwood Choreography Award, a Bonnie Bird New Choreography Award and The Place Prize 2006 Audience Award and was one of the first recipients of a Rayne Fellowship for Choreographers (2006).

As performer in *The Featherstonehaughs*, Silvestrini was singled out in press reviews for his nuanced performances, with one critic musing that he bore a marked resemblance to Schiele himself in *The Featherstonehaughs Draw on the Sketchbooks of Egon Schiele*.

227

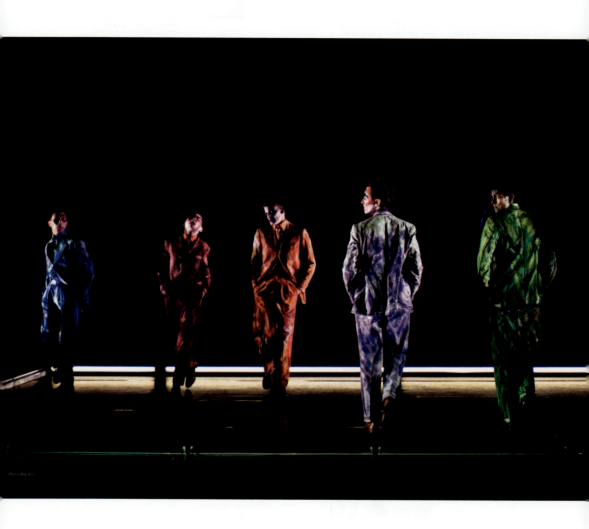

Inn Pang Ooi, Ronny Ming-hei Wong, Ryen Perkins-Gangnes, Sebastian Elias Kurth and Neil Callaghan.
Photo: Pau Ros

Suit photo: Rik Pennington

Notes

1. This brochure was comprised of commissioned photographs taken by photographer Rik Pennington and outlined the details of the provenance of the garment which I had documented as part of my research. The brochure is included at the end of this chapter. I compiled it with the help of designer David Caines.

2. Egon Schiele (1890–1918) was a renowned Viennese Expressionist Painter and protégé of Gustav Klimt.

3. Fashion designers have often drawn either literally or stylistically from visual art. In their 1993 Spring Summer collection, couture designers Dolce & Gabbana created a 'Venus Dress' which featured photo printed sections of Botticelli's *The Birth of Venus*. This dress was exhibited as part of the V&A's 2016 display *Botticelli Reimagined*.

https://www.vam.ac.uk/__data/assets/pdf_file/0018/261801/Botticelli-Reimagined-highlights.pdf (online). Accessed 15 January 2024.

4. The Lost Dances of Egon Schiele (2000) Directed by Lea Anderson and Kevin McKiernan. [Motion Picture, online] London: BBC & Arts Council England.
Available at: https://vimeo.com/129344200. Accessed 5 January 2024.

5. For the reconstruction of the work in 2010, the cast was comprised of: Neil Callaghan, Jacob Ingram-Dodd, Sebastian Elias Kurth, Ronny Ming-Hei Wong, Inn Pang Ooi (replaced by Gary Clarke in the second tour) and Ryen Perkins-Gangnes.

6. The business was established in 1960 as Len Wilton at 52 Berwick Street, London, where it remained for 50 years (eventually moving to 31 Berwick Street in 2010). In 1963 Eddie Kerr joined as an assistant cutter and by 1970 had been made partner, eventually buying the business in 1990. In 1997 Mr Eddie's son, Chris Kerr joined the business as an apprentice cutter under his father's tutelage and took over the business when he retired in 2002. Chris Kerr has cut suits for film and music stars including Brad Pitt, Johnny Depp and Nick Cave (Chris Kerr, online).

7. As with the production of *Smithereens*, no costume bible exists for this work, so some details are remembered or estimated at by the individuals involved in the production.

8. Guerrilla Girls is an anonymous group of feminist, female artists, who work to expose and resist gender and racial discrimination and inequality. The group was formed in 1985 in New York. 'The group employs culture jamming in the form of posters, books, billboards and public appearances to expose discrimination and corruption. To remain anonymous, members don gorilla masks and use pseudonyms that refer to deceased female artists' (TATE, online).

9. Star Wars is a media franchise which began with the original film *Star Wars* created by George Lucas in 1977. The franchise has since expanded into many avenues (theme parks, merchandise, books, etc).

10. In 2023 Powell was awarded an EE Fellowship at the Bafta Film Awards:

https://www.bafta.org/media-centre/press-releases/sandy-powell-to-be-honoured-with-bafta-fellowship. Accessed 15 January 2024.

11. These examples are chosen on the basis that the V&A has acquired or displayed items from famous works such as the Ballets Russes 1909 ballet, *Le Festin* (worn by Vaslav Nijinsky), and costumes designed by Coco Chanel for the 1924 work *Le Train Bleu* (featured in their 2010 exhibition *Diaghilev and the Golden Age of the Ballet Russes, 1909–1929*). There was also a display from 2001 to 2003 in the former V&A Theatre Museum (located in Covent Garden London, 1987–2007) which featured five of Fonteyn's costumes acquired by the V&A at the auction of Fonteyn's estate which took place at Christie's auction house on 12 December, 2000 (christies.com).

12. In early 2024, Sotheby's began operating a Popular Culture department once again.

13. An American online auction platform which facilitates consumer to consumer sales – it was founded in 1995 by Pierre Omidyar and has expanded to become a multinational corporation. www.ebay.co.uk. Accessed 15 January 2024.

14. Stormtroopers are fictional soldiers in the *Star Wars* films and franchise, who wear distinctive white helmets. These helmets are now seen by props and memorabilia experts as highly valuable artefacts for collectors.

15. Elvis Aaron Presley (1935–77), also known as Elvis, was an American singer, musician and actor. He was an iconic performer chiefly associated with Rock and Roll music.

16. James Bond films are a series of spy films (originally based on adaptations of spy novels written by Ian Fleming). The films are made by Eon productions and have been on-going production from 1962 to the present day.

Batman films are based on the fictional superhero Batman originally from American comic books (published by DC comics). There have been a large number of films and TV series based on the character, dating from the 1940s to the present day.

Harry Potter films are adaptations of a series of seven novels by author J. K. Rowling centred on a boy wizard. The subsequent franchise has expanded into a number of derivative productions and associated merchandise.

17. Princess Leia Organa is an iconic character in the *Star Wars* film franchise, originally played by American actress Carrie Fisher.

18. Edith Head (1897–1981) was a famed Hollywood costume designer who collaborated with directors such as Alfred Hitchcock, and was awarded eight Academy Awards (Oscars) during her career.

19. Dutch master painter Rembrandt (1606–69) for example, took on 50 students in his Amsterdam studio during the course of his lifetime. Discussing an iconic painting of Rembrandt's *The Standard Bearer*, of which there are nine variants of the work, John Hawley (Old Masters expert at Christie's auction house) noted that 'works by Rembrandt's pupils were frequently mixed with his own when entering the market, and various names would be posited to anonymous pictures when they changed hands' (Hawley 2018: n.pag.).

20. Fred Wilson (1954–present) is an American artist (who describes himself as being of 'African, Native American, European and Amerindian' descent (TATE online). At the time of writing he is represented by Pace Gallery New York. His quotes here are taken from 'Mining the Museum in Me' which formed part of a publication exploring the practice of collecting, and motivations to collect: *Pictures, Patents, Monkeys and More...On Collecting* edited by Lisa Cohen (2001).

21. In spring 2024, Lea Anderson was contacted by Sandy Powell to enquire about the possibility of acquiring Luca Silvestrini's suit from *The Featherstonehaughs Draw on the Sketchbooks of Egon Schiele* on loan, to use as a costume in an upcoming large budget Hollywood film. At the time of finalising this book, the suit awaits transportation to New York where it may appear in the film. Or, it may not. The after-life of the suit continues, and escapes the capacity of this book to capture it.

Overleaf: *Smithereens* exhibition, studio 1.1 (mask photos): Rik Pennington
Hand in Glove, V&A photos: Pau Ros

Display

If I don't move aside right now, I'm moments away from colliding with the approaching figure clad in Maoist overalls, who stares dead ahead and is taking no prisoners. For the past five minutes myself and my fellow spectators in the V&A's Raphael Court have been standing in a large square configuration, transfixed by the be-suited hip gyrations of several dancers performing *Elvis Legs* (1995) in the space among us. But now the music is scrambling, and out of nowhere it seems the next group of costumed performers are ploughing a determined path through the space, led by the Maoist figure (wearing a costume from Anderson's 1988 work, *Flag*). As if by mass kinaesthetic intuition the crowd shifts to allow the train of dancers through, whereupon they begin a section from *Flesh & Blood* (1989) sheathed in metallic floor-length gowns. This is Lea Anderson's *Hand in Glove* (2016). It is a performed exhibition of costume and it does just that: *performs* the costumes as a constantly evolving tableau which emerges in one area of the gallery only to fade away and be replaced by another troupe of fully costumed performers who have inserted themselves into the scene. Excerpts of work flare into brief cohesive choreographic life and then proceed in an orderly fashion elsewhere. The spectators traverse the gallery following the action where it occurs, and, for the most part, avoiding calamity. At one end, an area nicknamed, by Anderson, *The Beehive* is filled with rails of costumes. Jay Cloth, wardrobe mistress, is in situ here; costumed as the Door Whore from *Russian Roulette* (2008) he oversees the dancers changing in full view of the audience and is constantly at work sorting and replacing costumes on and off the rails. There are also some tall glass cases at this end of the gallery featuring static exhibits of costume accessories including wigs, false breasts and masks. These serve as a kind of lifeless 'wunderkammer' amid the frenzied activity. Items to stare at if you can take your eyes off the performers for a moment, which is no easy task. Over three hundred costumes and accessories from ten of Anderson's works feature in the exhibition. The sign bearers dressed in Maoist overalls patrol the space, holding signs aloft with the title and details of the works being performed. Dancers carve out yet another space to move in as the music echoes throughout the gallery, performed live by Steve Blake, Steve Beresford and Pat Thomas, in addition to recorded soundtracks. There is a feeling of perpetual motion at play and, undeniably, a sense of disappearance too as one set of costumes becomes elided by another before you have quite got to grips with them.

It is an alchemical display of highly choreographed surprises for the spectators, who stand around the edges and inadvertently cast long shadows across the mosaic floor when they walk past the banks of spotlights lined up along the periphery. And all the while, the exalted grandeur of the gallery itself with its aforementioned flooring, arched ceilings and walls of Raphael's Cartoons (1483–1520) provides the quasi-theatrical set, or the visual frame at least, for this distinctive hybrid of performance and exhibition.

The description I have just outlined, written from memory of an event now some years past, attempts to evoke the scene in which I found myself and the ways in which the performed exhibition functioned, technically and evocatively. *Hand in Glove* did something else of crucial interest for this book, however: it made an attempt to circumvent the stasis and severing of performance context which routinely occurs for costumes exhibited in traditional museum settings – trapped behind glass on mannequins, exiled from their theatrical liveness. Furthermore, *Hand in Glove* sought to achieve this circumvention, not by attempting any kind of constructed quasi-wholeness, but by fragmenting the costumes and their works even further. Just as one performance excerpt would find its stride in the gallery space it would sharply disintegrate, supplanted by another excerpt in a radically different choreographic and musical style. The spectators were thus catapulted from Elvis to *Ausdruckstanz* and on to the constructed nakedness of *Yippeee!!! Dead Skins* without time to draw breath. This chopping and changing, all unfolding within a precisely choreographed series of entrances and exits brought the spectator into relation with the costumes, yes, but more significantly, with their inherently fragmented nature. It communicated the sense that there is a catalogue of work on view which traverses different timeframes, aesthetic referents and musical styles – layer upon layer of performative sediment – the archival catalogue, in other words, of longstanding and multi-dimensional companies. A certain curatorial perspective on the archive was illustrated by *Hand in Glove*, that eschews the historical sequencing of display cabinets arranged in chronological order in favour of a choreographic mashup, which implicitly references the ticking past of years and accruing of works by layering them, one on top of another, as a performance rather than a static exhibition.

This chapter looks to *Hand in Glove* as a jumping-off point to explore the concept of display and what that could potentially mean in the wider context of creating alternative after-lives for performance remains. It will begin by looking at exhibitions created by Anderson with *Hand in Glove*, and by myself with the exhibition of Anderson's costumes, *Smithereens: A Collection of Fragments Considered as a Whole*, which I curated in 2021. The concept of display will then be further utilized as a shorthand for describing other modes through which the fabric remains of Anderson's archive can be seen to time-travel and shapeshift into new contexts. This chapter will therefore also include some brief discussion of the further smithereens which Anderson's fabric remains have morphed into: books, for example, and films for exhibition, and as conduits to choreographic reconstruction and remounting. Conceptualized in this fashion, Display serves as the final intervention undertaken with these fabric remains of performance; not as a static endpoint but more as an overarching and ongoing aim of keeping them visible and allowing their afterlives to expand and evolve. Held thus, within a conducive creative frame, they can continue to be refigured as (albeit partial) interlocutors, indicators of stubbornly persistent materialities and pointers to what is missing in terms of their surrounding legacy.

Dead butterflies

It is mid-March 2021 and I'm on the phone to Lea. The wretched one-year anniversary of the beginnings of the COVID-19 pandemic is turning, along with the calendar pages. The pandemic has caused mass loss of life and profound disruption to daily life on a global scale, and on a micro-level it has wrought chaos on the carefully planned infrastructure of my research and gallery exhibition. Exhibitions (my own included) and theatre performances in the United Kingdom are still largely on hold – postponed to an uncertain, imaginal future. Our call attempts to traverse the disorientating terrain of logistical exhibition planning amid wider existential questions concerning the role and function of artefacts and live performance in the current moment (in which museums and theatres are indefinitely closed to the public).[1] We speak of a *Cholmondeleys'* fortieth anniversary book project we have in the works, and of texts written feverishly during the pandemic lockdowns by an associate

Hand in Glove, V&A. Third Year Student Performers from London Contemporary Dance School. Costumes from 3. Photo: Pau Ros

of Lea's who remembers all sorts of details of the surrounding context of early *Cholmondeleys* days. Anecdotes and formative occurrences which had slipped Lea's mind. 'I want to put it all down', she says. 'I want to put the archive out there so it is safe'. The simplicity of this brings me up short. The assertion that by placing the knowledge, the evidence, the archive 'out there', there is a safety mechanism in place. An insurance policy against further and total loss. It is the opposite to the protection afforded by the archival cosseting of a cultural institution. We move on to discuss the recent grave news that the Theatre and Performance holdings at the V&A museum are to be vastly reduced. 'Thank God I never gave them a costume in the end', laughs Lea. This stirs a memory in me of an anecdote she had told me in the earliest days of the project. That the V&A had indeed once approached her about the possibility of her donating some costumes to their Theatre and Performance archive. They had visited the self-same lockup where I had first encountered the costumes. They had remarked on the suits as being a potential acquisition, or maybe a *Smithereens* dress. Initially flattered by the idea, Lea told me she soon had second thoughts.

> That was when I started to think about dead butterflies and whether we need to have them pinned in glass cases in museums [...] I understand it's important to know that a butterfly once existed. But it's not a butterfly anymore.

The outcome of those conversations with the V&A culminated in *Hand in Glove*. Acquisition of costumes was never broached again. At times I think Lea pondered whether she had done the right thing. After all, the V&A – a prestigious institution like that would surely be the absolute safest pair of hands. A refuge for the costumes. Yet this latest news shatters that illusion. Despite the trappings of prestige, the wonderful work rooms, the vast archives, they too are at the mercy of other forces at work: economic, political, sociocultural. Nothing stays the same. No path eludes the material transitions coming incrementally to us all, in the end.

The Latin roots of the term curate ('curatus, past participle of curare, "to take care of"') (Etymonline n.d.: online) can provide some helpful orientation for

Hand in Glove, V&A. Third Year Student Performer from London Contemporary Dance School. Costume from *Yippeee!!!*. Photo: Pau Ros

designing an exhibition of fabric remains. Bearing in mind those unavoidable material transitions and the loss of theatrical context and gradual vanishing of legacy and legibility (as described above) that attend garments such as these, how might one go about curating an exhibition which 'cares' for the costumes? What, in fact, might constitute 'caring' in the context of an archive which is suffering from an ongoing lack of visibility and increasing erasure of performance histories? For Anderson with *Hand in Glove*, the curation became about a bold re-animation of the costumes – putting them at material risk (of damage and further wear and tear) by remounting excerpts of the works and allowing the costumes to *dance* once more, albeit in a different presentational frame. Anderson explains:

> I thought about how once archived, costumes cannot be worn again. They can never be displayed in such a way that the viewer can see how the costume originally worked with the dancer's movements and the theatre lights, how the choreographer originally envisioned it for it to be seen. I got a little sad at my costumes not being seen in the way they were intended to be seen so I asked (Jane Pritchard)[2] [...] if she would ever consider doing a performed exhibition with real dancers. (Anderson 2016: n.pag.)

This curatorial approach opens up a new refiguring for the costumes – as remains of performance – fragmented and reanimated within a representational frame which is neither wholly theatrical nor wholly museological. As such it produces certain gains in terms of liveness and, equally, effects unavoidable alterations to the mode in which the costumes operate.

> **MKC:** Taking into account the performed management of the costumes and the live music etc., how did you feel about putting all of these together in one strange space within the museum?
>
> **LA:** Well it was worrying. There is so much in the exhibition and so much of the theatrical experience is immediately lost. *The Beehive* was an attempt to create the backstage, and Jay being there as wardrobe

Hand in Glove, V&A. Jay Cloth. Costume from *Russian Roulette*. Photo: Pau Ros

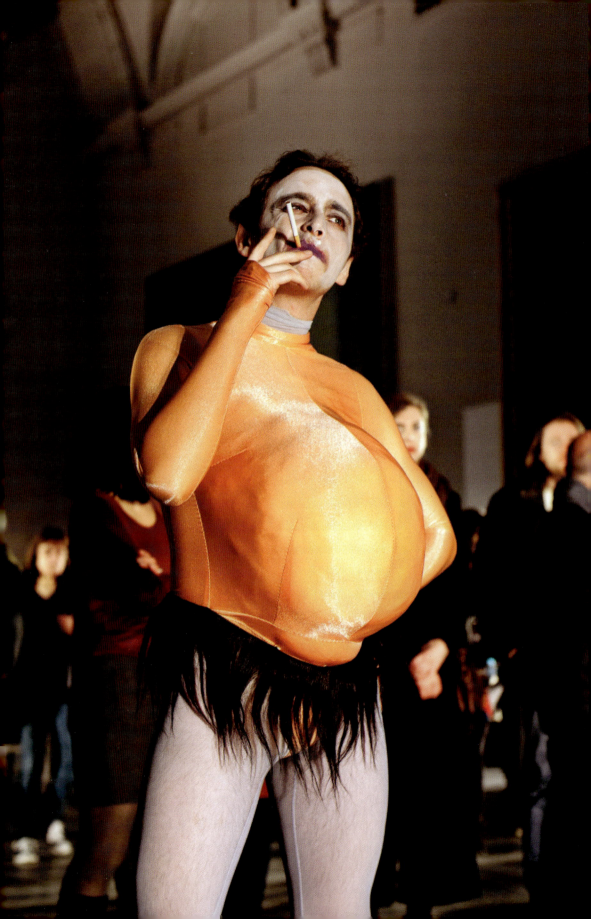

mistress was an attempt to have these things still present, but the meaning is completely different within an exhibition. The audience has more control over how they see it, and view it more in terms of industry. Some things worked – like the torch singer (from *Smithereens* [...]) being pushed along on the box with wheels (where you could see the dancer pushing the box). This worked well but on stage it worked very differently when things were hidden by the lights. But you can't have a show as a *show* in an exhibition.
(Connolly 2017a: 20)

LA: What really worked, and in an unexpected way, was the space. I would never have chosen that gallery, I would never have chosen that kind of grandiose renaissance splendour, with the altar-piece down the end.[...] It was so grand and on such an enormous scale that it gave the exhibition gravitas of a kind that I would never have chosen. But the good thing about such a big room is that it was easy to see the dancers in costume as objects within a space rather than something *about* the space. It wasn't a dance piece that had a relationship with the architecture, it was the context in which the audience viewed it, and it gave it a seriousness and a value that I never thought of. When I look at some of the photographs, I think 'that is really extraordinary'. Actually seeing it in that location and seeing what it brought to it. Having to look at it freshly (rather than my head being full of what I had wanted it to be), that's always a surprise. Realising it is *this* and not what I thought it was.
(Connolly 2017a: 24)

What Anderson signals here in terms of the particular visual relationships which the framing of the gallery space engendered is a significant element of how *Hand in Glove* functioned. In addition to the non-habitual and non-linear ways in which the performed elements of the exhibition conjured the shape of the archive as I have touched on earlier, the excerpts did indeed appear to be rendered as costumed choreographic *objects*.[3] Despite their liveness, they succeeded in functioning as performative artefacts or remains; visibly out of context and not fully recuperated in terms of their original performance lives, but which happened to be populating this temple of museological display at this particular moment. And, indeed, *Hand in Glove* was of a particular

Hand in Glove, V&A. Daniel Hay-Gordon. Costume from *Yippeee!!!*. Photo: Pau Ros moment in time. Once the exhibition ended the costumes returned once more to their archival packing boxes. The remains of the exhibition ended up being much like the ones left after traditional theatre performance: photographs, some video footage, online listings and the odd review. In avoiding the fate of dead butterflies which Anderson feared (with the costumes disappearing into museological storage or permanent static display), the live performed approach to exhibition sacrificed permanence and preservation of the garments in favour of curatorial fidelity to preserving performative liveness as a key element of their presentation.

Smithereens: A Collection of Fragments Considered as a Whole

The exhibition which I went on to curate took a different approach. Faced with the inherently partial and potentially ineloquent nature of these performance remains, my curation nonetheless held a similar instinct to Anderson's with *Hand in Glove* for using fragmentation as a means of illustrating the losses which these fabric shards point us towards, and expanding their potential for reimagining. I was conscious of the context in which I was operating – that of a largely invisible archive of fabric remains with limited funding and a small gallery space in which to work. Like the interventions of Disintegration, Preservation and Transaction which precede this one, I therefore go on to adopt an up close hands-on approach which looks to investigate ideas of visibility, legacy and material reality through 'doing things' with the costumes. In this case, as a means of opening them up to the public via display and dissemination.

The fundamental curatorial principle of 'taking care' of these fabric remains might seem at odds with my research methodology which has included active attempts to accelerate the material destruction of an artefact. However, in seeking to make visible within the gallery, the seemingly invisible forces at work in the after-lives of these garments, the exhibition is also putting forward alternative after-lives which respond to their material reality. My curatorial role is therefore bound up with the continual progression of their after-lives, as opposed to any imagined endpoint of achieving a gallery display. The exhibition, *Smithereens: A Collection of Fragments Considered as a Whole* (2021) represents another stage along the journey these artefacts are making into the imagined future.

The impulses at work in my selection of items for exhibition is not influenced solely by aesthetic or visually impactful grounds, but rather attempts to articulate the diffuse and shape-shifting nature of these smithereens. The curatorial choices arise from my material interactions with the costumes, their performance histories and their material nature. The exhibition also draws inspiration from a diverse collection of sources – musical, visual and textual – many of which have already been touched upon in the previous chapters: fleeting memories, images obscured by the passage of time, the snatched refrains of half-remembered tunes. In addition to these fragments, I find myself returning to the thematics of the ghost in my curatorial choices. I wish to highlight the layers of history, physical clues, traces of reciprocal bodily relationships and evidence of labour and craft (all as discovered during the interventions already carried out) in my display of the costumes. Ghosts and haunting provide helpful means of inculcating a specific kind of looking and *being-with* the materials in the gallery. Thematically housed within a framework of *conjuring a haunting through material encounter*, the exhibition looks to direct the gallery visitor's attention towards the traces and residues bound up in the costumes, and to approach these fabric remains as partial interlocutors of a somewhat obscured legacy.

Georgina Guy's book *Theatre, Exhibition, and Curation: Displayed & Performed* (2016) provides a nuanced investigation of the interplays and relations which arise between performance and display enacted within a gallery space. The ways, for example, in which 'Presenting what the gallery first seems unable to contain, the object lost or the performance past, exhibition events which operate in dialogue with performance [...] are specifically concerned with reimagining how the latter might function within contexts of display' (Guy 2016: 70). This could certainly be seen as a key element of how *Hand in Glove* operated within the V&A's Raphael Court. Guy is particularly engaged with exhibitions (such as Tate Modern, London's 2007 exhibition *The World Is a Stage*), which

> trouble models of performance founded on ephemerality. They exceed the form of the static object in perpetual display and the disappearing performance and might, therefore, be understood as expressions which

Hand in Glove, V&A. Third Year Student Performers from London Contemporary Dance School. Costumes from *Smithereens*. Photo: Pau Ros

Hand in Glove, V&A. Third Year Student Performers from London Contemporary Dance School. Costumes from *Russian Roulette*. Photo: Pau Ros

Hand in Glove, V&A. Third Year Student Performers from London Contemporary Dance School. Costumes from *Yippeee!!!*. Photo: Pau Ros

operate beyond both performed modes and object-centric display practices by occupying their interstice.
(Guy 2016: 24)

The exhibitions explored in Guy's book often take place in the blank white space of the contemporary gallery, as indeed did my own exhibition. This was in stark contrast to viewing the costumes amid the opulence of *Hand in Glove*'s museum setting. *Smithereens: A Collection of Fragments Considered as a Whole* was developed as a progression from my earliest encounters with the garments in the archive and the hands-on operations which were subsequently carried out. Whilst it was being mounted in a small white space venue (studio 1.1, London), I was nonetheless influenced by exhibitions such as *Hand in Glove* and other, more traditional largescale costume exhibitions mounted in costume/dress/performance-museum settings. In these ways my exhibition inhabited, if not an interstice, then certainly an odd netherworld between traditional costume and performance displays and the contemporary anonymity of a white-walled art space in which performance sometimes takes place.

Residues and ghosts on display

It seems helpful at this point to briefly survey some of those exhibitions which served as inspirational touchstones, or more accurately, dialogic counterparts for the ways in which I went about curating my own small-scale exhibition. Many of them deal thematically with haunting or residues of performance and the past lives of historical or well-worn garments. I was searching in this survey of adjacent exhibitions for ways in which haunting could be used as a refraction and curatorial invitation for encounter with a fractured set of fabric remains. 'Perhaps all costumes are for ghosts in one way or another?' suggests Aoife Monks in the epilogue of her book *The Actor in Costume* (Monks 2010: 141). Monks' chapter devoted to 'Dressing the Immaterial' traverses the ways in which costumes are unavoidably entangled with ghosts, ranging from the costume dilemmas which staging theatrical ghosts engender, to the hauntedness of costumes more broadly. Drawing on the work of Barbara Hodgdon (2006) to describe the liminal state of costumes post-performance as being in a way 'un-dead', Monks argues that 'Ghosts don't only appear onstage in armour; sometimes they haunt the theatre archive and museum in the form of leftover costume' (Monks 2010: 140).

Alongside the theoretical conceptions of haunting and the uncanny nature of costumes, the notion of garments as haunting or laying bare an absence (that of the body or the performance in which it lived) has been explored in various ways by fashion and dress curators. Exhibitions such as *Spectres: When Fashion Turns Back* (Victoria and Albert Museum, 2004–05), curated by Judith Clark, pivoted on the idea of 'recent fashion's haunting by history' (Clark 2005). Alongside exploring historical influences evident in contemporary garments, the exhibition's curation also employed imagery of haunting as a central visual effect. Shadows, partial face masks and low lighting evoked a sense of the garments themselves being haunted, enfolding traces of the past. This drawing attention to absence or the unseen (the phantoms of the physical bodies who made the garments and wore them) can be seen echoed in a number of fashion and dress exhibitions. Clark's subsequent curation of *The Concise Dictionary of Dress* at the Conservation Archives of the V&A Museum (at Blythe House, 2010) evoked absent physical forms and garments by exhibiting a wall into which garments had been moulded, leaving only their imprint (Clark and Phillips 2010). Although the imagery of haunting was employed to dramatic effect in both these exhibitions, it was deployed as a means of focusing on the ways in which previous fashions are reincarnated within contemporary design, and the conceptual absences evoked by garments.

Olivier Saillard has similarly drawn attention to the traces of the past enmeshed in garments, exploring alternative ways of exhibiting fashion and dress in his curatorial approach. Of most relevance to this research, in 2012 Saillard created *The Impossible Wardrobe*, performed at the Palais de Tokyo in Paris, which saw the actress Tilda Swinton perform with a range of garments from the historic archives of the Galliera (Paris museum of Fashion). Swinton carried, but never wore, garments ranging from a Coco Chanel designed tweed suit to a military jacket worn by Napoleon Bonaparte, interacting with the garments through actions such as smelling the jacket, or holding the tweed suit on hangers bunched at her hips, giving the illusion of a skirt (Saillard and Swinton 2015). Eschewing the traditional format of fashion exhibitions (which tend to be static and use mannequins), Saillard's curation gestured towards the presence of history within garments, the fragility of their material state, and the ways in which the body interacted with the garment in its lifetime. The use of Swinton's body was indeed innovative, but similarly the exhibition operated within a differing historical frame of reference to this book, handling the garments as objects of social and design history rather than investigating costumes within performance legacies.

Whilst scholars and curators involved with fashion and dress have approached the theorizing and display of garments in extended ways, the archival context of dance costumes (within larger museums, to-date) appears to operate within a mainly conventional museological format. Costumes, usually deemed historically valuable or rich in craftsmanship, and in the main from 'iconic' companies/performances are preserved within protected museum archives (such as the V&A) and exhibited in static formats (on mannequins in glass cases), as part of larger exhibitions of performance ephemera. The V&A's 2010 *Diaghilev and the Golden Age of the Ballets Russes 1909–1929*, which featured a large number of costumes worn by famous dancers such as Vaslav Nijinsky, is an illustrative example. Whilst undoubtedly much care was taken in the preservation and display of these items, there was little interrogation of the relationships between costume and dancing body. The popularity of this exhibition demonstrated the evocative power of performance ephemera to conjure narratives of performance and operate as totems or sacred relics within the mythology of performance. Encountering an elaborate beaded tunic worn by Nijinsky for example, enables the viewer to imagine the proportions and contours of Nijinsky's body. The sweat stains and evidence of repairs or alterations provide clues as to the labour and craft of performance. The trace remains held in the garments bring forth a particular narrative pertaining to the work which they were made for, and the body/bodies that inhabited them. Engaging with the garment in this way reveals a series of residues which can be contextualized within a wider framework, to articulate untold knowledge and reveal the ways in which costumes can be considered to haunt the stage post-performance. Looking at a costume known to be worn by Nijinsky, the viewer inescapably becomes conscious of Nijinsky's absence, regardless of curatorial intention of how to display the garment (as an object of craft for example, rather than a disembodied 'haunted' body). In the case of costumes worn by less well known or unknown performers however, this absence and haunted-ness may be less apparent to the viewer.

A smaller scale exhibition, *Present Imperfect: Disorderly Apparel Reconfigured*, exhibited at The Fashion Space Gallery, London College of Fashion (May 2017, curated by Amy De La Haye and Jeffrey Horsley), demonstrated extended possibilities both for exhibiting apparel that is worn or perished, and the potential for displaying dance costumes in inventive ways. The exhibition featured a costume designed by Suzanne Gallo, from a 1992 dance work *Touchbase*, which choreographer Merce Cunningham created for *Ballet Rambert*. The costume was comprised of a plain white sleeveless t-shirt sewn onto leotard pants. It showed obvious signs of wear and bore the crumpled handwritten name label of the dancer who wore it in the original work (Paul Old). In setting out to display this garment, De La Haye and Horsley laid it in an exhibition case which featured a life-size indent of a male dancer's body (created through scanning and laser-cutting). The costume was laid flat over this imprint, and underneath the glass case a recording of Merce Cunningham's voice as he taught company class could be faintly heard. The composition of this display immediately alerted the viewer to the absences which this flat, rather unprepossessing garment pointed towards. Alongside the material traces indelibly left in the fabric itself, the costume was positioned as interlocutor, conjuring up apparitions of absent choreographer, dancer and maker. The intentional highlighting of these aspects by the curators reflects a differing approach to that of exhibitions where the dislocated nature of the empty costume is papered over with the elegance and polish of the display of costume-as-object. However, despite the curatorial gesture towards the absent dancer's body and choreographer, *Present Imperfect* was unable to engage with the role of choreography in the history of the costume. The costume was exhibited as a standalone item within a costume and dress exhibition which disallowed any opportunity to compare several costumes from different works or pay close attention to the traces of choreography left on the garment. It has been an aspiration of the research in this book that close photographic documentation of the costumes in their current material states and in-depth interviews with dancers and choreographer might give clues as to particular elements of choreography or reciprocal relationships between choreography and costume which can then be traced within the garments themselves.

In a slightly different vein, but nonetheless of relevance aesthetically speaking, to my exploration of residues and ghosts on display, is visual artist Anselm Kiefer's exhibition *Walhalla* (White Cube London, 2016–17). This exhibition featured large scale sculpture and installation alongside paintings. The title referred to 'the mythical place in Norse mythology, a paradise for those slain in battle, as well as to the Walhalla neo-classical monument, built by Ludwig I King of Bavaria in 1842 to honour heroic figures in German history' (White Cube 2017). *Walhalla* evoked ideas of war, destruction and the detritus left behind. It featured a stark room akin to a field hospital with rows of beds. Of particular significance were two installations featuring items of clothing. One: a spiral staircase reaching to the ceiling on which clothes had been hung on hangers. Another: a large glass case filled with a rail of ceremonial garments. Frozen in arrested motion, the garments hung in a row. Christening robes and wedding dresses alike were all covered with a heavy impasto of paint, rubble, dust and in some instances, stains like rust and blood. Despite the substantial covering on the garments, the lace detailing and youthful/virginal connotations of them was unmistakable. One very large wedding dress flared at the bottom as if caught in movement – blown by wind, or billowed out by a bride running. The motion suggested by the garments was thus exaggerated by their entrapment.

The airlessness of the cabinet and suffocating failure of the garments (which ordinarily should float in a breeze) to move in any way, was staggering. This, and the name tags hanging from each garment spoke unavoidably of death, of life cut short; extinguished mid-breath. They were strongly evocative of the traces left in a garment. In creating a physical body (through the stiffening and encasement of the dress in paint), there was a sense of a hollow body 'standing-in' for the human one which had been obliterated in some way. This imagery, in addition to the expanded notions of display in exhibitions curated by Saillard and Clark, suggests creative possibilities for the ways in which costumes (post-performance) can potentially re-assert their visibility as fabric remnants of performance.

Anderson's costumes, if we follow the conceptual trends outlined so far, would require quite a particular curatorial gesture towards residues and haunting – one which specifically addresses the concerns of her archive and the wider aspirations of this project. Deploying the ghost as a curatorial theme can potentially be regarded as a conduit to foregrounding the visibility of these performance remains and gesturing towards the surrounding losses of performative context and erasure of legacy which attend them. This is realized via a continual fracturing, dispersal and display of archival fragments. Ghosts, or enacting a haunting is therefore used in my exhibition as a thematic strategy for directing the focus towards the materials at hand in their damaged, multi-layered and splintered materiality. The close encounters and alternative after-lives carried out in this project seek to develop costume as a site for interrogation via physical interactions and, also, to create alternative archival remnants. *Smithereens*, the gallery exhibition, carries forward these aims via multi-modal displays involving the costumes (Dead Skins, silver shoes and pubic hair from *Yippeee!!!*, the purple suit from *The Featherstonehaughs Draw on the Sketchbooks of Egon Schiele* and the *Smithereens* masks) alongside photographs and the short films made as part of the Disintegration and Preservation interventions. Enacting a haunting in the context of the exhibition provides a lens through which the gallery visitor might encounter these smithereens and the fractured histories which I am attempting to illuminate.

Despite this utilization of the ghost as a curatorial strategy, I haven't wished to wholly emulate a constructed haunted narrative – rather, I hope that the garments themselves can unfold these associations in their smallness, their decrepitude, and the minutiae of their physical details. A low-budget exhibition such as mine cannot afford the prestige effects of lighting and vast gallery space. It can, however, provide an intimacy of encounter with the objects rarely afforded in high-status venues. In this way, the uncanny nature of the fabric remains do not need amelioration. Their placement within a small gallery space which allows for a close reading of them does its own work. The intricacies of performance histories etched within smears of makeup, scrawled name tags and blobs of glue can be seen up close, alongside the inherent stillness of objects which once vibrated with the frenzy and peril of live performance.

On reverie and return

Adrian Heathfield, reflecting on the relations between museums, curatorial practice and live art, in dialogue with Branislava Kuburović, describes how he uses the work of Gaston Bachelard to think through the concept of reverie. 'a reverie is a reactivation of something nascent, unresolved or unassimilated in past experience, a revival of sorts. It's a return, release, and transformation of a buried or implicit historical force: a once felt-thought' (Heathfield and Kuburović 2016: 205). This sense of reverie speaks to the strategies underpinning the exhibition curation of Anderson's costumes. If 'spectacular' and closed narratives of performance and costume histories are to be avoided, then perhaps the partial nature of costume fragments (with their awkward material realities) can invite a spectatorship bound up with reverie. A return of sorts, but an implicitly incomplete one – an after-life, rather than a *remounting* of works already past.

Discussing his staging of a fashion and performance installation *Fashioning Embodiment* (2013) with designer Flora Zeta Cheong-Leen, Johan Stjernholm relates the use of visual repetition in the scenography of the exhibition to concepts of permeation and folding (borrowing from the work of Deleuze [2004; 2006]). Stjernholm argues that:

> [t]he process of permeation does not necessarily stop at my encounter with the fashion artifact. The curation of the exhibition allowed the visitors to study the exhibited artifacts in detail and close-up. Assuming again that I perceive a certain artifact as an instance of a series that permeates back to the dance [already seen in the installation]: If I were to take my time to study that artifact in more detail, additional layers of the design may start to take on connotative meaning to me [...] In this case, the details of the dress – [...] – begin to generate a much more complex series of incomplete narratives, microcosms of connotative meaning, where fragments of my past, perceptions of the world, and imagination all start to permeate and conflate in a multiplicity of directions.
> (Stjernholm 2019: 369)

The permeation and refraction of differing narratives and perception at work in the moment of encounter with the artefact Stjernholm describes, seems somewhat aligned to the idea of Simmel's 'echo', touched upon in Transaction (Simmel [1900] 2004: 73). For Simmel, the echo occurs due to an object having previously provided 'great pleasure or advantage', and he suggests that such remembered pleasure will evoke 'a feeling of joy at every later viewing of this object, even if any use or enjoyment is now out of the question' (Simmel [1900] 2004: 73). Whilst Simmel is relating these ideas to the perceived value of an object, and Stjernholm is unpicking the complex interplay of perception in the moment of encounter within the museum, these two perspectives are nonetheless helpful in considering how Anderson's costume objects might operate within a gallery exhibition. There is an implicit aim of inculcating a sense of reverie in the gallery visitor; allowing space for the permeation and refractions which Stjernholm describes to unfold, along with echoes and embodied memories which gallery visitors might hold in relation to experiencing the original performances in which these costumes lived.

The curation of the exhibition has also been influenced by an 'in-conversation' exchange I took part in with curator Jeffrey Horsley for an article published in *Studies in Costume and Performance*, 2018. We were discussing my research on Anderson's archive, in particular the Dead Skin costumes, and his work with Amy De La Haye on the curation of the 2017 exhibition *Present Imperfect: Disorderly Apparel Reconfigured* exhibited at The Fashion Space Gallery, London College of Fashion. I was particularly struck by Horsley's curatorial strategy (influenced by his work as a theatre designer) of responding associatively to an object, rather than being guided by the need to ensure legibility of the object. This associative approach was influential in the display of a partially burnt pair of eighteenth-century woman's kid leather gloves. Due to the singeing on the edges of the gloves they were neither aesthetically pleasing to look at, nor an intact example of a historical garment:

> with the gloves, it was an instant reaction for me – an instant reaction to think about how that singeing had happened on the glove. Why was it just around that top edge around the wrist? Why was the glove not burnt in its entirety? I guess as well I've got quite a visual mind and so I saw the glove, and instantly in my mind, saw images from Hitchcock's *Rebecca* (1940). It was an immediate connection! It was extraordinary to have those conversations with Amy, and for us then to decide as a team that, yes, we would follow that through because in many ways its very 'un-museum-like'. It's not a museum strategy to go off on this narrative path that is actually an invention around the object.
> (Horsley and Connolly 2018: 84)

Horsley cited a further source of inspiration – a catalogue essay by Michelle Nicol, in which Nicol described the curation of a Bernard Wilhelm exhibition as having assembled the objects as 'intelligent particles' (Nicol 2005: 228–30).

> And I thought I love this idea that when you go into an exhibition space everything is an intelligent particle. Whether it's the display case, whether it's the museum object, whether it's the chairs that have been put in there, whether it's the fire extinguisher in the corner. And I like this idea of particles as active things that vibrate and the vibration creates some kind of meaning. I guess when you were talking about Lea Anderson's costume as being part of a component part of performance, I would see that costume as one intelligent particle that aligns with lots of other intelligent particles in a particular situation.
> (Horsley and Connolly 2018: 85)

This image of particles has remained at the forefront of my thinking in conceiving the exhibition as a whole. The sense of a number of diffuse fragments which produce a series of meanings, both individually and through their interaction with each other and the space around them. This is helpfully conversant with the aim of allowing the incomplete nature of the items on display to be foregrounded in their presentation. Allowing them to refract and reflect back the partial histories which inhabit their material remains.

Musical influences

The musical scores from Anderson's works have also provided specific inspiration for the formation of the exhibition. The original scores of *Yippeee!!!* (2006) and *Smithereens* (1999) composed by Steve Blake are particularly significant – both in the stylistic features of the music and the fact that they provide the soundtracks to the two short films I created for the exhibition. Both of these musical scores operate in the realm of the liminal and the sentiment of reverie. Seemingly familiar refrains of music heralding from the era of Weimar cabaret echo throughout *Smithereens* – melodic enough just to catch the ear, before warping into discordant oblivion. The train of musical thought in both scores becomes repeatedly fragmented and thus complicated. They operate in the nether world of half-remembered melodies, yet disavow the opportunity for uncomplicated escapism and sentimentality. Within the original performances they provided a vital element in the creation of unsettling vignettes – the rictussed smiling showgirls of *Yippeee!!!* and the darkness of the failed cabaret acts in *Smithereens*. For the exhibition, the presence of the scores in the films provide an evocation of the original works, but furthermore, they successfully complicate the imagery of the films – illuminating once again the sense of the costumes being only one fragment of a wider absence of the work as a whole.

Selecting materials

The prospect of distilling the materials for display from the full collection of costumes and masks proves useful in clarifying the motivations behind the role of the exhibition within the wider alternative costume after-lives being created. As already outlined, there is a distinct aim of facilitating a close reading of the objects and allowing the complications of their materiality and partial nature to be foregrounded through their presentation. I realize on reflection, that there is also a discreet desire to somehow reflect the nature of my early encounters with the costumes in the lock-up. The ways in which those first lockup visits engendered a fundamental position towards the objects which was adopted more formally as the research progressed – that of encounter, listening and close reading.

The manner in which the dancers and makers spoke to the costumes, and more specifically, to the histories therein, seems key in my consideration. Trying on her mask nearly twenty years after she performed in the original production of *Smithereens* (1999), dancer Anna Pons Carrera remarks:

> Amazing […] it's so funny because it really is one of the glorious things about performance isn't it, that it's timeless. When you are there, time doesn't matter […] the relativity of time becomes very apparent in your experience. I feel like it could have been last year that we did [the show] – for me as far as I'm concerned, we could do it again next year!
> (Pons Carrera 2018: n.pag.)

The interviews with the creative individuals bound up with these fabric remains emphasize to me the ways in which they live on – as ciphers for memories and performances now vanished. The 'backstage' details betrayed by seeing the costumes at close quarters can be highlighted as an evocative site of memory rather than the diminishing of an illusion originally created by the costume when viewed onstage in performance. With these concerns in mind, assessing the items for inclusion in the gallery exhibition cannot be done on a hierarchical basis, or based on aesthetic merit and visual impact. Each item in and of itself is considered highly valuable within this context. There is an inherent risk in this approach of descending into Warholian levels of cataloguing and inclusion for display. Andy Warhol was famed for his creation of 'time capsules' – putting everything that had passed through his hands for a month into a labelled box and sending it away to a storage facility (Wollen 1993). Discussing Warhol's predilection for hoarding and collecting, Peter Wollen noted parallels between Warhol's non-hierarchical approach to storage and refusal to edit (films or audio recordings, for example), and that of composer John Cage in his compositions.

> For Cage, this refusal of selectivity had both an aesthetic and a spiritual, quasi-religious foundation, but with Warhol we can sense another dimension, a more social and psychological fear of rejection, which could express itself in the attempt to reintegrate the rejected.
> (Wollen 1993: 69)

Wollen cites examples of this non-selectivity such as when Warhol curated an exhibition in 1969 from the storage vaults of the Museum of Art at the Rhode Island School of Design:

> Back in his office, Robbins [the museum director] informed the curator of the costume collection that Warhol wanted to borrow the entire shoe collection. 'Well, you don't want it all', she told Warhol in a somewhat disciplinarian tone, 'because there's some duplication'. Warhol raised his eyebrows and blinked. In fact he wanted all the shoes, all the hatboxes (without taking the hats out), all the American Indian baskets and ceramics, all the parasols and umbrellas, all the Windsor chairs, and so on. 'All of them – just like that'.
> (Raid the Icebox [1969] in Wollen 1993: 66)

Wollen also suggested that Warhol's affection for the individuals associated with his famed 'Factory' in the 1960s also stemmed from this desire to 'reintegrate the rejected' (Wollen 1993: 66). He cites Warhol's saying 'the people I loved were [...] the leftovers of show business turned down at auditions all over town' (Warhol cited in Wollen 1993: 69). The line which Wollen draws between a non-hierarchical appreciation of material artefacts and a desire to celebrate the oft maligned or invisible, somehow resonates with my process of thinking through the mechanics of display for my exhibition. I am highly aware that the initial motivations behind this project have been to bring visibility to artefacts of performances now gone, and to allow an alternative after-life for these smithereens which runs counter to the exclusions of traditional archival, economic and museological contexts.

studio 1.1 gallery exterior. Photo: Mary Kate Connolly
Smithereens: A Collection of Fragments Considered as a Whole Private View, studio 1.1. Photo: Rik Pennington

260

Jay Cloth as Door Whore, *Smithereens* Exhibition Private View. Photo: Rik Pennington

Smithereens: A Collection of Fragments Considered as a Whole
Gallery exhibition
studio 1.1 gallery, Shoreditch
October 2021

It's early evening when you approach the gallery. Sun seeping through the gaps between the buildings of Redchurch St in East London. Yellow glow ebbing fast now, motoring on towards dusk. And it's cold. It has been in full swing for over an hour now, it's probably safe to assume that the early awkwardness greeting the first arrivals will have disappeared by this stage. There should be more of a crowd.

The location is betrayed by the minglers on the pavement – a small island of bodies on an otherwise quiet street. It is not possible to see the door from this initial vantage point. Soon, though, the distance is eaten up by your footsteps and the metal bars on the small window by the entry come into view. They seem somehow comical, these fortifications, set as they are onto the windows of a small ramshackle gallery. As the entryway draws closer, so too does the noise of the event, seeping outwards onto the pavement. The muffled hubbub of voices, some seemingly scratchy refrains of music which sound as if they can only be playing on a gramophone. The self-conscious choreography of people coming together plays out; the angled heads in thought, the emphatic nods of deep conversation, the air kisses of constructed familiarity.

At the doorway you come up abruptly against a figure, somewhat oval in shape, swathed in layers of flesh coloured fishnet mesh, appearing to peer in your direction, though it is impossible to tell, as, in lieu of a face there is only a mirror – it is your own perplexed reflection staring back which greets you. The figure turns, hunched, and sidesteps to make a turn inwards, back towards the gallery. The initial jolt of strangeness is assembling into coherence now – it is a figure in costume. Next there is the troubling fabric and tendrils of black hair which greet you. Obscuring your view, obstructing your entrance through the doorway. It seems that you will be forced to push through these dangling swathes which have been suspended from the ceiling, billowing downwards like inflated pillows; here a sleeve, there a row of poppered buttons. They are made from a slinky also meshy fabric that is blue. Or purple? They're faded. As you brush through them, they feel appealing and disgusting somehow, at the same time.

Smithereens masks on display with performer in costume from *Yippeee!!!*. Photo: Rik Pennington
Disintegration photographs and Dead Skins on display. Photo: Rik Pennington

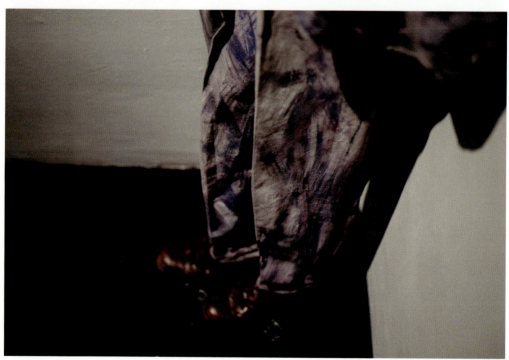

Dead Skins, pubic wigs and silver dancing shoes from *Yippeee!!!*. Photo: Rik Pennington
Schiele suit on display. Photo: Rik Pennington

It seems there are other costumed figures hovering on the fringes of the spectacle which greets you: a baboon squats on the floor with cocked head, and what appears to be a moving curtain edges its way elegantly along one wall, human arms protruding from it in a strange port de bras. There are exhibition catalogues, glasses of refreshments lined on a nearby table. All the usual armouries of the private view seem to be in attendance. Black concrete floor, white walls, uniform only in their imperfections – adorned with scuffs, cracks, minor holes. And yet, undeniably they state Gallery in their specificity of purpose. The lighting is softer than you might have imagined. Small uplighters punctuate the walls at intervals. There are words stencilled on to the wall to your left. Something about fragments, rupture, ghosts. Moving around to the right allows you to see that these suspended fabric bodies have been strung out across the ceiling, floating in limbo, covering most of the available area and snaking around the fluorescent strip lights.

Two television sets, vintage unknown but they are old and small with those slightly curved screens, sit atop white wooden plinths. Headphones hang expectantly alongside them. You recognize the fabric on the screen, and tight corkscrew curls of hair, as those that hang around you in the space. There are two short films to watch.

Photographs populate the space. Some large, unframed on thin boards filling one wall in its entirety. Some small and square, affixed to the wall in a long stiff paper concertina. Each photo angling towards the wall and away again, towards and away, as the concertina stretches out like a packet of postcards – the kind sold on racks outside souvenir shops of Continental Europe in a bygone age. In the catalogue which you hold in your hands, these pictures are also printed. Alongside the usual bumpf of biographical details and further musings on smithereens. But there are other images too – of performances now gone, in which you can recognize the costumes as being those around you. But how different they look in the publicity shots. Snatched moments of performance in flight.

There is a heavy black velvet curtain along one wall. Other than a sign telling patrons to watch their step, there is no other information. It is a touch precarious manoeuvring the curtain aside in order to slip through to the other side. One step down you go, plunged into relative darkness with dazzling spotlight beams momentarily disorientating you. A slight falter as you pass over the threshold, then you're in, and things settle as your eyes slowly adjust to the small space around you. It is even smaller than what has come before. Dark, save for those slightly blinding shafts of light streaming upwards from the floor. In the centre of the room there is movement. A large suspended structure like a child's mobile. Suspended as if in thin air, masks hang by single threads from flexing rods of bamboo. Slowly, slowly, the whole structure rotates. Round and round go the masks, bobbing slightly, their death mask shadows bobbing alongside them, traversing the walls of the space, catching the front of your jacket, the flesh of your hands. The shadows' journey across the walls alerts you to the presence of more masks – white ones, gaudily painted ones, collaged ones. They seem to be mounted in one continuous line along the walls at eye level. Mute and still as sentries. Keeping watch over the shadow dance taking place at the centre of the space. It is mesmerizing to watch, this steady, processional movement. Slightly mechanized in its uniformity of speed, and yet every now and then the new arrival of an onlooker or minor jostling for space amongst the visitors sets the masks moving with a sense of chaos. They seem abruptly, startlingly brought to life then; unpredictable. All of a sudden unknowable, uncanny. One more visitor through the curtain, and it is time to leave. There is no longer enough room for everybody. You push on, back through the curtain to the now seemingly garish light of the main gallery space with its suspended hollow fabric bodies, its images on the walls, a painted suit held up by rods in one corner of the space like the stick body from a game of hangman, the bustle of people. The smithereens.

Smithereens Exhibition Private View. Lewis Sharp in costume from *Yippeee!!!*. Photo: Rik Pennington
Smithereens Exhibition Private View. Elisa Vassena in costume from *Yippeee!!!*. Photo: Rik Pennington

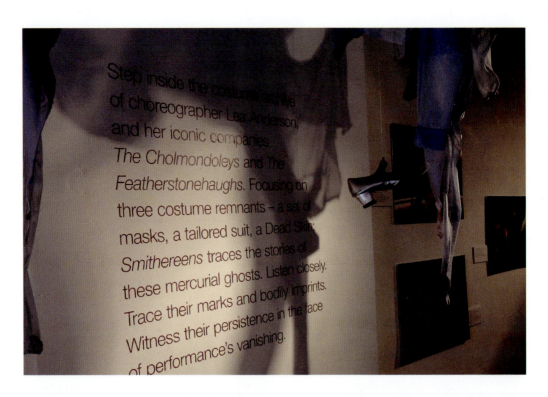

Smithereens Exhibition interpretation and Disintegration photographs on display. Photos: Rik Pennington

Smithereens masks on display with Stella Papi in costume from *Yippeee!!!*. Photos: Rik Pennington

This chapter has already questioned what might constitute 'caring' for the fabric remains of Anderson's archive in an exhibition context, and it has described two contrasting strategies to answer that question in the form of *Hand in Glove* (2016) and *Smithereens: A Collection of Fragments Considered as a Whole* (2021). Display, though, in the context of creating alternative afterlives for costume fragments can be considered not only in terms of gallery presentation, but in other forms of dissemination and fracturing. Replication, time-travel, transitions between material forms (from fabric to filmic, for example) can all be seen as constituting a continued attempt to articulate these smithereens within a representational frame, and in doing so, to persistently gesture towards the ruptured legacies which stand behind them. In light of this, I would like now to mention briefly the other provocations or calls to action which *doing-things* with the costume archive has given rise to in the context of Anderson's archive. It seems that the physical interventions which I undertook, borne out of the very pragmatic dilemma of the archive as outlined by Anderson, and the possible avenues to be explored – for creative destruction of performance detritus, careful preservation of totemic artefacts and transactional exchange of garments – somehow set in motion an evolving new perspective on the archive and suggested new ways forward for Anderson, towards representational repair and renewed visibility.

This book arguably stands as a first example of representational repair, but so too does a second book which I am currently developing with Anderson – an image-led celebratory publication incorporating the full catalogue of *Cholmondeleys* and *Featherstonehaughs* works stretching back across the 40 years which the book will commemorate. The crowdfunding campaign which has been used to fund this second book serves as illustrative testimony to the renewed awareness of, and support for the companies. It has been in the assembling of materials for both these publications that things have begun to get out of hand. During this period Anderson and I are to be found, not only lifting aged garments out of packing boxes, but also rifling through the paper archive; reading playbills, letters, handwritten notes, receipts for dance shoes. Then there are all the musical and film recordings in various antiquated analogue forms which we puzzle over and sort. Once more the uncomfortable question surfaces: what to do? What to do with all of this *stuff*? Attempting to find another partial answer to this dilemma we begin riffing on the concept of smithereens and the continued dispersal of fragments of performance.

We come up with a concept of viral archival droplets: short films which can incorporate interviews, images from the archive, music, and which will begin to populate the pages of Anderson's social media pages and replicate across platforms. This will serve as an alternative thread of archiving and putting information and imagery 'out there' in the public domain (as Anderson had wished to do back in 2021 when we spoke on the phone – an insurance policy against total erasure). Together with Steve Blake, Anderson begins to make these archival droplets and indeed they arise directly from, and speak back to, the archive – the times in which the *Cholmondeleys* performances were made, the artistic, social and cultural milieu that surrounded the work. The time-travelling that the performances did, and, in their fractured remains, still do, somehow. Old bus ticket stubs and Edinburgh festival playbills crop up in these short clips, alongside performance photographs, newspaper headlines from the 1980s and footage of the costume lockup as it is now, sound-tracked by snippets of conversation between Anderson and Blake, and the original show soundtracks.[4]

These archival droplets play with the idea of ever further fragmentation, followed by the crossover contagion and morphing of materials from the archive into something new, via their combination. All the material remains in the archive are considered admissible or up-for-grabs for this new endeavour. Gradually, this vein of work begins to suggest itself as a new pathway forward, or even a new form of intervention with the costumes. It is different from the streamlined themes of Disintegration, Preservation, Transaction and Display, but perhaps in some ways it emerges from these discreet operations as a natural progression – a tacit embracing of incompleteness, material transition and unavoidable contextual losses along the way, but which nonetheless presses on, gaining further visibility with each new form. Following on from the archival droplets, Anderson begins to develop plans for choreographic reconstructions, utilizing the costumes as key drivers of the reconstructive process – we discuss the possibilities of remaking works and updating the costumes using sustainable working processes. We also begin tentative conversations with a material culture museum about the possibility of donating costume items to be used as a living archive, where the costumes will be available to be touched, worn, and experimented with by gallery visitors until they materially degrade beyond feasible use.

I roughly sketch out these ongoing pathways forward here, not as an exhaustive or prescriptive list, but as an acknowledgement of the ongoing transition of the archive and the potential futures for its fabric remains as they continue to unfold. Despite this book and the interventions it outlines drawing shortly to a close, the smithereens are travelling on; fragmenting further but gaining further resonance and visibility as they do so. These developments are in step with increasing interest in alternative archival forms more broadly, and other archival projects among choreographers and dance organizations. *Siobhan Davies Dance* and their initiative Artist Archive (2023–24), for example, is a recently launched annual programme that 'questions what an archive can be and who gets to have one' (Siobhan Davies website 2023). Artist Archive 'gives precedence to artists and their past works that were unfunded or underfunded, had few opportunities to be presented, might otherwise be lost or forgotten or resist the mainstream' (Siobhan Davies website 2023).[5] In the 2023–24 programme, Artist Archive comprises material archives of Shannelle 'Tali' Fergus and Angel Zinovieff, a live archive featuring Angela Andres and Carol (Kavina) Pound and the digital archive of Adesola Akinleye. This is just one innovative example of new initiatives for dance archives which are currently developing at the time of writing this book.

To return to the idea of Display for a final moment however, I would like to conclude this chapter on display by suggesting that perhaps it is not the act of Display, after all, which is of utmost concern to this project. It is what is achieved by the display, or where the smithereens travel to next, that seems most important. All of the strategies outlined in this chapter, from putting bodies back into the costumes to signalling their incompleteness by refusing to do so (and, e.g. suspending them from the ceiling instead) seek to articulate these fractured remains, and moreover, to move towards a greater repair of their ruptured attendant legacies. Rather than an act of reassembly, this returns us to the idea of a salvage operation which picks through the remaining shards, acknowledges their incompleteness and uses them to draw attention to the other things whwich are not fully represented in the frame. Some of these attempts at further fragmentation hit some kind of mark – either of increased visibility (as with *Hand in Glove*) or associative resonance (as with *Smithereens: A Collection of Fragments Considered as a Whole*). Other attempts at fragmentation fall to the ground like dust, with equivalent weightlessness and invisibility – there are many unsuccessful funding bids and abandoned schemes in my work with Anderson and her costume archive. Nonetheless, these acts of display and fragmentation hold the thread of an earlier description of our work with these fabric remains (outlined in Beginning):

Our relationships to the materials to hand and the legacy which arguably lies therein, or elsewhere, are wholly different, but our impetus in what we attempt to mine these materials for is not so dissimilar. There is something at stake in these moments. We try to make the most of what we find. Make the most of what it can tell us, of how we might use it and where (if anywhere) it could travel to, for the future.

Notes

1. The United Kingdom went into official lockdown in mid-March 2020 following the outbreak of the COVID-19 pandemic. Whilst lockdown conditions eased some months later, by March 2021, the United Kingdom was in full nationwide lockdown with all schools and non-essential retail, performance and hospitality venues closed. Restrictions are detailed on a government COVID-19-dedicated website: https://www.gov.uk/coronavirus. Accessed 12 December 2023.

Whilst live performance was not possible under the full UK lockdown, many artists began finding ways of performing virtually, disseminating their work in online forums. Examples of this include Lea Anderson's crowdfunded film *Elvis Legs (Quarantine Mix)* released in July 2020 supported by Pavilion Dance South West. http://www.leaanderson.com/works/elvis-legs-quarantine-mix-2. Accessed 12 December 2023.

2. Jane Pritchard is Curator of Dance at the Victoria & Albert Museum, London.

3. For an in-depth exploration of the ways in which live performance in the contemporary museum can be considered as having become an object, see:

Casey, V. (2005), 'Staging meaning: Performance in the modern museum,' *The Drama Review*, 49:3, pp. 78–95.

4. At the time of writing, these archival droplets are available to view on Anderson's social media pages, including the Instagram account: @leaanderson'scholmondeleys.

5. Available at: https://www.siobhandavies.com/artist-archive/23-24/. Accessed 12 December 2023.

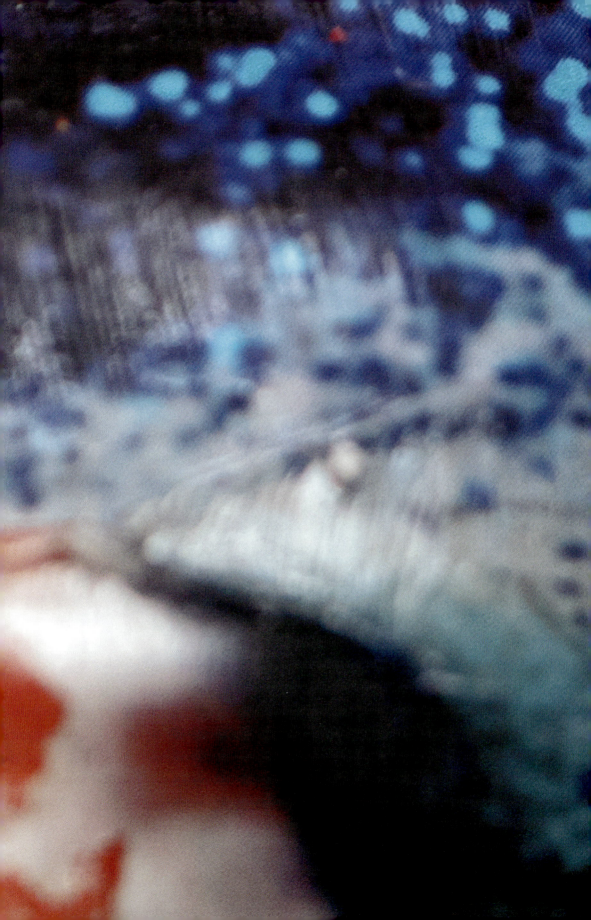

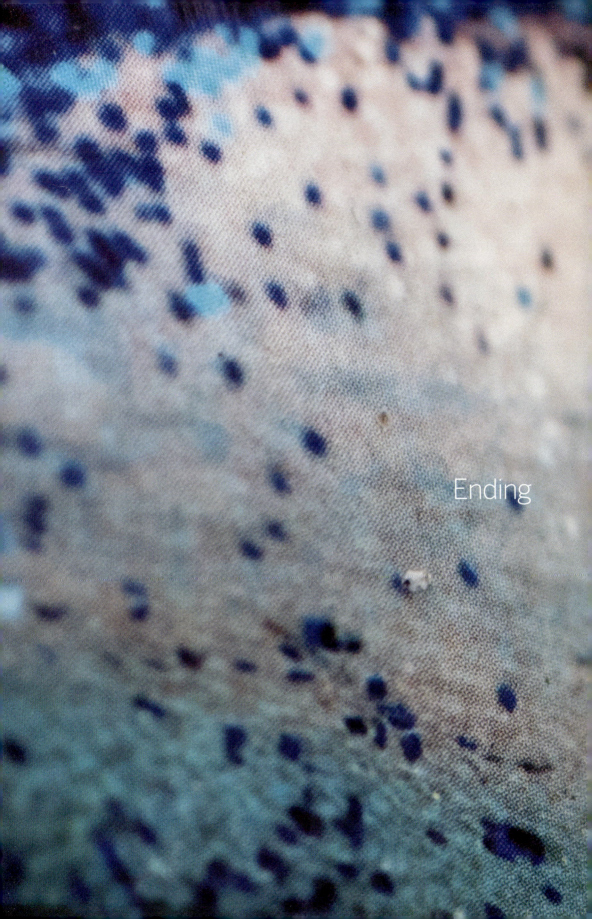
Ending

HAMM: You're a bit of all right, aren't you?
CLOV: A smithereen.
Endgame by Samuel Beckett ([1957] 2009: 10–11)

Perhaps 'Ending' is not what I mean. The work outlined in this book so far steers towards an inescapable conclusion that endings are not as they seem. Performances vanish, companies disband, memories fade and yet some *stuff* gets left behind. Not inconsequential stuff, it must be said, which takes all manner of material and immaterial form: fabric remains, defunct utilitarian objects, recollections, stains, rips in the structure of things, contradictions to the record laid down on paper, misremembered steps, hummed refrains, a lone thread snagged on a silver buckled shoe. *Smithereens*, they could be called. Things from 'there' and 'then', still *here* and *now*, and in fact travelling onwards towards another 'there' and 'then', which we are called to imagine. The question that has already cropped up in this book comes one last time: what to do? What to do with all of this *stuff*? This section which I have entitled Ending reflects briefly once again on the quandary of how best to regard time travelling objects and their interlinked immaterial counterparts – how best to care for them, really. It takes account for gestures which could arguably edge towards becoming disproportionate or even ridiculous – gestures which exceed themselves and, in doing so, illuminate both the inadequacy of the gesture itself and the warrant for care which motivates it.

How might these 'excesses' relate to the physical remains of performance, the degrading of memory around pre-digital theatre work, and the temporal material transitions of dance costumes? What might constitute an excessive or ridiculous gesture in those contexts? The attempted material destruction of an artefact in order to *protect* it from conceptually vanishing and materially declining could be considered thus. Attempts to fragment objects as a means of archival retrieval could also. These physical and conceptual actions (which have arisen from encounters with a set of material objects) indicate in essence that these are objects which *do*, in fact, more than merit the care.

Material realities and gradual vanishing

In starting to deal with unquantifiable erasures, persistent materialities and the partial futility always attached to gestures of care towards objects, it might be helpful to revisit an observation we have already encountered (from Hanna Hölling in conversation with Jorge Otero-Pailos) on the material transitions of artefacts and artworks:

> We have objects that are made of materials [...] And subsequently these materials transition, due to the process of decay or degradation, thus inevitably change[ing] the objects. Objects change because their constitutive material parts change, and nothing in this system inherits a fixed identity. It is an ecology of sorts that is full of intrinsic interdependencies and relations. Perhaps we could think of objects as temporal-material forms. Material transition is inherent to the entire material world as no single object is freed from it.
> (Otero-Pailos and Hölling 2019: 256)

This notion of an ecology with a series of interdependencies can be borrowed as a means to encapsulate the multidimensional nature of the fabric remains in this book. The decay and degradation which Hölling refers to foregrounds their materiality as well as altering it over time. Whether seeking to creatively accelerate these degradations through disintegration or stave off the ravages of time as much as possible through preservation, the sense of temporality and continual, gradual change nonetheless remains an immutable condition, and not just of these particular remains. As David Lowenthal unremorsefully puts it (cited in Disintegration), 'nothing can be preserved forever' (Lowenthal 2019: 17). 'Every inanimate object', he continues,

> like every living being, undergoes continual alteration, ultimately perishing. Cumulative corrosion extinguishes every form and feature. Things either morph into other entities, dismember into fragments or dissolve into unrecognizable components. Gradual change may be imperceptible within the span of a human lifetime or even longer, but it is eventually inexorable.
> (Lowenthal 2019: 17)

Accommodating the realities put forth by Otero-Pailos and Hölling and Lowenthal within this book is not to admit defeat, but rather to investigate specifically how *these* costumes may yet continue to live on in alternative after-lives, rather than proceeding invisibly towards their inevitable material decline in the lockup. If we concede that there is nothing so immutable as the inevitability of transition, alteration and vanishing (both material and otherwise), this reality can be harnessed as a companionable guide for navigating the predicaments faced by time-travelling precious remains which sit outside of traditional museological contexts.

In addition to the logistical and material concerns outlined, this book also gestures towards the conceptual ruptures and erasures being enacted upon the legacy of these costumes. The shattering of a coherent history of the performances in which the costumes lived, the erasure of a catalogue of choreography, and the inability for the companies which made these works originally to be sustained – to live on and continue making new work. Tracing the interdependencies of these garments becomes an act of conjuring, further fragmenting, and an attempt at interlocution. A looking backwards to the past and forwards to an indeterminate future all at once. These attempts have moved between the philosophical and sociological concerns bound up with fabric remains and the physical realities of the costumes themselves, which necessitate specific requirements for their care.

Hands-on interventions

With the Dead Skin, a close engagement with the specificities of its performance life and embodied history gives way to a mapping and attempted acceleration of the degradations brought about through the mutual influences of body, costume and choreography in the moment of performance. Filling the costume once more with the specific body which had previously inhabited it, and once more performing the specific choreographies which had vanished, utilizes this mutual decay as a gesture of illumination of the embodied histories bound up in the garment. Crucially, this act of destruction is equally an attempt at restoration – of bodily memories, reconstructed choreographies and the resurrection of performance histories which had slipped out of sight. A gesture of care. Additionally, there is an attempt at allowing a further alternative after-life through the creation of a short film. This film (viewed in the context of exhibition) allows the costume to shapeshift into another form, subject to alternate systems of dissemination, cataloguing, and ultimately also decay. Despite being unable to entirely avoid material decline, this alternative after-life does succeed in breaking free from the logistics of material storage and the particular decay specific to garments. In adopting an alternate material form, it is hoped that the film invites the viewer to re-engage with the materiality of the original Dead Skin, and to become aware of the potential vanishings engendered through storage and physical degradation. The film bears witness, and in doing so ignites awareness of the surrounding architectures – creative, material and socio-cultural, which influence its after-life.

Preservation witnesses a different attempt at restoration – physical gestures informed by museological expertise and the ethos of conservation – towards a material protecting and sustaining of the *Smithereens* masks. This gesture is not to suggest a priority (due to aesthetic or any other metrics) being given over to the masks as being superior or more valuable than the Dead Skin. It merely engages up-close with the masks and devises an after-life seemingly in step with their particular material nature. It was clear from the outset that they operate in the vein of a relic or totem (both to Anderson and her collaborators) and function distinctly as artefacts in and of themselves. To venture tentatively down a road of conservation in relation to these masks is, as suggested in Beginning, to 'dip toes' into a previously unknown (to myself and Anderson) world. With the masks, their material specificity means it has been physically and logistically possible to craft an intervention which could actually prove beneficial to their protection against destruction. This would not be possible in the context of the Dead Skin, or other materially-fragile costumes, which would require in-depth expertise, far beyond my capabilities or the remit of this project, to carry out any meaningful conservation.

Each intervention is a conjuring of sorts – a mapping and interlocution of the physical residues and tracks of history left on the surfaces and contours of the artefacts. The debates carried out (by myself and Anderson and the conservation experts I interviewed) as to whether to remove sticky name labels or packing noodles from the masks, demonstrate an awareness and sensitivity towards the catalogue of performance histories embedded therein. This is not dissimilar to the deliberate resurrection of specific choreographies (such as in the *Grid* sequence of *Yippeee!!!* as used in Disintegration) in order to exaggerate and accelerate the reciprocal degradation at work in the relationship between body and costume with the Dead Skin.

With the Schiele suit, attempts to summon lost histories were deployed as a means of creating an alternative after-life not only for the suit itself, but more broadly (in the production of economic gain), to facilitate new works and further performance lives. There was therefore less specific mapping of individual marks or residues on the suit than with the Dead Skin and the masks. The invoking of histories became more about focusing on the creative collaborations which had brought this suit into being – the network of individuals involved, the artistic influences, and the striking material nature of the garment. With the Schiele suit, a looking outwards informed my actions – towards auction houses, the canon of the visual art market, and the metrics of visibility and sale which influence the economic value placed on artefacts. The Schiele suit became a testbed; a garment to be weighed and measured against the caprices of value and heritage which confine the costumes in Anderson's archive to an invisible lockup in the first place. This was a costume that if auctioned successfully, might suffer from full irreversible disappearance into a private collection. Such a disappearance was also weighed up in this intervention and deemed a potentially unavoidable and not-quite-justifiable sacrifice in the face of nominal financial gain.

Erasures and recurrence

The continual erasure of surrounding context and knowledge of Anderson's works has become increasingly evident to me, even as this project has progressed over a time span of a few years. Press reviews and articles which had been openly available to access when I commenced my research, for example, are hidden behind newspaper pay-walls by the time of completing it a few years later. Whilst I can still access these articles because I know where to look, I have in mind the new researcher or undergraduate student performing similar searches and retrieving fewer results than I originally found. What then, *does* remain most prominently in these contexts? Often just words. The currency of negative press reviews (from, for example *Yippeee!!!* (2006)), which held sway over theatre programmers and theatre going public at the time of their writing, now form a historical narrative and in some cases may be all that is left visible (in a superficial search) of the legacy of these works (Jennings 2006; Mackrell 2006). During the process of writing the intervention chapters, when I finally turn to the relevant scholarship and press reviews of the works themselves I am newly conscious both of my impulse to fill out these partial narratives, and the rationale for why I should not do that. The capacity for my words to begin to 'stand-in' for the costumes themselves and to paper over the cracks in what persists of these performances, becomes apparent. There is a deliberate decision made at this point to avoid attempts at any 'filling-in' of history. The press reviews have instead been used in partnership with the costumes as evidence of how the costumes may have influenced the critical reception of the work at the time of its performance. What 'work' they may have done within the performance itself, and which traces we might now track of that, within their fibres. The findings thrown up by this approach operate as ciphers which reveal the incompleteness of the story and, in so doing, go some way towards highlighting (but not reversing) any continuing erasure.

I should also note that, of the works of Anderson's which I have been exploring, I have not seen all of them live. I never saw, for example, the original performance of *Smithereens* (1999), aside from some grainy, poor-quality video footage which Anderson retains of the work being performed during its original tour. I have viewed sections remounted by undergraduate dance students or as part of the performed exhibition *Hand in Glove* (2016). Whilst these encounters have been informative, they cannot be considered as wholly representative of the original performances – especially in cases like *Smithereens* (1999) where the masks were moulded to fit the original casts' faces. This does not entirely translate when transposed onto student casts of differing physiques (to that of the original cast) and performed as excerpts within mixed performance bills. Thus, for me, as for others latterly encountering these past works, the costumes remain as the site of primary encounter with the work. I do have the benefit of experiencing *Yippeee!!!* (2006) performed live as part of its original tour, but with *The*

Featherstonehaughs Draw on the Sketchbooks of Egon Schiele (1998 and 2010) my primary engagement with the work has been through film and aforementioned student-led remounts. These inconsistencies in knowledge account for some of the differing approaches in the intervention chapters. The information I have been piecing together – the questions I ask of the works' creators, the costume images I request the photographer to capture – emanate chiefly from my encounters with the costumes themselves. There is a certain usefulness in this perspective. It is foregrounded within a sense of ongoing erasure and awareness of not having the full story. It also tests the viability of the costumes as interlocutors for past performance histories.

This cognisance of erasure also inculcates a desire to *set things down*. Not in terms of filling-in conceptually or visually what has now vanished of the works – but attempting to gather together factual threads and minutiae. I catch myself quizzing Anderson for dates of performances, cast lists and subsequent revisions, musical details, titles, etc. which I then meticulously scribble down. The endnotes of this book begin to harbour an alternative kind of retrieval; of factual lists, explanations of lost costume bibles, addresses of tailors' shops, manufacturers' specifications for industrial props-making machinery. These lists have something of the excessive gesture in them too, or an implicit knowledge of the ways in which things will exceed or defeat this work temporally. The plastic masks may themselves outlive Anderson, me and all who were involved in their creation and performance life. The noting down of small details and crediting of dancers and makers comes then to be conceived as an archival leap of faith. A conviction that it is worth putting these things down *somewhere*, in order that they might lend legibility to the objects in an imaginal future. 'Testing', as Jorge Otero-Pailos puts it, 'our ability to believe in the reality of a temporality we call the future or to believe in the reality of a temporality we call the past' (Hölling and Otero-Pailos 2019: 262).

A sense of recurrence has permeated the journey described in this book. The costumes which I first encounter in the lockup return repeatedly – sometimes in new forms: photographs I have not previously seen, or films which I make, sentences which I write. The costumes thus transform along their journey, in minor and sometimes major ways. There have been other returns too: of artists, pop stars, science fiction characters and Hollywood sirens who crop up unannounced in relation to the fabric remains – they serve as markers of comparison for economic worth (in Transaction) or creative choreographic influences which inspired the original *Cholmondeleys* and *Featherstonehaughs* works (Disintegration). They return unexpectedly and begin to populate the endnotes of this text alongside all the other little bits. As if to say 'we are here too', in the landscape of 'there' and 'then' and *here* and *now* – travelling across time and context, just as Anderson's costumes do. Turning up again, as Gordon would describe it, 'when things are not in their assigned places […] when the people who are meant to be invisible show up without any sign of leaving, when disturbed feelings cannot be put away' (2008: xvi). Things thus unavoidably figured in relation to, or placed in perspective against, something else.

The unavoidable fact is that any gesture of care which is being attempted in this project through the writing of texts or material preservation or creative destruction, is being enacted from a position outside of the costume's own 'world'; at a significant temporal distance from their original incarnation, and by one who does not have all the facts, is not an expert. This project, and I, as researcher, come late to these remains. In a way, that is the point – it forces me to prioritize encounter first and follow any consequent paths of enquiry from there onwards and outwards. The slightly free-wheeling or adaptive nature of this kind of work feels keenly in step with the realities of dealing with an archive such as Anderson's which sits outside the protective mechanics of traditional museological preservation and cataloguing. A sense of agility gets baked into the endeavour from the start. The need to multitask and satisfy differing logistical needs and conceptual considerations (from mask storage to film making, and from early twentieth-century cultural critiques (Kracauer [1995] to the caprices of the art market; Degen [2013]) unavoidably shapes the project to be one which is willing to follow wherever discoveries lead. To attempt to round off this project as a closed narrative would do a disservice to its productively unruly elements. What could be naively marked as endings within this text are in fact continuances which exceed us – afterlives which continue to unravel in unique ways and sometimes unpredictable directions. Taking account for a series of gestures of care (ridiculous or excessive as they might be) in this context looks to suggest productive and novel modes to articulate archival remnants outside of traditional contexts as one potential means of staging partial representational repair for performance histories which are slipping beyond reach.

'What kind of case is a case of a ghost?' asks Gordon (2008: 24). 'It is' she offers, 'a story about what happens when we admit the ghost – that special instance of the merging of the visible and the invisible [...] the past and the present – into the making of [...] our accounts of the world' (Gordon 2008: 24). Throughout my work with Anderson's archive there has been a pervasive sense of the visible (material fragments) in dialogue with the invisible (vanished histories) – the aim that by engaging deeply and up close with the visible remains, somehow they could render conceptually (if not materially) visible the fragments which have been lost. 'Fragment' is a key descriptor here because it signals that the interlocution afforded is nonetheless unapologetically fragmentary. At no point has there been the aim of producing a conclusive, polished, or summative account. That would be to move into the realm of supplanting or creating a stand-in for the things which have been lost. The partial, the half-remembered, and the fragmentary are prioritized in this book.

Gordon borrows from the work of John Berger (1972) and Gayatri Spivak (1992) in forming her concept of haunting – building towards a case for the 'ghost as a social figure' (Gordon 2008: 25). She argues that the ghost is in fact 'often a case of inarticulate experiences, of symptoms and screen memories, of spiraling affects, of more than one story at a time, of the traffic in domains of experience that are anything but transparent and referential' (Gordon 2008: 25). These conceptions feel generative in the context of an archival project bound up with slippages, disappearances, and the viewing of a ruptured history through a veil of memory, the passage of time, and incomplete material remains. The approach which I used to access these inarticulate experiences, partial histories and body memories was an unashamedly practical one, led by the hunch that 'doing-something' physically with the fabric remains stowed away in the lockup could afford a wider, perhaps unexplored perspective on the visible and invisible frameworks which govern these garments and their degrading legacy. Each of the interventions in this book (towards disintegration, preservation, transaction and onwards towards exhibition display and further dissemination) serve as a means of conceptualizing a semi-vanished past and an uncertain alternative future, simultaneously held within the fibres of an aged garment. They attend closely to the encounter with mercurial fragmentary remains whilst bearing in mind that endings are not what they seem. The vanishing of mesh fabric slipping through fingers, the feather weight of a mask gingerly laid face up on a silk-covered table, the coarse heft of a waistcoat, unfurled slowly from the confines of a suitcase on a hot summer's day.

Smithereens, all of them. Fine things. A bit of all right.

Bibliography

Abel, R. and Holland, P. (eds) (2021), *Ghostly Fragments: Essays on Shakespeare and Performance by Barbara C. Hodgdon*, Ann Arbor, Michigan: University of Michigan Press.

Abraham, N. and Torok, M. (1994), *The Shell and the Kernel* (ed. N. T. Rand, trans. N. T. Rand), Chicago, IL: University of Chicago Press.

Adair, C. (1992), *Women and Dance: Sylphs and Sirens*, New York: New York University Press.

Allsopp, R. (2019), interviewed by M. K. Connolly, 27 November.

Anderson, L. (2016), interviewed by M. K. Connolly, 18 May.

Anderson, L. (2016), interview by *TILT Magazine*, 26 July, https://readymag.com/tribe/571718/3/. Accessed 12 January 2024.

Anderson, L. (2017), interviewed by M. K. Connolly, 17 August.

Anderson, L. (2018a), interviewed by M. K. Connolly, 11 April.

Anderson, L. (2018b), interviewed by M. K. Connolly, 21 June.

Anderson, L. and McKiernan, K. (2000), *The Lost Dances of Egon Schiele*, UK: BBC & Arts Council England.

Anderson, Z. (2010), 'The Featherstonehaughs draw on the Sketchbooks of Egon Schiele', *The Independent*, 11 November, https://www.independent.co.uk/arts-entertainment/theatre-dance/reviews/the-featherstonehaughs-draw-on-the-sketchbooks-of-egon-schiele-the-place-london-2130669.html. Accessed 5 May 2023.

Aoyama, M. (2017), interviewed by M. K. Connolly, 19 July.

Appadurai, A. (1994), 'Commodities and the politics of value', in S. Pearce (ed.), *Interpreting Objects and Collections*, London and New York: Routledge, pp. 76–91.

Arnold, N. (2017), 'Coping with costume', *Costume Culture and Dress International Conference*, 10–12 May, Birmingham: Gold Word Publishing, Birmingham City University, pp. 151–55.

Atkinson, P. and Silverman, D. (1997), 'Kundera's immortality: The interview society and the invention of the self', *Qualitative Inquiry*, 3:3, pp. 304–25.

Augello, M. (2020), 'Costume at the National Theatre: Wolfson Gallery National Theatre, London 4 October 2019–27 June 2020 exhibition review', *Studies in Costume and Performance*, 5:1, pp. 113–17.

Auslander, P. (2008), *Liveness: Performance in a Mediatized Culture*, 2nd ed., Abingdon and New York: Routledge.

Austin, J. L. (1962), *How to Do Things with Words: The William James Lectures Delivered at Harvard 1955*, London: Clarendon.

Bannerman, H. (2017), 'Making dance history live: Performing the past', in L. Nicholas and G. Morris (eds), *Rethinking Dance History: Issues and Methodologies*, 2nd ed., London: Routledge, pp. 94–106.

Barbieri, D. (2012), 'Encounters in the archive: Reflections on costume', *V&A Online Journal* 4, http://www.vam.ac.uk/content/journals/research-journal/issue-no.-4-summer-2012/encounters-in-the-archive-reflections-on-costume/. Accessed 25 January 2023.

Barbieri, D. (2017), *Costume in Performance: Materiality, Culture, and the Body*, London: Bloomsbury.

Barbieri, D. (2021), 'The body as the matter of costume: A phenomenological practice', in S. Pantouvaki and P. McNeil (eds), *Performance Costume: New Perspectives and Methods*, London: Bloomsbury, pp. 197–212.

Bari, S. (2019), *Dressed: The Secret Life of Clothes*, London: Jonathan Cape.

Barnard, M. (2007), *Fashion Theory: A Reader*, London: Routledge.

Beckett, S. ([1957] 2009), *Endgame*, London: Faber & Faber.

Berger, J. (1972), *Ways of Seeing*, London: British Broadcasting Corporation and Penguin Books.

Black, S., de la Haye, A., Entwistle, J., Root, R., Rocamora, A. and Thomas, H. (eds) (2013), *The Handbook of Fashion Studies*, London: Bloomsbury Academic.

Blake, S. (2017), interviewed by M. K. Connolly, 20 July.

Bleeker, M., Kear, A., Kelleher, J. and Roms, H. (eds) (2019), *Thinking Through Theatre and Performance*, London: Bloomsbury Methuen Drama.

Bradley, H. (1999), 'The seductions of the archive: Voices lost and found', *History of the Human Sciences*, XII:2, pp. 107–22.

Brennan, M. (1999), 'Smithereens is a smash', *Herald Scotland*, 14 October, https://www.heraldscotland.com/news/12211853.smithereens-is-a-smash/. Accessed 5 December 2019.

Briginshaw, V. A. (2009), *Dance, Space, and Subjectivity*, Basingstoke: Palgrave Macmillan.

Brown, I. (1999), 'A memorable disappearing act', *The Telegraph*, 25 October, https://www.telegraph.co.uk/culture/4718810/A-memorable-disappearing-act.html. Accessed 5 December 2023.

Brown, I. (2010), 'The Featherstonehaughs draw on the Sketchbooks of Egon Schiele', *The Arts Desk*, 8 November, https://theartsdesk.com/dance/featherstonehaughs-place?page=0,1. Accessed 5 February 2023.

Brown, M. (2016), 'Number of BAME arts workers must improve, says Arts Council report', *The Guardian*, 12 December, https://www.theguardian.com/society/2016/dec/12/number-of-minority-arts-workers-must-improve-arts-council-england. Accessed 20 November 2023.

Brown, M. (2020), 'UK theatre job losses rise by 2,000 in a month union figures show', *The Guardian*, 3 August, https://www.theguardian.com/stage/2020/aug/03/uk-theatre-job-losses-rise-2000-month-union-figures-show. Accessed 14 March 2023.

Bugg, J. (2014), 'Dancing dress: Experiencing and perceiving dress in movement', *Scene*, 2:1&2, pp. 67–80.

Bugg, J. (2020), 'Dressing dance – dancing dress: Lived experience of dress and its agency in the collaborative process', in H. Thomas and S. Prickett (eds), *The Routledge Companion to Dance Studies*, London and New York: Routledge, pp. 353–64.

Bugg, J. (2021), 'The body as site: Interdisciplinary approaches to dress in/as performance', in S. Pantouvaki and P. McNeil (eds), *Performance Costume: New Perspectives and Methods*, London: Bloomsbury, pp. 213–28.

Burt, R. (2007a), *The Male Dancer: Bodies, Spectacle, Sexualities*, London and New York: Routledge.

Burt, R. (2007b), 'Resistant identities in the work of Lea Anderson and Felix Ruckert', in S. Franco and M. Nordera (eds), *Dance Discourses: Keywords in Dance Research*, London and New York: Routledge, pp. 208–20.

Burt, R. (2016), 'Humming Edelweiss: Lea Anderson's Hand in Glove at the V&A', ramsayburt blog, 25 April, https://ramsayburt.wordpress.com/2016/04/25/humming-edelweiss-lea-andersons-hand-in-glove-at-the-va/. Accessed 10 December 2023.

Burt, R. and Briginshaw, V. A. (eds) (2009), *Writing Dancing Together*, Basingstoke: Palgrave Macmillan.

Busby, M. (2018), 'Shredded Banksy: Was Sotheby's in on the act?' *The Guardian*, 13 November, https://www.theguardian.com/artanddesign/2018/oct/13/shredded-banksy-was-sothebys-in-on-the-act. Accessed 5 January 2023.

Butt, G. (2008), 'Hoyle's humility: Interview with David Hoyle', *Dance Theatre Journal*, 23:1, pp. 30–34.

Carter, H. (2006), 'From Tiffany's to Christie's – dress fetches £467,200', *The Guardian*, 6 December, https://www.theguardian.com/uk/2006/dec/06/film.fashion. Accessed 5 February 2023.

Chris Kerr Tailors (2020), 'Bespoke tailoring Soho style', https://chriskerr.com/about/. Accessed 5 February 2023.

Christie's (2000), 'The Dame Margot Fonteyn Collection, Sale 9030', https://www.christies.com/lotfinder/Lot/margot-fonteyn-1975273-details.aspx. Accessed 5 February 2023.

Christie's (2006), 'Sale 4912 Film and Entertainment', https://www.christies.com/lotfinder/Lot/audrey-hepburn-breakfast-at-tiffanys-19614832498-details.aspx. Accessed 5 February 2023.

Clark, J. (2005), *Spectres: When Fashion Turns Back*, London: Victoria & Albert Museum.

Clark, J. (2017), 'Judith Clark costume', https://www.judithclarkcostume.com. Accessed 31 November 2023.

Clark, J. and Phillips, A. (2010), *The Concise Dictionary of Dress*, London: Artangel and Violette.

Clark, M. (2020), *Cosmic Dancer*, London: Barbican.

Clarke, P., Jones, S., Kaye, N. and Linsley, J. (eds) (2018), *Artists in the Archive: Creative and Curatorial Engagements with Documents of Art and Performance*, London: Routledge.

Cloth, J. (2017), interviewed by M. K. Connolly, 13 July.

Coffey-Webb, L. and Campbell, R. D. (2016), *Managing Costume Collections: An Essential Primer*, Lubbock, Texas: Texas Tech University Press.

Connolly, M. K. (2012), 'An audience with the other: The reciprocal gaze in Raimund Hoghe's theatre', in A. Lepecki (ed.), *Dance: Documents of Contemporary Art*, London: Whitechapel Gallery & MIT Press, pp. 120–21.

Connolly, M. K. (ed.) (2013), *Throwing the Body into the Fight*, London: Intellect.

Connolly, M. K. (2017a), 'Hand in Glove: Reflections on a performed costume exhibition and the stories behind the garments', *Studies in Costume & Performance*, 2:1, pp. 9–25.

Connolly, M. K. (2017b), 'Re-imagining the after-life of costumes post performance', *Presented at: Costume Culture and Dress International Conference*, Birmingham City University, 10-12 May.

Cotter, S. and Clark, M. (eds) (2011), *Michael Clark*, London: Violette.

Crawley, G. and Barbieri, D. (2013), 'Dress, time, and space: Expanding the field through exhibition making', in S. Black, A. de la Haye, J. Entwistle, R. Root, A. Rocamora and H. Thomas (eds), *The Handbook of Fashion Studies*, London: Bloomsbury, pp. 44–60.

Cvejić, B. (2019), 'How does choreography think "through" society?' in M. Bleeker, A. Kear, J. Kelleher and H. Roms (eds), *Thinking Through Theatre and Performance*, London: Bloomsbury Methuen Drama, pp. 270–83.

Cvejić, B. and Vujanovjić, A. (2012), *Public Sphere by Performance*, Berlin: books.

Daniel, J. (1998), 'The Featherstonehaughs Draw on the Sketchbooks of Egon Schiele', *Total Theatre*, 10:1, http://totaltheatre.org.uk/archive/reviews/featherstonehaughs-draws-sketch-books-egon-schiele. Accessed 5 February 2023.

Danjoux, M. (2013), 'Choreography and sounding wearables', *Scene*, 2:1&2, pp. 197–220.

Danjoux, M. (2020), 'Choreosonic wearables: Creative collaborative practices', in H. Thomas and S. Prickett (eds), *The Routledge Companion to Dance Studies*, London and New York: Routledge, pp. 157–76.

Daris, G. (2017), 'In praise and restitution of perished clothing', *The Costume Society Blog*, 8 September, https://www.costumesociety.org.uk/blog/post/in-praise-and-restitution-of-perished-clothing. Accessed 31 November 2023.

Dean, S. E. (2011), 'Somatic movement and costume: A practical, investigative project', *Journal of Dance & Somatic Practices*, 3:1&2, pp. 167–82.

Dean, S. E. (2021), '"Aware-wearing": A somatic costume design methodology for performance', in S. Pantouvaki and P. McNeil (eds), *Performance Costume: New Perspectives and Methods*, London: Bloomsbury, pp. 229–46.

Degen, N. (ed.) (2013), *The Market: Documents of Contemporary Art*, London: Whitechapel Gallery and MIT Press.

De la Haye, A. and Wilson, E. (eds) (1999), *Defining Dress: Dress as Object, Meaning and Identity*, Manchester: Manchester University Press.

Deleuze, G. (2004), *Difference and Repetition*, London: Continuum.

Deleuze, G. (2006), *The Fold: Leibniz and the Baroque*, London: Continuum.

Del Pilar Blanco, M. and Peeren, E. (eds) (2010), *Popular Ghosts: The Haunted Spaces of Everyday Culture*, London: Bloomsbury.

Del Pilar Blanco, M. and Peeren, E. (eds) (2013), *The Spectralities Reader: Ghosts and Haunting in Contemporary Cultural Theory*, London: Bloomsbury.

Derrida, J. ([1993] 1994), *Specters of Marx: The State of the Debt, the Work of Mourning and the New International* (trans. P. Kamuf), London: Routledge Classics.

Derrida, J. ([1995] 1996), *Archive Fever: A Freudian Impression* (trans. E. Prenowitz), London and Chicago, IL: University of Chicago Press.

de Waal, E. (2020), *Library of Exile*, London: The British Museum Press.

Dodds, S. and Adshead-Lansdale, J. (1997), 'Gesture, pop culture, and intertextuality in the work of Lea Anderson', *New Theatre Quarterly*, 13:50, pp. 155–60.

Donovan, T. (2010), 'The Featherstonehaughs draw on the Sketchbooks of Egon Schiele', *British Theatre Guide*, 9 November, https://www.britishtheatreguide.info/reviews/schiele-rev. Accessed 5 February 2023.

Droste, S. and Berber, A. ([1923] 2012), *Dances of Vice, Horror, and Ecstasy* (trans. and ed. M. Cole), Newcastle upon Tyne: Side Real Press.

Elgot, J. and Walker, P. (2021), 'England to enter toughest Covid lockdown since March', *The Guardian*, 4 January, https://www.theguardian.com/world/2021/jan/04/england-to-enter-toughest-covid-lockdown-since-march. Accessed 12 January 2023.

Elliot, R. (1994), 'Towards a material history methodology', in S. Pearce (ed.), *Interpreting Objects and Collections*, London and New York: Routledge, pp. 109–24.

Ezard, J. (2000), 'Fonteyn admirers horrified by sale of costumes and letters at auction', *The Guardian*, 5 December, https://www.theguardian.com/uk/2000/dec/05/johnezard. Accessed 5 February 2023.

Fajardo, S. (2018), interviewed by M. K. Connolly, 25 May.

Fashion Space Gallery (2017), 'Present Imperfect: Disorderly Apparel Reconfigured', https://www.fashionspacegallery.com/exhibition/present-imperfect. Accessed 31 November 2023.

Fatehi Irani, T. (2020), *Mishandled Archive*, London: Live Art Development Agency.

Fischer-Lichte, E. (2008), *The Transformative Power of Performance: A New Aesthetics*, New York: Routledge.

Foekje, B., Brokerhof, A.W., van den Berg, S. and Tegelaers, J. ([2000] 2007), *Unravelling Textiles: A Handbook for the Preservation of Textile Collections* (trans. B. Foekje, A.W. Brokerhof, S. van den Berg and J. Tegelaers), London: Archetype Publications.

Foster, S. L. (2009), 'Throwing like a girl, dancing like a feminist philosopher', in A. Ferguson and M. Nagel (eds), *Dancing with Iris: The Philosophy of Iris Marion Young*, Oxford: Oxford University Press, pp. 69–78.

Fraleigh, S. (1987), *Dance and the Lived Body: A Descriptive Aesthetics*, Pittsburgh, PA: University of Pittsburgh Press.

Franko, M. (2011), 'The dancing gaze across cultures: Kazuo Ohno's admiring La Argentina', *Dance Chronicle*, 34:1, pp. 106–31.

Freshwater, H. (2003), 'The allure of the archive', *Poetics Today*, 24:4, pp. 729–58.

Freud, S. ([1919] 2003), *The Uncanny* (trans. D. Mc Lintock), London: Penguin.

Gordon, A. F. and Radway, J. (2008), *Ghostly Matters: Haunting and the Sociological Imagination*, 2nd ed., Minneapolis, MN: University of Minnesota Press.

Gore, G., Rix-Lièvre, G., Wathelet, O. and Cazemajou, A. (2012), 'Elicitating the tacit: Interviewing to understand bodily experience', in J. Skinner (ed.), *The Interview: An Ethnographic Approach*, London: Berg, pp. 127–42.

Grampp, W. (1989), *Pricing the Priceless: Art, Artists and Economics*, New York: Basic Books.

Grew, R. (2019), 'Interplays of body and costume', *Studies in Costume and Performance*, 4:2, pp. 153–57.

Groom, A. (ed.) (2013), *Time: Documents of Contemporary Art*, London: Whitechapel Gallery and MIT Press.

Guerilla Girls (1989), 'Code of ethics for art museums', https://www.tate.org.uk/art/artworks/guerrilla-girls-guerrilla-girls-code-of-ethics-for-art-museums-p78795. Accessed 5 March 2024.

Guy, G. (2016), *Theatre, Exhibition, and Curation: Displayed & Performed*, London: Routledge.

Guerilla Girls (1990), *Guerilla Girls' Code of Ethics for Art Museums*, London: TATE.

Haight, L. (2006), 'Review: The Cholmondeleys and the Featherstonehaughs in Yippeee!!! at Sadler's Wells', *Londondance*, 15 November, http://ww.securedspace.net/articles/reviews/yippeee-2006-at-sadlers-wells-486/. Accessed 9 December 2023.

Hargreaves, M. (2007), 'Diseased dames in dancing shoes (Lea Anderson in conversation with Martin Hargreaves)', *Dance Theatre Journal*, 22:2, pp. 23–27.

Hawley, J. (2018), 'Flinck & Bol – Rembrandt's Star Pupils', https://www.christies.com/features/Flinck-and-Bol-Rembrandt-star-pupils-9134-1.aspx. Accessed 5 February 2023.

Heathfield, A. and Hsieh, T. (2009), *Out of Now; The Lifeworks of Tehching Hsieh*, London and Cambridge, MA: Live Art Development Agency and MIT Press.

Hencilla Camworth Insurance (2018), e-mail to Mary Kate Connolly, 16 March.

Reilly, R. (2019), e-mail to Mary Kate Connolly, 26 September.

Herrnstein Smith, B. (1988), *Contingencies of Value: Alternative Perspectives for Critical Theory*, Cambridge, Massachusetts: Harvard University Press.

Hesse, H. (2002), *Steppenwolf*, New York: Picador.

Hodgdon, B. (2006), 'Shopping in the archive: Material memories', in P. Hollander (ed.), *Shakespeare, Memory and Performance*, Cambridge: Cambridge University Press, pp. 135–68.

Hodgdon, B. (2016), *Shakespeare, Performance and the Archive*, Abingdon: Routledge.

Hodgson, S. (2019), interviewed by M. K. Connolly, 4 December.

Hölling, Bewer and Ammann (eds) (2019), *The Explicit Material: Inquiries on the Intersection of Curatorial and Conservation Cultures*, Leiden: Brill.

Hooper, K., Kearins, K. and Green, R. (2005), 'Knowing "the price of everything and the value of nothing": Accounting for heritage assets', *Accounting, Auditing & Accountability*, 18:3, pp. 210–33.

Horsley, J. and Connolly, M. K. (2018), 'Objects of transformation', *Studies in Costume & Performance*, 3:1, pp. 81–90.

Hudson, M. (2020), 'The arts are an essential service – as vital as health, education, defence', *The Independent*, 2 July, https://www.independent.co.uk/arts-entertainment/art/features/art-government-funding-lockdown-package-coronavirus-a9604541.html. Accessed 14 March 2023.

Hutera, D. (2011), 'Lea Anderson', in M. Bremser and L. Sanders (eds), *Fifty Contemporary Choreographers*, London: Routledge, pp. 29–35.

Ingold, T. (2012), 'Toward an ecology of materials', *Annual Review of Anthropology*, 41:1, pp. 427–42.

Janša, J. and Georgelou, K. (2017), 'What names (un)do', *Performance Research*, 22:5, pp. 1–3.

Jennings, L. (2006), 'Are the stars out tonight? No', *The Guardian*, 12 November, https://www.theguardian.com/stage/2006/nov/12/dance. Accessed 5 December 2023.

Jordan, S. (2011), 'The Featherstonehaughs Draw on the Sketchbooks of Egon Schiele', *The Daily Info*, 21 October, https://www.dailyinfo.co.uk/feature/6359/the-featherstonehaughs-draw-on-the-sketchbooks-of-egon-schiele. Accessed 5 February 2023.

Kelleher, J. (2015a), 'Recycling Beckett', in C. Lavery and C. Finburgh (eds), *Rethinking the Theatre of the Absurd: Ecology, the Environment and the Greening of the Modern Stage*, London: Bloomsbury Methuen Drama, pp. 127–45.

Kelleher, J. (2015b), *The Illuminated Theatre: Studies on the Suffering of Images*, London and New York: Routledge.

Kerr, C. (2018), interviewed by M. K. Connolly, 3 July.

Kickstarter Campaign (2016), 'Hand in Glove: A performed exhibition of costume and dance', 10 April, https://www.kickstarter.com/projects/hands-in-glove/hand-in-glove-a-performed-exhibition-of-costume-an. Accessed 5 February 2023.

Kneebone, R. (2020), *Expert: Understanding the Path to Mastery*, London: Penguin Viking.

Kvale, S. (1996), *InterViews: An Introduction to Qualitative Research Interviewing*, London: Sage Publications.

Landy, M. (2001), *Break Down*, London: C&A Oxford St.

Landy, M. (2010), *Art Bin*, New York: South London Gallery.

Lane, S. (2020), interviewed by M. K. Connolly, 13 February.

Lange-Berndt, P. (ed.) (2015), *Materiality: Documents of Contemporary Art*, London: Whitechapel Gallery and MIT Press.

Lawes, T. (2020), interviewed by M. K. Connolly, 13 February.

Leddy, D. (1999), 'The Cholmondeleys & the Featherstonehaughs with the victims of death, Smithereens', *Total Theatre*, 11:4, http://totaltheatre.org.uk/archive/reviews/cholmondeleys-featherstonehaughs-victims-death-smithereens. Accessed 5 December 2023.

Leese, E. (2012), *Costume Design in the Movies: An Illustrated Guide to the Work of 157 Great Designers*, New York: Courier Corporations.

Lehmann, A. (2017), 'Material literacy', *Bauhaus Zeitschrift*, 9, pp. 20–27.

Leonard, Z. (1992-1997), *Strange Fruit*, New York: Whitney Museum of American Art.

Lepecki, A. (2004), *Of the Presence of the Body: Essays on Dance and Performance Theory*, Middletown, Connecticut: Wesleyan University Press.

Lepecki, A. (2006), *Exhausting Dance: Performance and the Politics of Movement*, London: Routledge.

Lepecki, A. (2010), 'The body as archive: Will to re-enact and the afterlives of dances', *Dance Research Journal*, 42:2, pp. 28–48.

Levene, L. (1998), 'In the tortured steps of Egon Schiele', *The Independent*, 24 February, https://www.independent.co.uk/life-style/visual-arts-in-the-tortured-steps-of-egon-schiele1146676.html. Accessed 5 February 2023.

Live Performance and Film Dance Rebels: A Story of Modern Dance (2015), 13 December, BBC Four, https://www.bbc.co.uk/programmes/b06spm22. Accessed 11 May 2023.

Lowenthal, D. (2019), 'A sea-change rich and strange', in H. B. Hölling, F. G. Bewer and K. Ammann (eds), *The Explicit Material: Inquiries on the Intersection of Curatorial and Conservation Cultures*, Leiden: Brill, pp. 17–63.

Luckhurst, M. and Morin, E. (eds) (2014), *Theatre and Ghosts: Materiality, Performance and Modernity*, New York: Palgrave Macmillan.

Mackrell, J. (2006), 'Yippeee!!!', *The Guardian*, 6 November, https://www.theguardian.com/stage/2006/nov/06/dance. Accessed 9 December 2023.

Mackrell, J. (2017), 'A Kaleidoscope of legs: Busby Berkeley's flamboyant dance fantasies', *The Guardian*, 3 March, https://www.theguardian.com/stage/2017/mar/23/busby-berkeley-dance-42nd-street-choreography-film-musicals. Accessed 9 December 2023.

Maclaurin, A. and Monks, A. (2015), *Costume: Readings in Theatre Practice*, Basingstoke: Palgrave Macmillan.

Maler, L. (1982), *H2OMBRE*, New York: Center for Inter-American Relations.

Mangalanayagam, T. (2007), 'Lea Anderson Q&A', *Londondance*, 15 June, http://ww.securedspace.net/articles/interviews/lea-anderson-qanda/. Accessed 10 December 2023.

Manning, E. (1998), 'Movement well drawn: The Featherstonehaughs Draw on the Sketchbooks of Egon Schiele', *The Stage*, 5 March, n.p., LABAN Library & Archive Holdings.

Merewether, C. (ed.) (2006), *The Archive: Documents of Contemporary Art*, London: Whitechapel Gallery and MIT Press.

Merleau-Ponty, M. (1942), *La structure du comportement (The Structure of Behaviour)*, Paris: PUF.

Merleau-Ponty, M. ([1945] 2012), *Phenomenology of Perception* (trans. D. A. Landes), Abingdon: Routledge.

Mida, I. and Kim, E. (2015), *The Dress Detective: A Practical Guide to Object-based Research in Fashion*, London: Bloomsbury.

Monks, A. (2010), *The Actor in Costume*, Basingstoke: Palgrave Macmillan.

Monks, A. (2013), 'Collecting ghosts: Actors, anecdotes and objects at the theatre', *Contemporary Theatre Review*, 23:2, pp. 146–52.

Monks, A. (2019), *Costume at the National Theatre*, London: Oberon Books.

Monks, A. (2020), 'Costume at the National Theatre: A curator's talk', *Studies in Costume and Performance*, 5:1, pp. 101–11.

Monks, A. (2021), 'Curating costume: Reflection', in S. Pantouvaki and P. McNeil (eds), *Performance Costume: New Perspectives and Methods*, London: Bloomsbury, pp. 63–68.

Mui, A. (2010), 'Art becomes life for Egon Schiele', *Evening Standard*, 9 November, https://www.standard.co.uk/go/london/theatre/art-becomes-life-for-egon-schiele-7422462.html. Accessed 5 February 2023.

Nadoolman Landis, D. (2007), *Dressed: A Century of Hollywood Costume Design*, New York: Collins Design.

Nadoolman Landis, D. (2012), *Hollywood Costume*, London: V&A Publishing.

Nadoolman Landis, D. (2021), 'Hollywood costume: A journey to curation', in S. Pantouvaki and P. McNeil (eds), *Performance Costume: New Perspectives and Methods*, London: Bloomsbury, pp. 173–77.

Nebehay, C. M. (1989), *Egon Schiele: Sketchbooks*, London: Thames & Hudson.

Nicol, M. (2007), 'Shift & mix', in K. Debo (ed.), *Bernhard Willhelm: Het Totaal Rapell*, Antwerp: Fashion Museum Province of Antwerp, pp. 128–30.

Norman, N. (2010), 'The Featherstonehaughs Draw on the Sketchbooks of Egon Schiele Review, The Place Robin Howard Dance Theatre London', *The Stage*, 9 November, https://www.thestage.co.uk/reviews/2010/the-featherstonehaughs-draw-on-the-sketchbooks-of-egon-schiele-review-at-the-place-robin-howard-dance-theatre-london/. Accessed 5 February 2023.

Nothing Concrete (2020) 'Michael Clark's Creative World: Fashion with Stevie Stewart', Barbican, London, 18 December. https://www.barbican.org.uk/read-watch-listen/michael-clarks-creative-world-fashion-with-stevie-stewart. Accessed 14 March 2023.

O'Brien, C. (2009), 'Between the seams: The making of a princess', Master of Arts Thesis, Graduate Program in Interdisciplinary Studies, Ontario: York University, https://www.collectionscanada.gc.ca/obj/thesescanada/vol2/002/MR53745.PDF. Accessed 15 March 2023.

Ono, Y. (1961), *Painting for the Wind*, New York: MOMA.

Otero-Pailos, J. and Hölling, H. (2019), 'Materials, objects, transitions', in H. B. Hölling, F. G. Bewer and K. Ammann (eds), *The Explicit Material: Inquiries on the Intersection of Curatorial and Conservation Cultures*, Leiden: Brill, pp. 255–72.

Palladini, G. and Pustianaz, M. (eds) (2016), *Lexicon for an Affective Archive*, Bristol: Intellect.

Pantouvaki, S. and McNeil, P. (eds), *Performance Costume: New Perspectives and Methods*, London: Bloomsbury.

Parker, C. (1991), *Cold Dark Matter: An Exploded View*, London: TATE.

Pavis, P. (2003), *Analyzing Performance: Theater, Dance and Film* (trans. D. Williams), Ann Arbor, MI: University of Michigan Press.

Pearce, S. (ed.) (1994), *Interpreting Objects and Collections*, London and New York: Routledge.

Pearce, S. (ed.) (2000), *Researching Material Culture*, Leicester: Leicester University Press.

Peeren, E. (2014), *The Spectral Metaphor: Living Ghosts and the Agency of Invisibility*, Basingstoke: Palgrave Macmillan.

Peterson, J. (2018), interviewed by M. K. Connolly, 25 May.

Petitmengin, C. (2006), 'Describing one's objective experience in the second person: An interview method for the science of consciousness', *Phenomenology and the Cognitive Sciences*, 5:3, pp. 229–69.

Petitmengin, C. (2007), 'Towards the source of thoughts: The gestural and transmodal dimension of lived experience', *Journal of Consciousness Studies*, 14:3, pp. 54–82.

Phelan, P. (1993), *Unmarked: The Politics of Performance*, London and New York: Routledge.

Phelan, P. (2010), 'Haunted stages: Performance and the photographic effect', in J. Blessing (ed.), *Haunted: Contemporary Photography/Video/Performance*, New York: Guggenheim Museum, pp. 50–87.

Phillips, T. (2021), 'Global report: Coronavirus death toll reaches two million', *The Guardian*, 16 January, https://www.theguardian.com/world/2021/jan/15/global-coronavirus-death-toll-reaches-2-million-people. Accessed 20 January 2023.

Pons Carrera, A. (2018), interviewed by M. K. Connolly, 9 May.

Potter, M. (1993), '"A license to do anything": Robert Rauschenberg and The Merce Cunningham Dance Company', *Dance Chronicle*, 16:1, pp. 1–43.

Powell, S. (2018), interviewed by M. K. Connolly, 24 May.

Pritchard, J. (2010), *Diaghilev and the Golden Age of the Ballets Russes 1909–1929*, London: Victoria & Albert Museum.

Prown, J. (1994), 'Mind in matter: An introduction to material culture theory and method', in S. Pearce (ed.), *Interpreting Objects and Collections*, London and New York: Routledge, pp. 133–38.

Radnofsky, L. (2006), 'Yippeee!!! It's a Flop!' *The Guardian*, 7 November, https://www.theguardian.com/stage/theatreblog/2006/nov/07/post3. Accessed 12 December 2023.

Rapport, N. (2012), 'The interview as a form of talking-partnership: Dialectical, focussed, ambiguous, special', in J. Skinner (ed.), *The Interview: An Ethnographic Approach*. London: Berg, pp. 53–68.

Rauschenberg, R. (1953), *Erased De Kooning Drawing*, San Francisco; MOMA.

Reason, M. (2003), 'Archive or memory? The detritus of live performance', *New Theatre Quarterly*, 19:1, pp. 82–89.

Reason, M. (2006), *Documentation, Disappearance and the Representation of Live Performance*, Basingstoke: Palgrave Macmillan.

Retsikas, K. (2008), 'Knowledge from the body: Fieldwork, power and the acquisition of a new self', in N. Halstead, E. Hirsch and J. Okely (eds), *Knowing How to Know: Fieldwork and the Ethnographic Present*, Oxford: Berghahn Books, pp. 110–29.

Ricoeur, P. (2006), 'Archives, documents, traces', in C. Merewether (ed.), *The Archive: Documents of Contemporary Art*, London: Whitechapel Art Gallery, pp. 66–69.

Rottenberg, H. (2004). 'Hybrid relationships between dance and painting: A close examination of Lea Anderson's the Featherstonehaughs draw on the sketchbooks of Egon Schiele (1998)', Ph.D. thesis, Guildford: University of Surrey, http://epubs.surrey.ac.uk/854895/1/27557559.pdf. Accessed 2 February 2023.

Royal Opera House Collections online Fonteyn Collection. http://www.rohcollections.org.uk/SearchResults.aspx?searchtype=collection&person=margot%20fonteyn. Accessed 10 December 2023.

Saillard, O., Pinasa, D. and Sebillotte, L. (2010), *Le Défilé*, Taipei: Taipei Fine Arts Museum.

Saillard, O. and Swinton, T. (2015), *The Impossible Wardrobe and Other Couture*, Paris, New York and London: Rizzoli.

Schäffler, A. (2019), 'Out of the box', in H. B. Hölling, F. G. Bewer and K. Ammann (eds), *The Explicit Material: Inquiries on the Intersection of Curatorial and Conservation Cultures*, Leiden: Brill, pp. 176–85.

Schneider, R. (2001), 'Performance remains', *Performance Research*, 6:2, pp. 100–08.

Schneider, R. (2011), *Performing Remains: Art and War in Times of Theatrical Reenactment*, New York: Routledge.

Selsdon, E. and Zwingerberger, J. (2011), *Egon Schiele*, New York: Parkstone Press.

Shaw, J. L. (2017), *Exist Otherwise: The Life and Works of Claude Cahun*, London: Reaktion Books.

Silvestrini, L. (2018), interviewed by M. K. Connolly, 21 June.

Simmel, G. ([1900] 2004), *The Philosophy of Money* (trans. M. Bottomore and D. Frisby). London and New York: Routledge.

Sinclair, I. (2013), *Objects of Obscure Desire*, London: Goldmark.

Skinner, J. (2010), 'Leading questions and body memories: A case of phenomenology and physical ethnography in the dance interview', in P. Collins and A. Gallinat (eds), *The Ethnographic Self as Resource: Writing Memory and Experience into Ethnography*, Oxford: Berghahn Books, pp. 111–28.

Skinner, J. (ed.) (2012), *The Interview: An Ethnographic Approach*, London: Berg.

Sparshott, F. (1995), 'Some aspects of nudity in theatre dance', *Dance Chronicle*, 18:2, pp. 303–10.

Spatz, B. (2017), 'What do we document? Dense video and the epistemology of practice', in T. Sant (ed.), *Documenting Performance: The Context and Processes of Digital Curation and Archiving*, London: Bloomsbury Methuen Drama, pp. 241–52.

Spinney, L. (2021), 'Has Covid changed the price of a life?' *The Guardian*, 14 February, https://www.theguardian.com/world/2021/feb/14/coronavirus-covid-19-cost-price-life. Accessed 14 March 2023.

Spivak, G. C. (1985), 'The Rani of Sirmur: An essay in reading the archives', *History and Theory*, 24:3, pp. 247–72.

Stapleton, A. (2012), 'Introduction: Collectors and their collections', *The Journal of the Decorative Arts Society 1850-the Present*, 36, pp. 6–7.

Steedman, C. (2002), *Dust: The Archive and Cultural History*, New Brunswick: Rutgers University Press.

Steeds, L. (ed.) (2014), *Exhibition: Documents of Contemporary Art*, London: Whitechapel Gallery and MIT Press.

Steiner, J. (2018), interviewed by M. K. Connolly, 20 June.

Stewart, N. (2019), 'The erotic reduction: Crossed flesh in Lea Anderson's The Featherstonehaughs Draw on the Sketchbooks of Egon Schiele', in S. Grant, J. McNeilly-Renaudie and M. Wagner (eds), *Performance Phenomenology: To the Thing Itself*, Cham: Palgrave Macmillan, pp. 237–60.

Stjernholm, J. (2020), 'The scenography of choreographing the museum', in H. Thomas and S. Prickett (eds), *The Routledge Companion to Dance Studies*, London and New York: Routledge, pp. 365–80.

Stonard, J-P. (2017), *Anselm Kiefer: Walhalla*, London: White Cube.

Swinton, T. and Saillard, O. (2022), *Embodying Pasolini*, New York: Rizzoli.

TATE Gallery Biography of Fred Wilson, https://www.tate.org.uk/art/artists/fred-wilson-15855. Accessed 5 February 2023.

Taylor, D. (2003), *The Archive and the Repertoire: Performing Cultural Memory in the Americas*, Durham: Duke University Press.

Taylor, L. (2002), *The Study of Dress History*, Manchester: Manchester University Press.

Taylor, L. (2004), *Establishing Dress History*, Manchester: Manchester University Press.

The Guardian (2015), 'Judy Garland's sweat-stained *Wizard of Oz* dress sells for more than $1.5m', 24 November, https://www.theguardian.com/film/2015/nov/24/judy-garlands-sweat-stained-wizard-of-oz-dress-sells-for-more-than-15m. Accessed 5 February 2023.

Thomas, H. (ed.) (1993), *Dance, Gender and Culture*, London: Palgrave Macmillan.

Thomas, H. (2003), *The Body, Dance and Cultural Theory*, London: Palgrave Macmillan.

Thomas, H. and Prickett, S. (eds) (2020), *The Routledge Companion to Dance Studies*, London and New York: Routledge.

Thorpe, V. (2020), 'Arts bailout delay leaves jobs at risk in UK and theatre on brink of ruin', *The Guardian*, 4 October, https://www.theguardian.com/culture/2020/oct/04/arts-bailout-delay-leaves-jobs-at-risk-in-uk-and-theatres-on-brink-of-ruin. Accessed 14 March 2023.

Tolentino, J. (2017), 'Past/upcoming works', http://www.julietolentino.com/TOLENTINOPROJECTS/Performance/Performance.html. Accessed 31 November 2023.

Tomić-Vajagić, T. (2014), 'The dancer at work: The aesthetics and politics of practice clothes and leotard costumes in ballet performance', *Scene*, 2:1–2, pp. 89–105.

Tomić-Vajagić, T. (2021). 'Shapeshifters and Colombe's folds: Connective affinities of Issey Miyake and William Forsythe', in K. Farrugia-Kriel and J. Nunes Jensen (eds), *Oxford Handbook of Contemporary Ballet*, Oxford: Oxford University Press, pp. 438–56.

V&A Interview with John Cowell (1998), http://www.vam.ac.uk/content/articles/i/the-textile-painter-john-cowell/. Accessed 14 March 2023.

Vincenzi, S. (2017), interviewed by M. K. Connolly, 14 September.

Von Rosen, A. (2020), 'Costume in the dance archive: Towards a records-centred ethics of care', *Studies in Costume and Performance*, 5:1, pp. 33–52.

Vermersch, P. (1994), *L'entretien, d'explicitation*, Paris: ESF.

Vermersch, P. (2015), 'Explicitation interview and memory', *Expliciter*, 106, pp. 38–43, English translation, http://www.entretienavecpierre.fr/2015/04/explicitation-interview-and-memory-1-english-translation-from-french-2015-expliciter-106-38-43/. Accessed 10 September 2023.

Warhol, A. (2007), *The Philosophy of Andy Warhol (From A to B and Back Again)*, London: Penguin.

Watson, K. (1999), 'Heart of the grotesque', *The Guardian*, 23 October, https://www.theguardian.com/stage/1999/oct/23/dance.artsfeatures. Accessed 5 December 2023.

Weinstock, J. A. (2004), 'Introduction: The spectral turn', in J. A. Weinstock (ed.), *Spectral America: Phantoms and the National Imagination*, Madison, Wisconsin: University of Wisconsin Press, pp. 3–18.

Whatley, S. (2017), 'Tools, frameworks and digital transformation', in T. Sant (ed.), *Documenting Performance: The Context and Processes of Digital Curation and Archiving*, London: Bloomsbury Methuen Drama, pp. 283-304.

Whatley, S. (2020), 'Digital preservation of dance, inclusion, and absence', in H. Thomas and S. Prickett (eds), *The Routledge Companion to Dance Studies*, London and New York: Routledge, pp. 311-22.

White Cube (2017), '*Anselm Kiefer Walhalla*', https://www.whitecube.com/exhibitions/anselm_kiefer_bermondsey_2016. Accessed 31 October 2023.

Wilcox, C. (2020), *Patch Work: A Life Among Clothes*, London: Bloomsbury.

Wilkinson, S. (2011), 'The Featherstonehaughs Draw on the Sketchbooks of Egon Schiele Review, Riverside Studios', *The Stage*, 24 November, https://www.thestage.co.uk/reviews/the-featherstonehaughs-draw-on-the-sketchbooks-of-egon-schiele-review-at-riverside-studios-london. Accessed 14 March 2023.

Wilson, E. (2009), *Adorned in Dreams: Fashion and Modernity*, London: I B Tauris & Co Ltd.

Wilson, F. (2001), 'Mining the museum in me', in L. Cohen (ed.), *Pictures, Patents, Monkeys and More…On Collecting*, New York: Independent Curators International, pp. 54-55.

Wolfreys, J. (2002), *Victorian Hauntings: Spectrality, Gothic, the Uncanny and Literature*, Basingstoke: Palgrave.

Wollen, P. (2008), *Raiding the Icebox: Reflections on Twentieth-Century Culture*, London: Verso.

Wood, C. (2004), 'Let me entertain you', *Afterall*, 9, pp. 36-44.

Wulff, H. (2012), 'Instances of inspiration: Interviewing dancers and writers', in J. Skinner (ed.), *The Interview: An Ethnographic Approach*, London: Berg, pp. 163-78.

Zuniga-Shaw, N. (2011), 'Synchronous objects, choreographic objects, and the translation of dancing ideas', in G. Klein and S. Noeth (eds), *Emerging Bodies: The Performance of Worldmaking in Dance and Choreography*, Bielefeld: Transcript Verlag, pp. 207-22.

Biographies

The Cholmondeleys and *The Featherstonehaughs*

The Cholmondeleys were originally founded by Lea Anderson, with Teresa Barker and Gaynor Coward, in 1984, following their graduation from the Laban Centre for Movement and Dance (now Trinity Laban Conservatoire for Music and Dance). In 1987 Anderson established an all-male company *The Featherstonehaughs*. The companies made over 87 works, both live and on film. They performed throughout the UK and internationally. While initially the companies performed separately, many works were made that featured both companies together. These works include *Yippeee!!!* (2006) and *Smithereens* (1999), featured in this publication, while *The Featherstonehaughs Draw on the Sketchbooks of Egon Schiele* (1998 and 2010) is an example of a work made only for *The Featherstonehaughs*. Some works were later cross-cast on the sibling company. *Flesh & Blood*, for example, was created for *The Cholmondeleys* in 1989 and remounted on *The Featherstonehaughs* in 2010. A full list of the companies' works is available on Lea Anderson's website: www.leaanderson.com and in *Lea Anderson's The Cholmondeleys and The Featherstonehaughs: 40 Years of Style and Design*, published by *The Cholmondeleys* (2024).

Mary Kate Connolly

is a writer, editor and curator based in London, UK. Her longstanding collaboration with Lea Anderson continues today, finding new ways in which embodied objects and garments can live on beyond the performances in which they first took flight. The year 2024 sees the launch of *Lea Anderson's The Cholmondeleys and The Featherstonehaughs: 40 Years of Style and Design*, a celebratory publication charting the companies' histories and collaborators, edited by Mary Kate. In 2021, she curated *Smithereens: A Collection of Fragments Considered as a Whole* – a multimedia exhibition of *Cholmondeleys* and *Featherstonehaughs* costumes at studio 1.1, London.

Previous edited publications include *Throwing the Body into the Fight: A Portrait of Raimund Hoghe* (2013) and *People Show: Nobody Knows but Everybody Remembers* (2016).

Mary Kate is former Programme Leader of the MA and MFA creative practice at Trinity Laban Conservatoire of Music and Dance. She has written exhibition catalogue essays for visual artists David Caines, Angela Hogg and Margarita Zafrilla Olayo, among others. Mary Kate presents her research internationally and has performed at conferences and festivals including Prague Quadrennial, Brut Wien and SPILL, UK.

Lea Anderson was born in London and trained at St Martin's School of Art and The Laban Centre for Movement and Dance while performing as a singer in a post-punk band. Lea cofounded *The Cholmondeleys* company after graduation from The Laban Centre, London in 1984 and has been making work for the company ever since. Lea makes work for theatre, film, TV, cabaret, site specific and social media platforms, and has also been regularly commissioned to make work for other companies including *The National Dance Company of Cuba, National Folk Dance Company of Peru, Compania Danza PUCP Peru* and *National Dance Company Wales*. Lea has a special interest in performed exhibitions and misconstructions of forgotten performance works using scores. In 2002 Lea was awarded an MBE for her services to dance, and in 2006 was awarded an honorary doctorate by Dartington College of Arts. In 2014 Lea was appointed Regents Professor at the University of California, in Los Angeles.

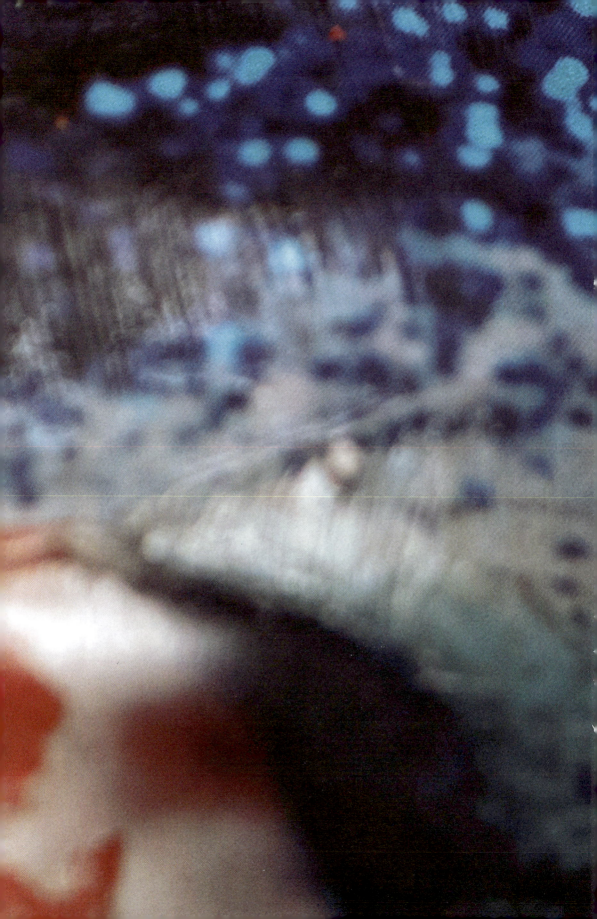